LATTER-DAY PROPHETS

THEIR LIVES, TEACHINGS, AND TESTIMONIES

with Profiles of Their Wives

by

EMERSON ROY WEST

Covenant Communications, Inc.

97 98 99 00 01 02 03   10 9 8 7 6 5 4 3 2 1

Latter-Day Prophets: Their Lives, Teachings, and Testimonies
Covenant Communications, Inc.
ISBN 1-55503-133-3
Cover photos © The Church of Jesus Christ of Latter-day Saints
Used by Permission

ACKNOWLEDGMENTS

Grateful appreciation is expressed to the following people who have contributed to this book:

To my loving wife, Gloria, whose love, counsel, encouragement, and personal sacrifices made this book possible. She was very helpful in preparing of the charts, researching material, typing the manuscript, formatting, editing, and proofreading and she offered constructive criticism and suggestions.

To my children who proofread and evaluated the material— Jennifer, Julie, Janelle, and Jon. Special thanks to my son Jerry who proofread the entire manuscript, prepared the title page, and gave very helpful suggestions, especially with formatting.

To Dr. Dale Mouritsen, Cupertino, California Institute Director, who was a constant source of information and strength.

To Joy Hulme, J. Robert Driggs, Marilyn Parks, and Dean Rigby for their editorial assistance.

To Church scholars Larry C. Porter, Susan Easton Black, James B. Allen, Leonard Arrington, Donald Cannon, Carol Cornwall Madsen, Glen R. Stubbs, Robert J. Matthews, Larry E. Dahl, Dale LeBaron, Clyde Williams, Glen M. Leonard, and Brent L. Top, for evaluating the material and offering helpful suggestions.

To James Kimball and Grant Allen Anderson of the Church Historical Department, to Carl Johnson of the Church Copyright Department and to Michael Watson and Don Staheli, secretaries to the First Presidency, for their helpful assistance.

To family members of the Presidents: Robert McKay, Reed Benson, Richard Hunter, Helen Lee Goates, Edward Kimball, Joseph F. McConkie, and various other relatives for their assistance.

To William W. Slaughter, photograph archivist for The Church of Jesus Christ of Latter-day Saints, and to Ron Evans of the LDS Church Museum, for providing the pictures.

To Nancy Wudel, Rose Mary LeBaron, Max Parker, Dianne Montgomery, Barbara Davis, Kirk Waldron, and Wayne Covington for their helpful assistance.

To JoAnn Jolley and Valerie Holladay of Covenant Communications for their professional and editorial assistance, and to Mike Johnson for designing the cover.

To the Utah State Historical Society for the photographs of Minnie Snow, Leonora Cannon Taylor, and Sophia Whitaker Taylor. Used by permission. All rights reserved.

To the LDS Church Visual Resources for "The Second Coming" and "Christ and the Apostles" by Harry Anderson ©The Church of Jesus Christ of Latter-day Saints. Used by permission.

Notes: Under the "Teachings" section for each President, quotation marks have been omitted, although the exact words of the President have been used.

Under the category "Baptism" in the biographical section for each President, the age, date and location are given only for Joseph Smith, Brigham Young, John Taylor, Wilford Woodruff and Lorenzo Snow.

ABOUT THE AUTHOR

An educator and author, Emerson Roy West was born in Logan, Utah, the son of Roy and Geneva West. His background and interest in Church history and presidents stems from his teaching in the Church and his family association with his father, who worked in the Church Department of Education for more than forty-five years.

Mr. West holds a bachelor's degree in sociology, history, and Spanish and a master's degree in speech and counseling from Brigham Young University. He was a high school and junior college teacher in San Jose, California, for thirty-five years. He taught English, Spanish, speech, and debate and was also a debate coach. He is the author of the books *When You Speak in Church, Vital Quotations, Profiles of the Presidents,* and *How to Speak in Church.*

He served a mission for The Church of Jesus Christ of Latter-day Saints in Uruguay and Paraguay and served with the U.S. Army in Germany as an assistant chaplain. He has held many teaching and executive positions in ward and stake auxiliaries. He and his wife, the former Gloria Kay Driggs, are now residing in Provo, Utah. They are the parents of five children: Jerry, Jennifer (Mitchell), Julie Ann, Janelle and Jonathan.

KEY TO ABBREVIATIONS

AGQ	Answers to Gospel Questions	IE	Improvement Era
CN	Church News	JD	Journal of Discourses
CR	Conference Report	JI	Juvenile Instructor
DBY	Discourses of Brigham Young	MF	Miracle of Forgiveness
DN	Deseret News	MS	Millennial Star
DNW	Deseret News Weekly	NE	New Era
DS	Doctrines of Salvation	RSM	Relief Society Magazine
DWW	Discourses of Wilford Woodruff	SGO	Sharing the Gospel with Others
EnM	Encyclopedia of Mormonism	SYHP	Stand Ye in Holy Places
FPM	Faith Precedes the Miracle	TGAS	Teachings of George Albert Smith
GBH	Go Forward With Faith: The Biography of Gordon B. Hinckley	THBL	Teachings of Harold B. Lee
		TLS	Teachings of Lorenzo Snow
GD	Gospel Doctrine	TPJS	Teachings of the Prophet Joseph Smith
GI	Gospel Ideals	TETB	Teachings of Ezra Taft Benson
GK	Gospel Kingdom	TPC	The Presidents of the Church
GS	Gospel Standards	TSWK	Teachings of Spencer W. Kimball
HC	History of the Church	YALW	Ye Are the Light of the World

★★★★★★★★★★★

TABLE OF CONTENTS

Charts and Additional Information

From the beginning of time, men and women have searched for the answers to life's most bewildering questions:

- Who am I?
- Where did I come from?
- What is life's purpose for me?
- Does our Heavenly Father have a plan for me?
- What does the life and mission of Jesus Christ mean to me?
- How can I find peace and happiness?

Who, living in this world of confusion and uncertain values, would not like a clearer sense of the meaning of life? Who does not want to find a peace and happiness that will transcend the trials and the tragedies of life?

My purpose in life has been to find God's mission for me. My church and my beliefs have been central in my life. I believe in the divinity of Jesus Christ. I believe that The Church of Jesus Christ of Latter-day Saints is the restoration of Christ's original church and gospel. It offers the blessing of ongoing revelation. The organization, authority, and ordinances of the Church are once again on the earth. The teachings and revelations of Jesus Christ have been restored in their fulness in modern times.

God the Father has acted through prophets to achieve these purposes, just as He has always spoken to His children on earth throughout history. (See 2 Chr. 29:25-27; Jer. 7:25; Eph. 4:11; Acts 15:32.) God has said He will "do nothing" until He reveals His words through "His servants the prophets." (Amos 3:7; Eph. 2:19-20; 1 Cor. 12:28.) Thus, in modern times, our Heavenly Father has again spoken through His prophets to His children on earth. Joseph Smith, the first prophet of this dispensation, was the instrument through which God effected this restoration.

Our first parents, Adam and Eve, choosing to exercise their God-given agency, partook of the fruit of the tree of knowledge of good and evil, thus disobeying God and becoming mortal. Consequently, they and all of their descendants became subject to both mortal and spiritual death. Mortal death is the separation of body and spirit; spiritual death is the separation of the spirit from the presence of God and being unaware of spiritual things.

Because all human beings after Adam and Eve have in some way been disobedient to divine law, they cannot regain the presence of God without an atonement for this disobedience. God's divine plan provided a redeemer to pay for those sins, to break the bonds of death, and to make possible the reunion of the spirits and bodies of all persons who have ever dwelt on earth or who may yet come to this earth.

Jesus Christ was designated by Heavenly Father, before the earth was created, to redeem humankind and to conquer death. During His mortal ministry, Jesus taught the eternal plan of salvation, served others, exemplified love, testified of His Father, and organized His church. As Paul told the Ephesians, the church of Jesus Christ was "built upon the foundation of the apostles and prophets, Jesus Christ himself being the chief corner stone." (Eph. 2:20.) This organization would endure until "all come in the unity of the faith, and of the knowledge of the Son of God, unto a perfect man." (Eph. 4:13.) In other words, as long as humankind exists in its fallible state, the identifying characteristic of Jesus Christ's church will be its organization with a foundation of apostles and prophets, Jesus Christ Himself being the chief cornerstone. Since the Church was established by Christ during His ministry, we must assume that it is essential, not optional.

For a time, this original organization perpetuated itself, with a new apostle (Matthias) being chosen to take Judas' place. (See Acts 1:23-26.) Though we do not have the record of their selection, Barnabas and Paul are referred to as apostles in Acts 14:14. Paul, in his epistles, introduces himself as an apostle of divine commission. However, the Savior and the apostles prophesied that an apostasy and falling away would occur. (See Matt. 24:5, 9-12, 23-24; 2 Thess. 2:3.) Although Christianity survived as a religion, it was doctrinally and organizationally different from the original church, and the authority to act in the name of God was lost.

Early apostles promised a restoration of what had been lost, including the restoration of the offices of apostles and prophets. (See Acts 3:20-21; Eph. 1:10.) This restoration has occurred. The key figure in the Lord's restoration was the first of the modern prophets, Joseph Smith, Jr. (See *JS-H*, Pearl of Great Price.)

A religion stagnates if it relies only on ancient revelation. The Bible testifies that God is a living, revealing, and communicating being. Revelation is an ongoing process to modern prophets. The Church of Jesus Christ of Latter-day Saints has the answers to life's vital questions, and the gospel found therein provides faith and hope for life's challenges.

Some important aspects of The Church of Jesus Christ of Latter-day Saints include:

- Faith in God as our Eternal Father, faith in Jesus Christ as our Savior and Redeemer, and faith in the Holy Ghost as the Comforter, Testifier, and Revelator. We receive the companionship of the Holy Ghost when we are baptized and confirmed members and it will remain with us thereafter if we keep our gospel covenants.

- Each member of the Godhead (God the Father, Jesus Christ, and the Holy Ghost) is an independent personage, separate and distinct from the other two, the three being in perfect unity and harmony with each other.

- God speaks His will through His living prophets.

- We lived as spirits before we were born, and we will live after death. As a result, we can eternally continue to progress and learn. We are blessed in this life and the next for our obedience to the commandments, for the Lord has said, "There is a law irrevocably decreed in heaven before the foundation of this world, upon which all blessings are predicated." (D&C 130:20.)

- Important records of God's dealings with the human family are preserved in the scriptures. Two volumes dealing with ancient times are the Bible, a record of happenings in the Old World, and the Book of Mormon, a New World record. Revelations to Joseph Smith and his successors appear in the Doctrine and Covenants and the Pearl of Great Price.

- The Church of Jesus Christ of Latter-day Saints has the same organization as that found in the New Testament, with prophets, apostles, bishops, elders, seventies, and other officers.

- Each individual may gain a personal testimony of the truthfulness of the gospel and the Church.

- Each individual possesses agency, allowing him or her to choose what to believe, do, and become.

- The priesthood, or the authority to act in God's name, is available to every worthy male member twelve years and older. The Church is staffed by lay people.

- Members of the Church pay tithing both as a spiritual law and as the basic means of financing the programs of the Church. As in the Old Testament, tithing is ten percent of an individual's annual interest, which is understood to mean income.

- The family unit becomes eternal when marriages are solemnized for time and eternity, and where vicarious works are performed for the dead in temples dedicated for that purpose.

- The Church teaches the importance of genealogy—or tracing one's family history into the past. The saving ordinance of baptism can be performed for those who died without the opportunity of hearing the gospel, and family units can be sealed together for time and eternity.

- Tens of thousands of members serve voluntarily as missionaries.

- The Word of Wisdom, a divine law containing dietary and health guidelines, promises both temporal and spiritual blessings. (D&C 89.)

- The Church provides opportunities for service and responsibility for each member.

- Monday night is set aside for family home evening, and families are encouraged to meet together to pray, share experiences, teach and learn the gospel, sing together, play together, and strengthen family unity.

- Through the Relief Society organization, women develop their skills, talents, and spirituality. They cultivate special interests and friendships with other women and provide compassionate service to the sick and needy. Each month, women fellowship each other through a program called "visiting teaching." Pairs of "visiting teachers" visit other women to provide a spiritual message and offer needed assistance at times of crisis. Women also serve in many leadership capacities in Church organizations.

- "Home teachers," who are male representatives of the bishopric, visit assigned families each month.

- The Church emphasizes the pursuit of truth, including obtaining a good education or vocational training. An important scriptural admonition is "The glory of God is intelligence." All members are encouraged to acquire the skills to become physically, emotionally, financially, and spiritually self-reliant.

- The welfare plan meets the short-term temporal needs of members having financial difficulty.

- Young people receive religious education through seminaries and institutes of religion at buildings near their high school, college and university campuses. The Church owns and operates some elementary and high schools in foreign countries.

It also operates institutions of higher learning (Ricks College in Rexburg, Idaho; Brigham Young University in Provo, Utah; and BYU-Hawaii in Laie, Oahu).

- The Church emphasizes recreation and cultural development, including a youth program of sports, drama, speech, music, and dance.

- The gospel produces a hopeful, buoyant, and happy attitude toward life. "Men are that they might have joy." (2 Ne. 2:25.)

The Prophet Joseph Smith said, "We don't ask any people to throw away any good they have got; we only ask them to come and get more." *(HC* 5:258.)

As stated by President Joseph F. Smith, "The Church of Jesus Christ of Latter-day Saints is the only true and living church upon the face of the whole earth. The Church of Jesus Christ of Latter-day Saints is no partisan Church. It is not a sect. It is The Church of Jesus Christ of Latter-day Saints. It is the only one today existing in the world that can and does legitimately bear the name of Jesus Christ and his divine authority." (*GD*, p. 137.)

President Howard W. Hunter stated, "To answer affirmatively the question, 'Am I a living member?' confirms our commitment. It means that we now and always will love God and our neighbors as ourselves. It means our actions will reflect who we are and what we believe. It means that we are every day Christians, walking as Christ would have us walk. . . .

Living members give heed to the Spirit, which quickens the inner life. They pray for strength to overcome difficulties. Living members put Christ first in their lives, knowing from what sources their lives and progress come. . . . Living members recognize the need to put into action their beliefs. . . .

As members of the living church we have a belief in the living God. We have a firm belief . . . that this is the true and living church of the true and living God. The question we have yet to answer is: Am I dedicated and committed, a true and living member?" (*Ensign*, May 1987, pp. 17-18.)

ROLE OF THE PRESIDENT

From Joseph Smith, personally called by Jesus Christ as the first prophet of the Restored Church, to the current prophet and President of the Church, members acknowledge prophets as men called of God to perform His work on earth.

". . . to be a seer, a revelator, a translator, and a prophet, having all the gifts of God. . . . " (D&C 107:92.)

The duties, responsibilities, and blessings enumerated in this verse of describe the role of the President of the Church. Verse 91 refers to him the "President of the office of the High Priesthood," emphasizing the Church as the entity through which the priesthood operates. As President of the High Priesthood, the President of the Church is "to preside over the whole church, and to be like unto Moses." The Lord, in summarizing those duties, comments tellingly, "Behold, here is wisdom." (D&C 107:91-92.)

The prophet is called of God to be the Lord's oracle, lawgiver, seer, and representative on earth. It is through the living prophet that continuing revelation comes from the Lord. (See D&C 21:4-5.)

The prophet is the only person who possesses all of the keys of the priesthood and is the only one authorized to receive revelation for the entire Church, either new or amendatory. He alone can present the authoritative interpretation of scriptures that is binding on the Church. He is a teacher of truth and possesses the inspired capacity to discern between truth and error for the Church. Consequently, he identifies mistaken beliefs and movements within the Church and in the world, seeking to correct them and teaching correct principles. Spiritual safety lies in heeding the voice of the prophet when he gives direction concerning principles, doctrine, beliefs, and behavior. It is part of each member's testimony that the prophet speaks with authority from the Lord. When speaking as the prophet, what he says is considered scripture.

The President of the Church receives revelation on all matters pertaining to the Church. (See D&C 107:65-67; 91-92.) Three important examples follow:

- **Revelation on Church Organization.** Receiving a personal visitation the night after President Woodruff's death, the Savior instructed President Snow to immediately organize the presidency of the Church. (See Romney, *The Life of Lorenzo Snow*, p. 421.) In 1961, President McKay ordained members of the First Council of the Seventy to the office of high priest, which gave them the privilege of presiding at stake conferences, which eased the growing administrative burdens of the Quorum of the Twelve. President Kimball organized the First Quorum of the Seventy on October 3, 1975. President Benson discontinued stake seventies quorums throughout the Church on October 4, 1986, and organized the Second Quorum of the Seventy on April 1, 1989. In 1995, President Hinckley released all Regional Representatives and created the new local office of Area Authority, a move meant to decentralize the leadership of the Church. In April 1997, those who were serving in the office of Area Authority became Area Authority Seventies and members of the Third, Fourth, and Fifth Quorums of Seventies. President Hinckley said, "With these respective quorums in place, we have established a pattern under which the church may grow to any size." (*CN*, April 12, 1997, p. 6.) The Area Authority Seventies preside at stake conferences, train stake presidencies, create and organize stakes, set apart stake presidencies, tour missions, and train mission presidents. If needed, more quorums may be added.

- **Revelation on Church Doctrine.** Joseph Smith stands preeminent in revealing Church doctrine since he restored the fulness of the gospel, including all essential ordinances and principles for the salvation and exaltation of mankind. The Lord, however, gives additional revelations as He deems appropriate and "in case of difficulty respecting doctrine or principle, if there is not a sufficiency written to make the case clear to the minds of the council, the President may inquire and obtain the mind of the Lord by revelation." (D&C 102:23.) One example is the revelation received on June 8, 1978, by President Kimball, indicating that all worthy male members of the Church were eligible for the priesthood. (See

D&C Declaration 2.) In 1976, Church membership accepted Joseph Smith's vision of the celestial kingdom and Joseph F. Smith's vision of the redemption of the dead as additions to the Pearl of Great Price, becoming Sections 137 and 138 of the Doctrine and Covenants on June 6, 1979).

■ **Revelation on Contemporary Issues.** Our world is complex, and we face critical questions and problems with significant moral implications. The President gives counsel on issues such as pornography, abortion, homosexuality, sexual immorality, gambling and government-sponsored lotteries, spouse and child abuse, violence, Sabbath day observance, family unity, and the role of women in the Church. He avoids addressing partisan and political issues.

The President's official prophetic declarations to the Church are usually announced at general conferences or sent by letter to local units with the signature of the First Presidency.

In addition to receiving revelation, the President of the Church has the following general duties:

- He holds the "keys of the kingdom" (D&C 65:1-2), that is, the governing power and authority to administer in all spiritual and temporal affairs of the Church. By delegation, General Authorities, temple presidents, mission presidents, stake presidents, bishops, and others receive keys pertaining to specific offices in their own areas. Thus, through the President's authority, salvation becomes available to all people.

- He acts as sole spokesman of the Lord to the Church.

- He has the gift of prophecy through the Holy Ghost.

- He has full responsibility for the welfare of the Church, authorizing and receiving reports pertaining to its progress and problems. He also preserves order in the Church.

- He holds all the keys to the sealing ordinances of the temple, and he may delegate them to his counselors and to members of the Quorum of the Twelve. Only the prophet can grant cancellation

of a sealing. All temples are under his direct supervision.

- He is trustee-in-trust for the Corporation of the President, which holds, or may hold, title to all properties of the Church.

- He acts as chairman of the Church Board of Education.

- He is responsible for the preparation and procedure of general conference.

The President is assisted by at least two counselors, and together they form the First Presidency. They meet regularly with the Quorum of the Twelve Apostles in the Salt Lake Temple, usually on Thursday, to make decisions concerning the affairs of the Church. The President, his two counselors, and the quorum act in concert. (See D&C 90:12-18; 107:22, 79.)

The President often addresses the public. He speaks at general conferences, priesthood meetings, regional conferences, solemn assemblies, area seminars, stake conferences, firesides, special satellite broadcasts, funerals, youth conferences, women's conferences, and missionary meetings. He also speaks at civic, governmental, and patriotic assemblies, as well as at universities, colleges, and schools. He often answers questions on points of doctrine and policy. The *Church News* covers his travels and often prints his remarks.

He dedicates temples, chapels, and other Church buildings. He ordains and sets apart various Church officers. He meets with many people in his extensive travels and greets the notables of the world who visit Salt Lake City. He also meets with educators and civic and government leaders.

Current conference addresses are heard by millions of people throughout the world via radio and television. The President's messages are translated into many languages and printed in Church publications distributed worldwide. He also writes quarterly articles for the *Ensign*. During times of crisis or disaster, he makes decisions for the Church that affect people all around the world.

The President willingly welcomes the challenges of Church growth. Approximately 400 buildings worldwide are under construction at any point in time. The Church currently has more members outside the United States than within.

The President attends regional conferences throughout the world to become acquainted, on a personal basis, with local leaders and members. His role is to bring men to God and God to men. Like the Savior, who epitomizes what all prophets strive to be, the President does not merely point the way to the divine presence, but leads the way just as Moses led the children of Israel to the Promised Land. The prophet and his followers tread the same path, there being only one road to God. Each man, woman, and child must travel that road, and in so doing, will be entitled to the same endowment of divine power. All who wish may obtain the fulness of gospel blessings by complying with gospel laws.

The President gives guidance with regard to virtually every potential problem or societal challenge that may arise either institutionally or individually. Those who listen and follow his counsel will avoid many of the problems that plague the world, and they will become stronger and be better able to withstand the tests of mortality.

An example of Church members not following the counsel of the President occurred during President Heber J. Grant's administration, when there was a national effort to repeal the 18th Amendment to the Constitution of the United States. A repeal would allow the legal sale of liquor once again. Utah disregarded President Grant's counsel, voted for the repeal, the deciding vote in the successful repeal of the 18th Amendment.

A prophet exemplifies Christlike character. He humbly admits his limitations and imperfections, but his "humanness" never overpowers his divine calling to provide inspired direction. His life reflects commitment, courage, moral excellence, knowledge, patience, humility, temperance, kindness, long-suffering, charity, love, faith, hope, and godliness. He follows the Savior's admonition to "turn the other cheek." He teaches reverence and respect for the priesthood of God. He demonstrates total commitment to the Savior's work and bears testimony

of divine truths. He oversees the preaching of the gospel to "every nation, kindred, tongue and people" and teaches that each convert is to be treated as an equal.

While no one is guaranteed safety from all physical harm in the world today, there is a safety that is much more significant—spiritual safety. The inspired counsel of the Lord's prophet—the President of The Church of Jesus Christ of Latter-day Saints—if followed, will lead individuals back to the presence of Heavenly Father and His Son Jesus Christ. While serving as an apostle, George Albert Smith said, "When we are instructed by the President of the Church, we believe he tells us what the Lord would have us do. To us it is something more than just the advice of man." (*CR*, Oct. 1930, p. 66.) The Lord also emphasized this principle in D&C 1:38. Part of the prophet's role is to teach and encourage members to steadfastly press forward in their quest for eternal life and exaltation. All of the Lord's prophets have experienced the adversities of mortality, struggled with temptations and challenges, and suffered grief as inevitable losses have come to them. In so doing, they have learned obedience and met life's hardships with courage and strength. They have been victorious over their environments because they have, as they have testified, centered their lives upon the only source of spiritual strength, Jesus Christ. The President nourishes his own spirituality by spending time in prayer, meditation, and scripture study in order to be attuned to the promptings of the Spirit.

God speaks to His people through the prophet. President Harold B. Lee explained this role: "In each dispensation when His gospel has been upon the earth and His church has been established, the Lord has appointed and has vested authority in one man at a time in each dispensation who has borne the title of President of the Church, or Prophet, seer, and revelator to the Church. Such titles, or the conferring of such authority, do not make of one "head of the Church," which title belongs to Jesus Christ. It does make of him, however, God's mouthpiece and the one who acts in God's stead and through whom He speaks to His people by way of instruction, to give or to withhold principles and ordinances, or to warn of judgments." (*THBL*, pp. 528-29.)

SUCCESSION IN THE PRESIDENCY

"Each President has been uniquely selected for the time and situation which the world and Church needed. All were 'men of the hour'. . . . Contemplate the miracle of that foreordination and preparation! Though called and given keys years prior to the time that the mantle fell upon him, the President was always the right man in the right place for the times." (*TETB*, p. 142.)

The procedures governing succession in the presidency are divinely inspired. It is the Master who chooses the President. The succession procedure is here summarized.

• When the President of the Church dies, the First Presidency is dissolved and the counselors are automatically released and returned to their former quorums of priesthood activity.

• The presiding power then resides in the Quorum of the Twelve, and during that interim period they constitute the presiding quorum. The President of the Quorum of the Twelve is the presiding officer of the Church.

• Seniority begins automatically when a man is set apart as a member of the Quorum of the Twelve and is based on length of continuous service, not age.

• The new President, who is the senior apostle in the Quorum and also President of the Quorum of the Twelve, is selected "by prophecy and by the laying on of hands by those who are in authority." (Articles of Faith 1:5.) This is accomplished in a temple meeting where members of the Quorum of the Twelve, dressed in the robes of the holy priesthood, assemble in prayer and fasting. Each man, guided by inspiration, declares his belief, judgment, and testimony relating to the man who should be the next President of the Church. Usually the apostle next in seniority to the President of the Twelve nominates the President of the Twelve as the new prophet. The nomination must be seconded and unanimously approved.

• The senior apostle is then set apart as President, with the laying on of hands by the Twelve acting as a body. The next senior member of the Twelve is the voice for this sacred occasion.

This succession procedure will continue as the order of the Church unless the Lord changes it by revelation to the senior apostle or to the President before his death.

Usually at the first general conference following the setting apart of the new President, the body of the Church votes, in a solemn assembly, to sustain the new President as Prophet, Seer, and Revelator, and as President of the Church, promising to "uphold" him with its "confidence, faith, and prayers." (D&C 107:22.)

Thus, to become President of the Church, a man must have been called of God, ordained an apostle and set apart as a member of the Quorum of the Twelve, sustained by the Quorum of the Twelve and by members of the Church in solemn assembly.

At general conference on April 2, 1995, President Gordon B. Hinckley explained the events of March 12: "With President Hunter's passing, the First Presidency was dissolved. Brother Monson and I, who had served as his counselors, took our places in the Quorum of the Twelve, which became the presiding authority of the Church.

"Three weeks ago today all of the living ordained Apostles gathered in a spirit of fasting and prayer in the upper room of the [Salt Lake] temple. Here we sang a sacred hymn and prayed together. We partook of the sacrament of the Lord's supper, renewing in that sacred, symbolic testament our covenants and our relationships with Him who is our divine Redeemer.

"The presidency was then reorganized following a precedent well established through generations of the past.

"There was no campaigning, no contest, no ambition for office. It was quiet, peaceful, simple, and sacred. It was done after the pattern which the Lord Himself had put in place . . . .

"Yesterday morning members of the Church across the world met together in a solemn assembly. You raised your hands, without compulsion and of your own free will, to confirm the action taken by the Apostles three weeks ago and to sustain those called to serve." (*Ensign*, May 1995, p. 69.)

How, then, do we support the new President of the Church? We sustain him by accepting changes in leadership as they occur, by withholding adverse criticism, and by abstaining from murmuring. We sustain him by listening to and obeying his counsel. We sustain him with our daily prayers and genuine love and concern.

At the solemn assembly where President Gordon B. Hinckley was sustained as the fifteenth President of The Church of Jesus Christ of Latter-day Saints, President Thomas S. Monson conducted the business of the solemn assembly, giving instructions for the procedures to be used. In turn, members of the First Presidency and the Quorum of the Twelve sustained the First Presidency. They were followed by members of the First and Second Quorums of the Seventy and the Presiding Bishopric.

Next, stake patriarchs, high priests, and elders of the Melchizedek Priesthood participated in the sustaining, followed by members of the Aaronic Priesthood—deacons, teachers, and priests. They were followed by members of the Relief Society—women eighteen years of age and older—and all young women—ages twelve to eighteen—in turn, who stood and sustained the First Presidency.

Finally, the entire congregation, including those who had already participated, and all members of the Church throughout the world participating at stake centers, meeting houses, and homes receiving the conference proceedings by television or satellite transmission, stood and raised their hands to sustain the First Presidency.

God controls succession in the presidency. Before a man is called to be an apostle, the Lord knows whether he will eventually be the President of the Church, and if so, when. President Ezra Taft Benson said, "God knows all things, the end from the beginning, and no man becomes President of the Church of Jesus Christ by accident, nor remains there by chance, nor is called home by happenstance." (*Report of the Seoul Korea Area Conference*, 1975, p. 52.)

President Gordon B. Hinckley, speaking as the President of the Quorum of the Twelve Apostles and as a counselor to President Howard W. Hunter, testified about prophetic succession: "Let it be understood by all that Jesus Christ stands at the head of this church which bears His sacred name. He is watching over it. . . . His is the prerogative, the power, the option to call men in His way to high and sacred offices and to release them according to His will by calling them home. . . . I do not worry about the circumstances in which we find ourselves. I accept these circumstances as an expression of His will." (*Ensign*, May 1994, p. 59.)

LINE OF AUTHORITY

THE LORD JESUS CHRIST

PETER, JAMES, AND JOHN
were ordained apostles by the Lord Jesus Christ.

JOSEPH SMITH, JR., and OLIVER COWDERY
received the Melchizedek Priesthood and apostleship in 1829 from Peter, James and John.

THE THREE WITNESSES
were called by revelation to choose the Twelve Apostles and on February 14, 1835, were blessed by the First Presidency to ordain the Twelve Apostles.

BRIGHAM YOUNG
was ordained an apostle by the Three Witnesses, Oliver Cowdery, David Whitmer, and Martin Harris.

JOSEPH F. SMITH
was ordained an apostle by Brigham Young.

DAVID O. MCKAY
was ordained an apostle by Joseph F. Smith.

GORDON B. HINCKLEY
was ordained an apostle by David O. McKay.

JOSEPH SMITH, JR.
1805-1844
First President

- **Born**: December 23, 1805, in Sharon, Vermont

- **Family**: Joseph Smith was the son of Joseph, Sr. and Lucy Mack Smith, the fourth of eleven children. At age 21, Joseph married Emma Hale on January 18, 1827 (she died on April 30, 1879); they had eleven children. After the Lord revealed the principle of plural marriage, other wives were sealed to Joseph.

- **Baptism**: May 15, 1829, age 23, in the Susquehanna River near Harmony, Pennsylvania

- **Missions**: Missouri (1831-32); Canada (1833); Michigan (1835); Eastern States (1836); Canada (1837).

- **Education**: Grammar schools, heavenly tutors, School of the Prophets, self-educated by study and prayer.

- **Occupation**: Farmer, builder, banker, merchant, city builder.

- **Apostle**: Ordained by Peter, James, and John in 1829 (served 3 years; age 23-26)

- **First Elder**: April 6, 1830, to January 25, 1832 (served 1 year, 9 months; age 24-26)

- **Church Callings:** Apostle, First Elder, and missionary

- **President of the Church**: January 25, 1832, to June 27, 1844 (served 12½ years; age 26-38)

- **General Authority**: 14 years

- **Temple Dedicated**: Kirtland (1836)

- **Favorite Hymn**: "A Poor Wayfaring Man of Grief" (Not a hymn during Joseph's day, but a popular song with the tune name "Duane Street.")

- **Hymns About Joseph Smith**: "Joseph Smith's First Prayer," "Praise to the Man," "We Thank Thee, O God, for a Prophet," "Come, Listen to a Prophet's Voice," "Come, Sing to the Lord," "Now, We'll Sing with One Accord," "The Seer! Joseph the Seer," and "Truth Eternal."

- **Special Interests and Hobbies**: Wrestling, jumping at a mark, pulling sticks, horseback riding, and ice skating

- **Selected Teachings**: *History of the Church, Teachings of the Prophet Joseph Smith, The Words of Joseph Smith* and *Teachings of Joseph Smith*

- **Other Responsibilities While President**: President of Kirtland Stake (1834-38), City Councilman and Mayor of Nauvoo, editor of the *Times and Seasons*, and Lieutenant General in the Nauvoo Legion

- **Priesthood and Keys Restored**: (1) Keys of the Book of Mormon by **Moroni** (D&C 27:5.); (2) Keys of the Aaronic Priesthood by **John the Baptist**, 1829; (3) Keys of the Dispensation of the Fulness of Times, and Melchizedek Priesthood by **Peter, James** and **John**, 1829; (4) Keys of the Sealing Power by **Elijah**, 1836; (5) Keys of Gathering of Israel and the Restoration of the Lost Tribes by **Moses**, 1836; (6) Dispensation of the gospel of Abraham (Celestial Marriage) by **Elias**, 1836. (Other unspecified keys were given. See D&C 128:21.)

- **Significant Contributions**: The prophet re-established the doctrine and practice of continuous revelation; he clarified the following: the true nature of God, the personage of the Holy Ghost, human potential, the nature and purpose of the Fall of Man, man's redemption from Adam's fall, mankind's premortal existence in a spirit form, the true purpose of life, how to attain eternal happiness, the eternal nature of family relationships, an understanding of life after death, the doctrine of the resurrection, and an understanding of the concept of Zion. He translated the Book of Mormon and received the revelations contained in the Doctrine and Covenants. He also translated the Book of Abraham and received the revelations contained in the Books of Moses and Matthew (chapter 24) which compose the Pearl of Great Price and Articles of Faith, and he established the true Church again on the earth in 1830. (D&C 58:7, 119:2.)

- **Legacy of Papers**: He kept ten record books containing diary material and wrote or dictated approximately 400 letters and documents, covering the last fifteen years of his life. In 1838, he began to write, dictate, supervise and prepare a history of the Church. After his death in 1844, other capable people continued the project, completing it in 1856. The work is a six-volume, 2,000-page history. Sacred writings include the Book of Mormon, the books of Moses and Abraham (found in the Pearl of Great Price, which also contain extracts from his personal history), a revision of the Bible, and revelations which are published in the Doctrine and Covenants.

- **Appearance, Personality, and Qualities**: He stood six feet tall, weighed 200-210 pounds, had an athletic build, light brown hair, and a distinguished appearance; he was charismatic, cheerful, warm, vigorous, resourceful, compassionate, loyal, and was noted for his spiritual gifts. He was innovative, imaginative, and aggressive leader. He freely forgave prodigals, some of whom had caused him much misery and pain. He was known for his love for all and had the ability to establish a bond with people of all ages and circumstances.

- **Died**: June 27, 1844, from gunshot wounds at the hands of a mob (martyred) in Carthage, Illinois (age 38).

- **1844** Members: 26,000 Stakes: 1
  (June) Missions: 3 Temple: 1
  Missionaries: 586 (set apart in 1844)
  General Authorities: 23

Biographical Highlights

Joseph Smith was raised a farm boy. His parents moved often and were poor. Joseph loved his parents, worked with his family, and suffered during their hardships. He was stricken at age seven with typhoid fever and had surgery on his left leg that left him with a limp for the remainder of his life.

In 1820, near Palmyra, New York, Joseph sought religion and harmony with God. In answer to a prayer for guidance, he received a remarkable vision of God the Father and His son, Jesus Christ. (*JS-H* 7:20.) He also had a series of angelic visitations that prepared him for his prophetic calling. He was visited several times by the Angel Moroni from 1823 to 1827. In 1829, he received the Aaronic Priesthood from John the Baptist and the apostleship and Melchizedek Priesthood from Peter, James, and John.

By 1830, he had translated and published the Book of Mormon. He also restored and organized the Church of Christ (officially named by revelation in 1838 as "The Church of Jesus Christ of Latter-day Saints"). He established and filled its offices and received revelation to guide the Church. Missionary work began under his direction. He defined doctrines, set forth principles for living in a Christian society, and encouraged people to better themselves, gain an education, and improve their family life. Despite his great accomplishments, those who found his teachings offensive assassinated him and feared his political power. He spent his life bringing forth a new dispensation of religious knowledge at great personal cost. About a year before his death, he said the following to a congregation of listeners in Nauvoo, "If I had not actually got into the work and been called of God, I would back out. But I cannot back out: I have no doubt of the truth." (*HC* 5:336.)

Joseph Smith never claimed that he had established a new religion. Rather, he testified that his work was a restoration of the everlasting gospel of Jesus

Christ and a restoration of Christ's lost church. As the prophet of God, Joseph Smith was favored of God, but his divine calling did not spare him from adversity. He spent months in prison, was pursued as a fugitive, was tarred, feathered, and beaten, and was betrayed to his enemies. His strong body endured this abuse. Many times throughout his life, the Prophet lost most of his material possessions due to imprisonments, the treachery of false friends, and frequent lawsuits. Despite immense difficulties in his life, he was a happy, robust, optimistic man. Those who knew him felt his strength and courage, even in the darkest times. His enlightened spirit eased his brief bouts of discouragement.

Though not worshipped by Church members, Joseph Smith is revered in his calling as prophet, seer, revelator, and first President of the Church in the latter days.

"Leadership of the Church set Joseph Smith's life on a new course. Up to that time he had been a young man with a divine gift and a mission to translate the Book of Mormon; now, without any previous organizational experience, he was responsible for organizing a church and leading a people. He had to rely on revelation. . . . They [the revelations] range from instructions on mundane details of administration to exalted depictions of life hereafter. Typically, when problems had to be solved, whether administrative or doctrinal, the Prophet sought divine guidance and by virtue of this help led the Church." (Bushman & Jessee, "Joseph Smith: The Prophet," *EnM* 3:1335.)

Visions

As a boy of fourteen, in the spring of 1820, Joseph Smith was sincerely interested in determining which of the many religions was the most correct and which church he should join. One day while struggling to find the truth, he read a passage in James: "If any of you lack wisdom, let him ask of God, that giveth to all [men] liberally, and upbraideth not; and it shall be given him." (James 1:5.) Determined to ask of God, he entered a secluded quiet grove of trees and prayed with faith. "I saw two Personages, whose brightness and glory defy all description, standing above me in the air. One of them spake unto me, calling me by name

and said, pointing to the other—'This is My Beloved Son. Hear Him!'. . .

"I asked the Personages who stood above me in the light, which of all the sects was right (for at that time it had never entered into my heart that all were wrong)—and which I should join.

"I was answered that I must join none of them, for they were all wrong." (*JS-H* 1:17-19.)

Joseph also learned that he had been chosen to be an instrument in God's hands. After this marvelous experience, Joseph returned to his home and told his family and others about the manifestation. His family accepted his testimony; others, however, rejected his story and harassed him.

Over three years later, on September 21, 1823, Joseph prayed to know concerning his status before the Lord. An angel appeared. "He called me by name, and said unto me that he was a messenger sent from the presence of God to me, and that his name was Moroni; that God had a work for me to do. . . . He said there was a book deposited, written upon gold plates, [and] . . . that the fulness of the everlasting Gospel was contained in it, as delivered by the Savior to the ancient inhabitants." (*JS-H* 1:33-34.)

In 1829, Joseph and Oliver Cowdery, who had joined Joseph in the work, received the Aaronic Priesthood from John the Baptist. Joseph recorded: "We on a certain day went into the woods to pray and inquire of the Lord respecting baptism for the remission of sins. . . . While we were praying and calling upon the Lord, a messenger from heaven descended in a cloud of light, and having laid his hands upon us, he ordained us." (*JS-H* 1:68.)

So great was Joseph's mission that holy prophets foresaw his ministry thousands of years before his birth. Joseph of Egypt even prophesied about Joseph Smith's life. (See 2 Ne. 3:6, 14-15.)

Recognition

Josiah Quincy, the mayor of Boston, visited Joseph Smith in the summer of 1844 in Nauvoo, Illinois. He was able to observe the Prophet closely and said: "It is by no means improbable that some future textbook for the use of generations yet unborn will contain a question something like this: What historical American of the nineteenth century has exerted the most powerful influence upon the destinies of his countrymen?' And it is by no means impossible that the answer to that interrogatory may be thus written: 'Joseph Smith, the Mormon Prophet.' And the reply, absurd as it doubtless seems to most men now living, may be an obvious commonplace to their descendants. History deals in surprises and paradoxes quite as startling as this.

"Born in the lowest ranks of poverty, without book-learning, and with the homeliest of all human names, he had made himself at the age of thirty-nine a power upon the earth. Of the multitudinous family of Smith, none had so won human hearts and shaped human lives as this man Joseph. His influence, whether for good or evil, is potent today, and the end is not yet.

"It is no small thing, in the blaze of this nineteenth century, to give to men a new revelation, found a new religion, establish new forms of worship, to build a city with new laws, institutions, and orders of architecture—to establish ecclesiastical, civil, and military jurisdiction, found colleges, send out missionaries, and make proselytes on two hemispheres. Yet all this has been done by Joe Smith, and that against every sort of opposition, ridicule, and persecution." (Evans, *Joseph Smith: An American Prophet*, pp. 3-4.)

"In his book *Churches in North America: An Introduction*, Jesuit scholar Gustave Weigel wrote of Joseph Smith: 'His productivity marks him as a man of genius. He had very little schooling . . . yet he was a combination of practical wisdom, great daring and imagination. He was clearly a leader of men, with a great confidence in himself which repeated failures could not destroy.'" (Edwin O. Haroldsen, "Good and Evil Spoken Of," *Ensign*, Aug. 1995, p. 10.)

Achievements

By direct commission from Jesus Christ, Joseph Smith restored the original Church of Christ, including its same basic offices, powers, ordinances, and doctrines. By revelation, Joseph Smith learned the correct name of the church, clarified the true

concept of Deity, received the keys of salvation and saving ordinances for both the living and the dead, and authorized the building of the first temples in this dispensation in Kirtland, Ohio, and Nauvoo, Illinois.

Joseph Smith alone has added 900 new pages of revealed scripture in our day. He published new scripture (the Book of Mormon and the Book of Abraham) from records and papyri he translated through the gift and power of God, received the Book of Moses by revelation, received revelations for the latter days recorded in the Doctrine and Covenants, and corrected at least 3,410 verses in the Bible.

The Prophet commissioned the writing of the history of the Church, dictating extensive passages and helping with its editing. He wrote the "Articles of Faith" (a summary of Latter-day Saint beliefs) and organized the Relief Society organization for women. He established and taught the divine law of consecration and stewardship and received by revelation a health code called the Word of Wisdom.

"It was not uncommon to see him involved in sports activities with the young and vigorous men of a community. He is known to have wrestled, pulled sticks, engaged in snowball fights, played ball, slid on the ice with his children, played marbles, shot at a mark, and fished." (Bushman & Jessee, *EnM* 3:1338.)

He was a leader in education, organizing the School of the Prophets (one of the first adult schools in America). He also established several social, economic, cultural, and educational institutions. Under the Prophet Joseph's leadership, the Church moved from New York to Ohio, from Ohio to Missouri, and from Missouri to Illinois.

Joseph Smith's vision of the celestial kingdom received in the Kirtland Temple on January 21, 1836, was canonized on April 3, 1976, by the General Conference of the Church. It is now Section 137 of the Doctrine and Covenants.

Larry Porter, BYU Professor of Church History and Doctrine, said, "Within the Church every member is a partaker of the great blessings associated with the restored gospel of Jesus Christ. Under the auspices of the Holy Priesthood, the Prophet Joseph Smith fulfilled the predictions of the prophets of ages past and met the expectations of his eternal commission." (*CN*, Jan. 30, 1993, p. 12.)

Joseph Smith's Family

A precious part of Joseph's life and a contributing factor to his spiritual strength was his relationship with his wife and children. They, too, passed through much physical and spiritual hardship for his sake. In 1827, before the publication of the Book of Mormon, Joseph married a loyal and capable woman, Emma Hale. He later wrote of her: "Many were the reverberations of my mind when I contemplated for a moment the scenes we had been called to pass through, the fatigues and the toils, and sorrows and sufferings, and the joys and consolations, from time to time, which had strewed our paths and crowned our board." (*HC* 5:107.)

Joseph and Emma had eleven children—nine boys and two girls—two of them included the Murdock twins whom they adopted—a boy and a girl. Of these children, only five lived to maturity. Emma gave birth to their last child four months after Joseph's death.

In his journal, Joseph wrote of taking his family to concerts, the theater, circus performances, and excursions on Mississippi River boats. The family often enjoyed evenings around the fireside, playing games, and reading and studying together. Despite the many duties and persecutions that took Joseph away from home, his family was very important to him, and he deeply loved them.

Orson Pratt's Testimony of the Character of Joseph Smith

Orson Pratt, a member of the Quorum of the Twelve Apostles, had a keen intellect and was one of the early Church's leading tract writers. He was closely associated with Joseph Smith for fourteen years. He commented:

"I then became intimately acquainted with him [Joseph Smith]. I had the great privilege, when I was in from my missions, of boarding most of the time at his house, so that I not only knew him as a public teacher, but as a private citizen, as a husband and father. I witnessed his earnest and humble devotions both morning and evening in his family. I heard the words of eternal life flowing from his mouth, nourishing, soothing and comforting his family, neighbors, and friends. I saw his countenance lighted up as the inspiration of the Holy Ghost rested upon him, dictating the great and most precious revelations now printed for our guide. I saw him translating, by inspiration, the Old and New Testaments, and the inspired book of Abraham from Egyptian papyrus.

". . . [My testimony] is the same today as it was when I first received the testimony that he was a Prophet. I knew that he was a man of God. It was not a matter of opinion with me, for I received a testimony from the heavens concerning that matter. . . ." (*JD* 7:176-77.)

Personal Experience Showing Forgiveness

Joseph Smith's capacity to love was often revealed through his capacity to forgive. During the hostile days of persecutions in Missouri, William W. Phelps apostatized, signed his name to a false affidavit that brought much suffering to Church members and was instrumental in the imprisonment of the Prophet. Phelps was excommunicated on March 17, 1839, but later repented and asked for forgiveness.

Joseph wrote to him: "Believing your confession to be real, and your repentance genuine, I shall be happy once again to give you the right hand of fellowship, and rejoice over the returning prodigal. . . . Come on, dear brother, since the war is past, For friends at first are friends again at last." (*TPJS*, p. 166.)

William Phelps came back into the Church in 1841. He was noted for his valuable musical contributions. He wrote many hymns, including "The Spirit of God," "Praise to the Man," and "Now Let Us Rejoice."

Elder Dallin H. Oaks' Testimony of the Integrity of the Prophet Joseph

Elder Dallin Oaks of the Quorum of the Twelve said that through his extensive personal study and legal research, his findings shed new light on the events that led to the martyrdom of Joseph Smith and the closing of an opposition newspaper by the city of Nauvoo.

"Mormon historians, including Elder B. H. Roberts, had conceded that this action was illegal, but as a young law professor pursuing original research, I was pleased to find a legal basis for this action in the Illinois law of 1844. The amendment to the United States Constitution that extended the guarantee of freedom of the press to protect against the actions of city and state governments was not adopted until 1868, and it was not enforced as a matter of federal law until 1931." (See Dallin H. Oaks, "The Suppression of the *Nauvoo Expositor*," *Utah Law Review* 9 [1965]: 862.) "We should judge the actions of our predecessors on the basis of the laws and commandments and circumstances of their day, not ours."

Elder Oaks pointed out two other areas of personal research in little-known areas that shed light on the character and integrity of Joseph Smith. Studying the lengthy trial of the assassins of Joseph and Hyrum, he said, "Nothing in our discoveries . . . showed anything that reflected dishonor on the men whom they murdered."

Elder Oaks referred to the financial activities of Joseph during the panic and depression of the 1840s. "The enemies of Joseph charged him with fraud in various property conveyances, mostly in behalf of the Church. A succession of court proceedings that extended for nearly a decade examined these claims in meticulous detail. Finally, in 1852, long after the Saints' exodus from Illinois (so there was no conceivable political or other cause for anyone to favor the Prophet), a federal judge concluded this litigation with a decree that found no fraud or other moral impropriety by the Prophet." (See Dallin H. Oaks and Joseph I. Bentley, "Joseph Smith and Legal Process: In the Wake of the Steamboat *Nauvoo*," *BYU Law Review* [1976]:735.) "Independent of the decree, as one who has examined the hundreds of pages of allegations and evidence in these proceedings, I testify to the Prophet's innocence of the charges against him."

"Like other faithful Latter-day Saints, I have built my life on the testimony and mission of the Prophet Joseph Smith. In all of my reading and original research, I have never been dissuaded from my testimony of his prophetic calling and of the gospel and priesthood restoration the Lord initiated through him." (Dallin H. Oaks, "Joseph, the Man and the Prophet," *Ensign*, May 1996, pp. 72-73.)

President Gordon B. Hinckley's Testimony of the Mission of the Prophet Joseph

On June 27, 1993, the 149th anniversary of the martyrdom of the Prophet Joseph Smith, after extensive renovation, the Joseph Smith Memorial Building (formerly the Hotel Utah) was dedicated in Salt Lake City by President Gordon B. Hinckley. Originally to be named the Utah Building, President Hinckley was inspired that the building should memorialize the Prophet Joseph Smith. The First Presidency met with the Quorum of the Twelve Apostles, and they also agreed that it should be named for the Prophet Joseph. The building is intended to preserve and enhance the memory of Joseph Smith. The First Presidency's desire is that those who visit the building will want to become better acquainted with the Prophet Joseph's life and his works.

President Hinckley said, "I think the Lord wanted this building named the Joseph Smith Memorial Building." He referred to the nine-feet tall, heroic-size statute standing in the lobby of the building, saying, "It reminds me of the words I love: 'Praise to the man who communed with Jehovah! Jesus anointed that Prophet and Seer. Blessed to open the last dispensation, Kings shall extol him, and nations revere.'" (*Hymns*, 1985, no. 27.)

"I think of the great words of section 122 of the Doctrine and Covenants, written when the Prophet was in Liberty Jail, after spending five months of that terrible, bitter winter in a dungeon cell. He cried out to the Lord in an hour of distress, 'Oh God, where art thou?' (D&C 121:1.)

"And among the words which came in response to that cry were these: 'The ends of the earth shall inquire after thy name, and fools shall have thee in derision, and hell shall rage against thee;

'While the pure in heart, and the wise, and the noble, and the virtuous, shall seek counsel, and authority, and blessings constantly from under thy hand.

'And thy people shall never be turned against thee by the testimony of traitors.' (D&C 122:1-3.)

"This is another day of fulfillment for that prophecy, my brothers and sisters. I love the Prophet Joseph Smith. I love the Prophet Joseph Smith.

"I bear testimony of the divinity of his calling. There is not a shadow of doubt in my mind of the fact that he was called of God. I know that the conversation which took place in the grove was as intimate and as real and as personal as is my conversation with you this night. I know that. I thank the Prophet for his testimony, for his work, for his life, for his sacrifice, for his witness of the living reality of God our Eternal Father and the risen Lord Jesus Christ." ("A Heroic Figure," *Ensign*, Sept. 1993, p. 38.)

Martyrdom

The last hours of Joseph Smith's life were spent in the Carthage Jail. Joseph asked John Taylor, a fellow inmate, to sing, "A Poor Wayfaring Man of Grief." Hyrum Smith, the prophet's brother, and Willard Richards were also present. The narrative hymn contains a message Joseph wanted the Saints to remember and to follow—to embrace the concept of charity of which Christ spoke by caring for one's neighbor and caring for the poor and needy. Hyrum asked Elder Taylor to sing the song yet again. Shortly after Elder Taylor finished, the mob attacked the jail, murdering the Prophet and his brother on June 27, 1844. (See *HC* 7:101-102.)

Evaluation of Joseph Smith's Mission

It is impossible to weigh the impact of Joseph Smith's life and mission upon the Church and the world. Perhaps he gave the best summary when he said, "I calculate to be one of the instruments of setting up the kingdom of Daniel by the word of the Lord, and I intend to lay a foundation that will revolutionize the whole world . . . be by sword or gun that this kingdom will roll on: the power of truth is such that all nations will be under the necessity of obeying the Gospel." (*HC* 6:365.)

Joseph Smith's Testimony

Joseph Smith was an instrument in the hands of the Lord in opening a new gospel dispensation. He claimed to be—a prophet of the living God. His testimony of the Lord and Savior Jesus Christ stands today as one of the most beautiful and powerful scriptural passages in the Doctrine and Covenants. Speaking of a vision he and Sidney Rigdon had witnessed, he said:

"And now, after the many testimonies which have been given of him, this is the testimony, last of all, which we give of him: That he lives!

"For we saw him even on the right hand of God; and we heard the voice bearing record that he is the Only Begotten of the Father—

"That by him, and through him, and of him, the worlds are and were created, and the inhabitants thereof are begotten sons and daughters unto God." (D&C 76:22-24.)

As Joseph Smith bore testimony of Jesus Christ, so others have testified of him. From the hearts of his mourning people came what might have been his epitaph, but which is a testimony that thousands have echoed since: "Joseph Smith, the Prophet and Seer of the Lord, has done more, save Jesus only, for the salvation of men in this world, than any other man that ever lived in it." (D&C 135:3.)

Teachings of Joseph Smith

Anger. If a spirit of bitterness is in you, don't be in haste. (*HC* 6:315.)

Atonement. That man was not able himself to erect a system or plan with power sufficient to free him from a destruction which awaited him, is evident from the fact that God . . . prepared a sacrifice in the gift of His own Son who should be sent in due time, to prepare a way, or open a door through which man might enter into the Lord's presence, whence he had been cast out for disobedience. From time to time these glad tidings were sounded in the ears of men in different ages of the world down to the time of the Messiah's coming. By faith in this atonement or plan of redemption, Abel offered to God a sacrifice that was accepted, which was the firstlings of the flock. Cain offered of the fruit of the ground and was not accepted, because he could not do it in faith, he could have no faith or could not exercise faith contrary to the plan of heaven. It must be by shedding the blood of the only Begotten to atone for man; for this was the plan of redemption; and without the shedding of blood was no remission. (*HC* 2:15.)

Baptism. Baptism is a sign to God, angels, and to heaven that we do the will of God, and there is no other way beneath the heavens whereby God had ordained for man to come to Him to be saved and enter into the kingdom of God, except faith in Jesus Christ, repentance, and baptism for the remission of sins, and any other course is in vain; then you have the promise of the gift of the Holy Ghost. (*HC* 4:554-555.)

Book of Mormon. I told the brethren that the Book of Mormon was the most correct of any book on earth, and the keystone of our religion, and a man would get nearer to God by abiding by its precepts, than by any other book. (*TPJS*, p. 194.)

Constitution. The Constitution of the United States is a glorious standard; it is founded in the wisdom of God. (*TPJS*, p. 147.)

Eternal Progression. God himself, finding he was in the midst of spirits and glory, because he was more intelligent, saw proper to institute laws whereby the rest could have a privilege to advance like himself. (*HC* 6:312.)

Faith. Faith comes by hearing the word of God through the testimony of the servants of God; that testimony is always attended by the Spirit of prophecy and revelation. (*HC* 3:379.)

Genealogy. The greatest responsibility in this world that God has laid upon us is to seek after our dead. (*TPJS*, p. 356.) Those saints who neglect it in behalf of their deceased relatives, do it at the peril of their own salvation. (*TPJS*, p. 193.)

God the Father. God himself was once as we are now, and is an exalted man, and sits enthroned in yonder heavens! That is the great secret. If the veil were rent today, and the great God who holds this world in orbit, and who upholds all worlds and all things by His power, was to make himself visible—I say, if you were to see him today, you would see him like man in form—like yourselves in all the person, image, and very form as a man, for Adam was created in the very fashion, image and likeness of God, and received instruction from, and walked, talked and conversed with Him, as one man talks and communes with another. . . . It is the first principle of the gospel to know for certain the character of God, and to know that we may converse with Him as one man converses with another, and He was once a man like us, yea, and that God himself, the Father of us all, dwelt on an earth, the same as Jesus Christ Himself did. (*HC* 6:305.)

God the Father. If you wish to go where God is, you must be like God, or possess the principles which God possesses, for if we are not drawing towards God in principle, we are going from Him and drawing towards the devil. Yes, I am standing in the midst of all kinds of people. Search your hearts, and see if you are like God. I have searched mine, and feel to repent of all my sins. (*TPJS*, p. 216.)

Happiness. Happiness is the object and design of our existence; and will be the end thereof, if we pursue the path that leads to it; and this path is virtue, uprightness, faithfulness, holiness, and keeping all the commandments of God. But we cannot keep all the commandments without first knowing them. (*TPJS*, p. 255-56.)

Holy Ghost. The gift of the Holy Ghost by the laying on of hands cannot be received through the medium of any other principle than the principle of righteousness, for if the proposals are not complied with, it is of no use, but withdraws. (*HC* 3:379.)

Human Rights. If it has been demonstrated that I have been willing to die for a "Mormon," I am bold to declare before heaven that I am just as ready to die in defending the rights of a Presbyterian, a Baptist, or a good man of any other denomination; for the same principle which tramples upon the right of the Latter-day Saints would trample upon the right of the Roman Catholics, or of any other denomination who may be unpopular and too weak to defend themselves. It is the love of liberty which inspires—civil and religious liberty to the whole of the human race. Love of liberty was diffused into my soul by my grandfathers while they dangled me on their knees. (*HC* 5:498.)

Knowledge. A man is saved no faster than he gets knowledge. (*HC* 4:588.)

Knowledge. I could explain a hundred fold more than I ever have of the glories of the kingdoms manifested to me in the vision, were I permitted, and were the people prepared to receive them. (*TPJS,* p. 305.)

Liberty. Sacred is the memory of that blood which bought for us our liberty. (*HC* 3:9.)

Love. Love is one of the chief characteristics of Deity, and ought to be manifested by those who aspire to be the sons of God. A man filled with the love of God, is not content with blessing his family, but ranges through the whole world, anxious to bless the whole human race. (*HC* 4:227.)

Loving Others. It is a duty which every Saint ought to render to his brethren freely—to always love them, and ever succor them. To be justified before God, we must love one another; we must overcome evil; we must visit the fatherless and widow in their affliction, and we must keep ourselves unspotted from the world; for such virtues flow from the great fountain of pure religion, strengthening our faith by adding every good quality that adorns the children of the blessed Jesus, we can pray in the season of prayer; we can love our neighbor as ourselves, and be faithful in tribulation, knowing that the reward of such is greater in the kingdom of heaven. What a consolation! What a joy! Let me live the life of the righteous, and let my reward be like his! (*TPJS*, p. 76.)

Missionary Work. No unhallowed hand can stop the work from progressing; persecutions may rage, mobs may combine, armies may assemble, calumny may defame, but the truth of God will go forth boldly, nobly, and independent, till it has penetrated every continent, visited every clime, swept every country, and sounded in every ear, till the purposes of God shall be accomplished, and the Great Jehovah shall say the work is done. (*HC* 4:540-41.)

Obedience. I made this my rule: When the Lord commands, do it. (*HC* 2:170.)

Persecution. Those who cannot endure persecution, and stand in the day of affliction, cannot stand in the day when the Son of God shall burst the veil, and appear in all the glory of His Father, with all the holy angels. (*HC* 1:468.)

Plan of Salvation. At the first organization in heaven we were all present, and saw the Savior chosen and appointed and the plan of salvation made, and we sanctioned it. (*TPJS*, p. 181.)

Prayer. Seek to know God in your closets, call upon him in the fields. Follow the directions of the Book of Mormon, and pray over, and for your families, your cattle, your flocks, your herds, your corn, and all things that you possess; ask the blessings of God upon all your labors and everything that you engage in. Be virtuous and pure; be men of integrity and truth; keep the commandments of God; and then you will be able more perfectly to understand the difference between right and wrong—between the things of God and the things of men. (*TPJS*, p. 247.)

Priesthood, Melchizedek. [The Melchizedek Priesthood] is the channel through which all knowledge, doctrine, the plan of salvation and every important matter is revealed from heaven. (*HC* 4:207.)

Principles. I teach the people correct principles and they govern themselves. (Quoted by John Taylor, *JD* 10:57-58.)

Progression. When you climb up a ladder, you must begin at the bottom, and ascend step by step, until you arrive at the top; and so it is with the principles of the Gospel—you must begin with the first, and go on until you learn the principles of exaltation. But it will be a great while after you have passed through the veil before you will have learned them. (*TPJS*, p. 348.)

Repentance. Daily transgression and daily repentance is not that which is pleasing in the sight of God. (*HC* 3:379.)

Resurrection. All your losses will be made up to you in the resurrection, provided you continue faithful. By the vision of the Almighty I have seen it. (*DC* 5:362.)

Revelation. A person may profit by noticing the first intimation of the spirit of revelation; for instance, when you feel pure intelligence flowing into you, it may give you sudden strokes of ideas, so that by noticing it, you may find it fulfilled the same day or soon; (i.e.) those things that were presented unto your minds by the Spirit of God, will come to pass; and thus by learning the Spirit of God and understanding it, you may grow into the principle of revelation, until you become perfect in Christ Jesus. (*HC* 3:381.)

Salvation. When we have power to put all enemies under our feet in this world, and a knowledge to triumph over all evil spirits in the world to come, then we are saved. (*HC* 5:387.)

Satan. All beings who have bodies have power over those who have not. The devil has no power over us only as we permit him. The moment we revolt at anything which comes from God, the devil takes over. (*TPJS*, p. 181.)

Sealing. When a seal is put upon the father and mother, it secures their posterity, so that they cannot be lost, but will be saved by virtue of the covenant of their father and mother. (*HC* 5:530.)

Service. All I can offer the world is a good heart and a good hand. (*HC* 5:498.)

Smith, Hyrum. Brother Hyrum, what a faithful heart you have got! Oh may the Eternal Jehovah crown eternal blessings upon your head, as a reward for the care you have had for my soul! O how many are the sorrows we have shared together; and again we find ourselves shackled with the unrelenting hand of oppression. Hyrum, thy name shall be written in the book of the Law of the Lord, for those who come after thee to look upon, that they may pattern after thy works.

I could pray in my heart that all my brethren were like unto my beloved brother Hyrum, who possesses the mildness of a lamb, and the integrity of a Job, and in short, the meekness and humility of Christ; and I love him with that love that is stronger than death, for I never had occasion to rebuke him,

nor he me, which he declared when he left me today. (Smith, *DS* 1:219-220.)

Spirit. The spirit is a substance; that it is material, but that it is more pure, elastic and refined matter than the body; that it existed before the body, can exist in the body; and will exist separate from the body, when the body will be mouldering in the dust; and will in the resurrection, be again united with it. (*HC* 4:575.)

Spirits. We may look for angels and receive their ministrations, but we are to try the spirits and prove them, for it is often the case that men make a mistake in regard to these things. God has so ordained that when He has communicated, no vision is to be taken but what you see by the seeing of the eye, or what you hear by the hearing of the ear. When you see a vision, pray for the interpretation; if you get not this, shut it up; there must be certainty in this matter. An open vision will manifest that which is more important. Lying spirits are going forth in the earth. There will be great manifestations of spirits, both false and true. (*HC* 3:391.)

Testimony. The fundamental principles of our religion are the testimony of the Apostles and Prophets, concerning Jesus Christ, that He died, was buried, and rose again the third day, and ascended into heaven; and all other things which pertain to our religion are only appendages to it. (*HC* 3:30.)

Tolerance. We claim the privilege of worshiping Almighty God according to the dictates of our own conscience, and allow all men the same privilege, let them worship how, where, or what they may. (Eleventh Article of Faith.)

Truth. We should gather all the good and true principles in the world and treasure them up, or we shall not come out true "Mormons." (*HC* 5:517.)

Women. Our women have always been signalized for their acts of benevolence and kindness. They have always been ready to open their doors to the weary traveler, to divide their scant pittance with the hungry and from their robbed and impoverished wardrobes, to divide with the more needy and destitute. (*HC* 4:567.)

BRIGHAM YOUNG
1801-1877
Second President

- **Born**: June 1, 1801, in Whitingham, Vermont

- **Family**: Brigham Young was the son of John and Abigail Howe Young, the ninth of eleven children. Brigham married Miriam Works, Mary Ann Angell, and twenty-three other women, sixteen of whom bore a total of fifty-seven children. (Arrington, *Brigham Young: American Moses*, pp. 420-21.)

- **Baptism**: At age 30, on April 14, 1832, in his own mill pond near Mendon, New York

- **Missions**: New York and Canada (1832-33), New York (1835), Canada and New England (1836); Great Britain (1839-41), and the Eastern States (1843).

- **Education**: Self-educated, School of the Prophets, apprenticeship

- **Occupation**: Carpenter, glazier, painter, landscaper, pioneer, colonizer, Governor of Utah Territory (1850-1857), businessman (mills, farms).

- **Church Callings:** Apostle, missionary, Church business agent

- **Apostle**: Ordained by the Three Witnesses on February 14, 1835 (served 12½ years; age 33-46)

- **President of the Quorum of the Twelve**: April 14, 1840, to December 27, 1847 (served 7 years)

- **Senior Apostle**: June 27, 1844, to December 27, 1847 (3½ years)

- **President of the Church**: December 27, 1847, to August 29, 1877 (served 30 years; age 46-76)

- **General Authority**: Served 42½ years. He served the shortest period of time as an apostle before becoming President (12 years) and the longest period as President (30 years). He ordained three of his sons apostles: Brigham Young, Jr. (1864),

who was sustained to the Quorum of the Twelve (1868), and served as an additional or assistant counselor in the First Presidency; Joseph Angell Young (1864), though not a member of the Quorum of the Twelve; John W. Young (1864), though not a member of the Quorum of the Twelve, was sustained as an additional or assistant counselor, and later as First Counselor in the First Presidency.

- **Temples Dedicated**: Two: Nauvoo (1846) and St. George (1877).

- **A Favorite Hymn**: "O Ye Mountains High"

- **Selected Teachings**: *Journal of Discourses* (contains 400 of his addresses) and *Discourses of Brigham Young*

- **Special Interests and Hobbies**: acting in plays, attending Salt Lake Theatre, dancing, and singing duets with his brother Joseph

- **Other Responsibilities While President**: Served as governor from 1849 when the provisional State of Deseret was organized; served as Governor of the Territory of Utah (1850-1857), and served as Superintendent of Indian Affairs of Utah.

- **Appearance, Personality, and Qualities**: He was five-feet, ten inches tall, weighed 185-200 pounds, wore a beard after the 1850s, and had a rugged and stocky physique. He was a stickler for self-discipline and self-control; was humble, modest and loyal; had a great talent for selecting men and women who would be useful in the kingdom. He had a marked ability for organization, and his courageous steadfastness earned for him the title "Lion of the Lord." Biographer Leonard J. Arrington calls him an "American Moses." Brigham Young emphasized the connection between religion, happiness, and the quality of one's daily labor, encouraged kind treatment of Indians, and respected animals and nature. His dramatic power and sincerity made him a natural and forceful speaker.

- **Note**: In 1940, Twentieth Century Fox produced a movie, *Brigham Young—Frontiersman*, starring Dean Jagger as Brigham Young. Mr. Jagger became a Church member in 1971, thirty-one years later. Brigham Young's statue is in the National Statuary Hall in the Capitol Building, Washington, D.C. He is recognized as one of the great American colonizers of the nineteenth century.

- **Died**: August 29, 1877, of ruptured appendix, Salt Lake City, Utah (age 76)

- **1877**: Members: 115,065 Stakes: 20
  Missions: 8 Temples: 2
  Missionaries: 250
  General Authorities: 26

Biographical Highlights

Born into a poor family, Brigham Young received only eleven days of formal schooling, but through hard work became a skilled craftsman in the building trades. After studying the Book of Mormon for two years, he was baptized in 1832. He traveled to Kirtland to meet the Prophet Joseph Smith, whom he found chopping firewood. "Here my joy was full at the privilege of shaking the hand of the Prophet of God, and receiving the sure testimony by the spirit of prophecy, that he was all any man could believe him to be as a true prophet." (*HC* 1:297.) This was the beginning of a great friendship and love he had for the Prophet Joseph Smith. The testimony he received was never shaken despite many difficult experiences.

Brigham Young provided dynamic leadership in

Kirtland during the apostasy of 1838. The Saints had just survived the winter exodus from Missouri to settle on a bend of the Mississippi River in Illinois, where they contended with hunger, disease, poverty, and a shortage of materials. Brigham Young and his fellow apostles were called to leave their destitute families to preach the gospel in Great Britain. Brigham reported: "My health was so poor I was unable to go thirty rods without assistance. I left my wife sick, with a babe only ten days old, and all my children sick and unable to wait upon each other." (*MS* 25:646.)

In 1846, when 16,000 Latter-day Saints were driven from Nauvoo, Illinois, Brigham Young led them to the Salt Lake Valley. Wagon trains and handcart companies moved more than 70,000 Saints to the Great Basin between 1847 and 1869. Brigham is ranked as one of the great American colonizers; nearly 360 LDS settlements were founded during his administration. He was the founder of many enterprises, industries, and factories in the West, and he encouraged the building of roads, canals, railroads, schools, temples, hospitals, mills, theaters, and railroads.

Brigham Young took a strong interest in the Native Americans among whom the Saints had settled. His theme was patience and forbearance. He called missionaries to establish Indian farms, and he took orphaned Indian children into his own home. He advocated a policy of feeding the Indians and befriending them and held periodic meetings with Indian chiefs. "The main elements in these attempts to make the Indians more civilized included— besides farming and religion—living in houses, literacy, paying for what they received, and adopting Christian morals." (Arrington, *Brigham Young: American Moses*, p. 220.)

He encouraged excellence and refinement in every aspect of the lives of his followers, encouraged the arts, and founded the Salt Lake Theatre. He promoted fine craftsmanship of temples, tabernacles, public buildings, and homes.

In 1850, he established the University of Deseret in Salt Lake City (later the University of Utah); in 1875, he established Brigham Young Academy in Provo (later Brigham Young University); in 1876, he founded Brigham Young College (Logan, Utah) and the Latter-day Saints College in Salt Lake City (now LDS Business College).

Other accomplishments include the organization of the State of Deseret, 1849; the establishment of the Perpetual Emigrating Fund, 1849; the territory-wide organization of the Sunday School, 1849; the public announcement of plural marriage, 1852; the Salt Lake Tabernacle, 1867; and the founding of organizations for Mormon youth (YWMIA in 1869 and YMMIA in 1875). In 1874 he promoted the United Order movement in an effort to encourage cooperation, home production, and consumption. Among the first to receive an endowment in 1842, Brigham continued the Prophet Joseph's program of temple ordinances as a high priority among the people. (Endowments were given outside the temple until December 1845 and in Salt Lake at the Endowment House until 1876.)

"Brigham's most obvious achievements were the product of his lifelong talent for practical decision making. He instituted patterns of Church government that persist to this day. In leading the Saints across the Iowa plains, he issued detailed instructions that were followed by the hundreds of companies that crossed the plains to the Salt Lake Valley in succeeding years. In the Great Basin he directed the organization of several LDS settlements; set up several hundred cooperative retail, wholesale, and manufacturing enterprises; and initiated the construction of meetinghouses, tabernacles, and temples. While doing all this, he carried on a running battle with the United States government to preserve the unique LDS way of life.

"His overriding concern was to build on the foundation begun by Joseph Smith to establish a commonwealth in the desert where his people could live the gospel of Jesus Christ in peace, thereby improving their prospects in this life and in the next. He loved the Great Basin because its harshness and isolation made it an ideal place to 'make Saints.'" (Arrington, "Brigham Young," *EnM* 4:1609.)

President Young inaugurated changes directly affecting the operation of the Church on the local level. He released members of the Council of the Twelve from presiding over local units, reorganized stakes, defined the duties of the Apostles, mandated that a bishopric consist of high priests, and ex-

tended the Aaronic Priesthood systematically to teenage boys. In 1877, the First Presidency issued a guidebook that was the codification of priesthood principles necessary to operating stakes, wards, and quorums. It was the most comprehensive policy statement about priesthood practices since the Doctrine and Covenants was first published. It served then much like the bishops' and stake presidents' handbooks serve today and was carefully and often referred to by local leaders. (See William G. Hartley, "The Priesthood Reorganization of 1877: Brigham Young's Last Achievement," *BYU Studies*, Fall 1979, pp. 20-21.)

Brigham Young taught that home and family were not the only ways women could contribute. He actively encouraged women to develop their talents in some professional field such as medicine, journalism, law, physics, and bookkeeping. Jill Mulvay Derr, a research historian at BYU, wrote: "Young showed an interest in involving women in higher education. . . . Young never stopped prescribing a sphere of activity for women, but over a period of years, the sphere he prescribed became wider and wider. . . . The status of women decidedly improved during the administration of President Brigham Young. His reorganization of the Relief Society launched women into an era of public activity that involved them in business and gave them new economic status in a community that was itself concerned with economic identity." (Jill Mulvay Derr in *Lion of the Lord*, pp. 330-331; see also quotations on women by Brigham Young in this section under "Teachings.")

Brigham Young saw the advantage of the railroad and through his efforts brought rail service to the Mormon communities of Utah and Idaho. The railroad helped missionary travel and convert emigration and transported large granite blocks to the building site of the Salt Lake Temple. The living standards of the Saints improved as furniture, machinery, and other commodities were thus transported more quickly and cheaply. (John J. Stewart, "The Railroad Builder," in *Lion of the Lord*, ed. Black and Porter, p. 289.)

Evaluation of Brigham Young

"The true stature of Brigham Young emerges if one seeks to compose a list of his peers. He led a ragged and impoverished band, stripped of virtually all their earthly goods, into an unknown territory. His critics and biographers note that the man was unique among the leaders of modern history for he alone, without any political and financial backing, established from scratch in the desert an ordered and industrious society, having no other authority than the priesthood and the spiritual strength with which he delivered his teachings. By constant exhortations and instructions, he drew his people together and inspired them in carrying out the divine mandate to build up the kingdom of God on earth." (Hugh W. Nibley, "Teachings of Brigham Young," *EnM* 4:1611.)

While serving a mission to England, he arrived there without money, but his mission was a great success. "But through the mercy of God we have gained many friends, established churches in almost every noted town and city in the kingdom of Great Britain, baptized between seven and eight thousand souls, printed five thousand Books of Mormon, three thousand hymnbooks, twenty-five hundred volumes of the Millennial Star, and six thousand tracts, and emigrated to Zion one thousand souls. (*MS* 6:7.)

Training to Become the Leader of the Church

The Prophet Joseph said, "The time will come when Brother Brigham Young will preside over the Church." (*JD* 3:51.) Brigham Young was a man of great faith, courage, and optimism, and he was willing to endure many hardships for the gospel. These experiences trained him to assume leadership of the Church.

Brigham was given leadership positions early, and his responsibilities, which continually increased, included being a captain in Zion's Camp, a confidant of the Prophet Joseph, a member of the Twelve, the organizer of the Missouri exodus, the President of the Twelve, and the presiding elder of the English mission.

Brigham Young's Speeches

During his extensive service as President of the Church, he delivered hundreds, if not thousands, of extemporaneous speeches on a wide range of topics—such as how to utilize the untapped re-

sources and talents given to us by the Lord; the atonement of Christ; women's fashions; recollections of Joseph Smith; how to form a righteous society; and how to return to the presence of God. His consistent purpose was to motivate the Saints to action and inspire them to live their religion.

Brigham Young's Testimony

"I testify that there is a God, and that Jesus Christ lives, and that he is the Savior of the world. Have you been to heaven and learned to the contrary? I know that Joseph Smith was a Prophet of God, and that he had many revelations. Who can disprove this testimony? Anyone may dispute it. I have had many revelations; I have seen and heard for myself, and know these things are true, and nobody on earth can disprove them. The eye, the ear, the hand, all the senses may be deceived, but the Spirit of God cannot be deceived. When inspired with that Spirit the whole man or woman is filled with knowledge, he can see with a spiritual eye, and he knows that which is beyond the power of man to controvert. What I know concerning God, concerning the earth, concerning government, I have received from the heavens, not alone through my natural ability, and I give God the glory and the praise. Men talk about what has been accomplished under my direction, and attribute it to my wisdom and ability; but it is all by the power of God, and by intelligence received from him." (*JD* 16:46.)

Teachings of Brigham Young

Agency. All intelligent beings are . . . endowed with certain inalienable rights, privileges, and powers inherent in them. When God organized intelligent beings, He organized them as independent beings to a certain extent, as He is Himself. And whether we see an evil act or a good act performed by an intelligent being, that being has performed the act by his will, by his own independent organization, which is capable of doing good or evil, of choosing light or darkness. (*JD* 6:146.)

Anger. If you find passion coming on you, go off to some place where you cannot be heard; let none of your family see you or hear you, while it is upon you, but struggle till it leaves you; and pray for strength to overcome. (*JD* 11:290.)

Atonement. I ask, is there a reason for men and women being exposed more constantly and more powerfully, to the power of the enemy, by having visions than by not having them? There is and it is simply this—God never bestows upon his people, or upon an individual, superior blessings without a severe trial to prove them, to prove that individual, or that people, to see whether they will keep their covenants with Him, and keep in remembrance what He has shown them. Then the greater the vision, the greater the display of the power of the enemy. And when such individuals are off their guard they are left to themselves, as Jesus was. For this express purpose the Father withdrew His spirit from His son, at the time he was to be crucified. Jesus had been with his Father, talked with Him, dwelt in His bosom, and knew all about heaven, about making the earth, about the transgression of man, and what would redeem the people, and that he was the character who was to redeem the sons of earth, and the earth itself from all sin that had come upon it. The light, knowledge, power, and glory with which he was clothed were far above, or exceeded that of all others who had been upon the earth after the fall, consequently at the very moment, at the hour when the crisis came for him to offer up his life, the Father withdrew Himself, withdrew His Spirit, and cast a veil over him. That is what made him sweat blood. If he had the power of God upon him, he would not have sweat blood; but all was withdrawn from him, and a veil was cast over him, and he then plead with the Father not to forsake him. "No," says the Father, "you must have your trials, as well as others." (*JD* 3:205-206.)

Children. Bring up your children in the love and fear of the Lord; study their dispositions and their temperaments, deal with them accordingly, never allowing yourself to correct them in the heat of passion; teach them to love you rather than to fear you. (*DBY*, p. 207.)

Death. We shall turn round and look upon it (the valley of death) and think, when we have crossed it, why this is the greatest advantage of my whole existence, for I have passed from a state of sorrow, grief, mourning, woe, misery, pain, anguish and disappointment into a state of existence, where I can enjoy life to the fullest extent as far as that can be done without a body. My spirit is set free, I thirst no more, I want to sleep no more, I hunger no more, I tire no more, I run, I walk, I labor, I go, I come, I do this, I do that, whatever is required of me, nothing like pain or weariness, I am full of life, full of vigor, and I enjoy the presence of my Heavenly Father, by the power of His Spirit. . . .The spirits of the living that depart this life go into the world of spirits, and if the Lord withdraws the veil it is much easier for us then to behold the face of our Father who is in heaven than when we are clothed upon with this mortality. (*JD* 17:142.)

Duty. For heaven's sake, for your own sake, and for the sake of Him who died for us, never let us falter in our duty. While we live, it is our duty to love the Lord with all our might, and with all our strength, and with all our souls. This is our duty first and foremost: we ought to love Him better than our wives, children, and brethren and sisters, and all things besides. Is this our duty? Verily yes. Let the heart love God, and serve Him, without any division of feeling: never suffer it to wander to the right or to the left for one moment. (*JD* 1:32.)

Education. Education is the power to think clearly, the power to act well in the world's work, and the power to appreciate life. (*IE*, July 1920, p. 831.)

Endowment. Your endowment is to receive all those ordinances in the House of the Lord which are necessary for you, after you have departed this life, to enable you to walk back to the presence of the Father, passing the angels who stand as sentinels, being enabled to give them the key words, the signs and tokens, pertaining to the holy priesthood and gain your eternal exaltation in spite of earth and hell. (*DBY*, p. 416.)

Environment. Beautify your gardens, your homes, your farms; beautify the city. This will make us happy, and produce plenty. This earth is a good earth, the elements are good if we will use them for our own benefit, in truth and righteousness. Then let us be content, and go to with our mights to make ourselves healthy, wealthy, and beautiful, and preserve ourselves in the best possible manner, and live just as long as we can, and do all the good we can. (*DBY*, p. 302.)

Eternal Progression. We do not expect to cease learning while we live on earth, and when we pass through the veil, we expect still to continue to learn. (*JD* 6:286.)

Gifts of the Spirit. The gifts of the Gospel are given to strengthen the faith of the believer. (*JD* 10:324.)

God the Father. But the Lord is our God and it is He whom we serve; and we say to the whole world that He is a tangible Being. We have a God with ears, eyes, nose, mouth; He can and does speak. He has arms, hands, body, legs and feet; He talks and walks; and we are formed after His likeness. The good book—the Bible, tells us what kind of a character our Heavenly Father is. In the first chapter of Genesis and the 17th verse, speaking of the Lord creating men, it reads as plain as it can read, and He created man in His own image and likeness; and if He created Adam and Eve in His own image, the whole human family are like Him. (*JD* 13:308.)

Good/Evil. People are liable in many ways to be led astray by the power of the adversary, for they do not fully understand that it is a hard matter for them to always distinguish the things of God from the things of the devil. There is but one way by which they can know the difference, and that is by the light of the spirit of revelation, even the spirit of our Lord Jesus Christ. Without this we are all liable to be led astray and forsake our brethren, forsake our covenants and the Church and kingdom of God on earth. . . . Consequently, it becomes us, as Saints, to cleave to the Lord with all our hearts, and seek unto Him until we do enjoy the light of His Spirit, that we may discern between the righteous and the wicked, and understand the difference between false spirits and true. (*JD* 3:43-44.)

Gospel. What is this work? The improvement of the condition of the human family. This work must continue until the people who live on this earth are prepared to receive our coming Lord. (*JD* 19:46.)

Happiness. When man is industrious and righteous, then is he happy. (*JD* 9:244.)

Holy Ghost. Cast all bitterness out of your own hearts—all anger, wrath, strife, covetousness, and lust, and sanctify the Lord God in your hearts, that you may enjoy the Holy Ghost. (*JD* 8:33.)

Honesty. Simple truth, simplicity, honesty, uprightness, justice, mercy, love, kindness, do good to all and evil to none, how easy it is to live by such principles! A thousand times easier than to practice deception! (*JD* 14:76.)

Jesus Christ. The greatest and most important of all requirements of our Father in heaven and of his son Jesus Christ . . . is to believe in Jesus Christ, confess him, seek to him, cling to him, make friends with him. Take a course to open a communication with your Elder Brother or file-leader—our Saviour. (*JD* 8:339.)

Money. If you wish to get rich, save what you get. A fool can earn money; but it takes a wise man to save and dispose of it to his own advantage. (*JD* 11:310.)

Mortality. The whole mortal existence of man is neither more nor less than a preparatory state given to finite beings, a space wherein they may improve themselves for a higher state of being. (*JD* 1:334.)

Motherhood. Woman has her influence, and she should use that in training her children in the way they should go; if she fails to do this she assumes fearful responsibilities. (*JD* 14:106.)

Music. We cannot preach the gospel without good music. (Cornwall, *A Century of Singing—The Salt Lake Tabernacle Choir*, p. 25.)

Obedience. The Lord has sent forth his laws, commandments, and ordinances to the children of men, and requires them to be strictly obeyed, and we do not wish to transgress those laws, but to keep them. We do not wish to change his ordinances, but to observe them; we do not wish to break the everlasting covenant, but to keep that with our fathers, with Jesus, with our Father in Heaven, with holy angels, and to live according to them. (*DBY*, p. 220.)

Parents (example for children). My remarks will be to parents as well as to children. I will commence by saying that if each and every one of us who are parents will reflect upon the responsibilities devolving upon us we shall come to the conclusion that we should never permit ourselves to do anything that we are not willing to see our children do. We should set them an example that we wish them to imitate. Do we realize this? How often we see parents demand obedience, good behavior, kind words, pleasant looks, a sweet voice and a bright eye from a child or children when they themselves are full of bitterness and scolding! How inconsistent and unreasonable this is! If we wish our children to look pleasant we should look pleasant at them; and if we wish them to speak kind words to each other, let us speak kind words to them. We need not go into detail, but we should carry out this principle from year to year in our whole lives, and do as we wish our children to do. I say this with regard to our morals and our faith in our religion. (*JD* 14:192.)

Perfection. We can alter the phraseology of the sentence [Matt. 5:48] and say, "Be ye as perfect as ye can" for that is all we can do, though it is written, be ye as perfect as your Father who is in heaven is perfect. . . . The sin that will cleave to all the posterity of Adam and Eve is, that they have not done as well as they know how. (*JD* 2:129.)

Prayer. It matters not whether you or I feel like praying, when the time comes to pray, pray. If we do not feel like it, we should pray till we do. . . . You will find that those who wait till the Spirit bids them pray, will never pray much on this earth. (*JD* 13:155.)

Priesthood. If anybody wants to know what the priesthood of the Son of God is, it is the law by which the worlds are, were, and will continue forever and ever. It is that system which brings worlds into existence and peoples them, gives them their revolutions—their days, weeks, months, years, their seasons and times and by which they are rolled up as a scroll, as it were, and go into a higher state of existence. (*JD* 15:127.)

Recreation. Recreation and diversion are as necessary to our well-being as the more serious pursuits of life. There is not a man [or woman] in the world but what, if kept at any one branch of business or study, will become like a machine. Our pursuits should be diversified as to develop every trait of character and diversity of talent. (*DBY*, p. 238.)

Self-Control. The greatest mystery a man ever learned, is to know how to control the human mind,

and bring every faculty and power of the same in subjection to Jesus Christ; this is the greatest mystery we have to learn while in these tabernacles of clay. (*JD* 1:46-47.)

Smith, Joseph. Joseph Smith holds the keys of this last dispensation, and is now engaged behind the veil in the great work of the last days. . . . No man or woman in this dispensation will ever enter into the celestial kingdom of God without the consent of Joseph Smith. . . . He holds the keys of that kingdom for the last dispensation—the keys to rule in the spirit-world; and he rules there triumphantly. (*JD* 7:289-90.)

Trials. The lifetime of man is a day of trial, wherein we may prove to God, in our darkness, in our weakness, and where the enemy reigns, that we are our Father's friends and that we receive light from him and are worthy to be leaders of our children. (*JD* 8:61.)

Truth. "Mormonism," so-called, embraces every principle pertaining to life and salvation, for time and eternity. No matter who has it. If the infidel has got truth it belongs to "Mormonism." The truth and sound doctrine possessed by the sectarian world, and they have a great deal, all belong to this Church. As for their morality, many of them are, morally, just as good as we are. All that is good, lovely, and praiseworthy belongs to this Church and Kingdom. "Mormonism" includes all truth. There is no truth but what belongs to the gospel. It is life, eternal life; it is bliss; it is the fulness of all things in the gods and in the eternities of the gods. (*DBY*, p. 3.)

Women. We have sisters here who, if they had the privilege of studying, would make just as good mathematicians or accountants as any man; and we think they ought to have the privilege to study these branches of knowledge that they may develop the powers with which they are endowed. We believe that women are useful, not only to sweep houses, wash dishes, make beds, and raise babies, but that they should stand behind the counter, study law or physic, or become good bookkeepers and be able to do the business in any counting house, and all this to enlarge their sphere of usefulness for the benefit of society at large. (*JD* 13:61.)

JOHN TAYLOR
1808-1887
Third President

- **Born**: November 1, 1808, in Milnthorpe, England

- **Family**: John Taylor was the son of John and Agnes Taylor, the second of ten children. John married Leonora Cannon, Elizabeth Kaighin, Jane Ballantyne, Mary Ann Oakley, Sophia Whitaker, Harriet Whitaker, and Margaret Young; had a total of thirty-five children.

- **Baptism**: May 9, 1836, at age 27, baptized along with Leonora in Black Creek at Georgetown, Ontario, Canada

- **Missions**: Great Britain (1839-41); France and Germany (1849-52); Utah (1854-55); Eastern States (1855-57)

- **Education**: English private schools, School of the Prophets, self-educated

- **Occupation**: Farmer, woodturner, publisher, writer

- **Church Callings:** Supervision of the Church in Canada, apostle, missionary, mission president

- **Apostle**: Ordained by Brigham Young on December 19, 1838 (served 41 years; age 30-71)

- **President of the Quorum of the Twelve**: October 6, 1877, to October 10, 1880 (served 3 years)

- **Senior Apostle**: August 29, 1877, to October 10, 1880 (3 years)

- **President of the Church**: October 10, 1880, to July 25, 1887 (served 7 years; age 71-78). First President to assume office at an advanced age.

- **General Authority**: Served 48½ years. He set apart his son William W. Taylor as a member of the First Council of Seventy (1880); he ordained his son John W. Taylor an apostle (1884).

- **Temple Dedicated**: Logan (1884)

- **Motto**: The Kingdom of God or nothing.

- **Favorite Hymns**: "A Poor Wayfaring Man of Grief." He wrote two hymns: "Go, Ye Messengers of Glory" and "Go, Ye Messengers of Heaven" (He had a beautiful singing voice.)

- **Selected Teachings**: *The Gospel Kingdom; The Mediation and Atonement of Our Lord and Savior Jesus Christ;* and *The Government of God*

- **Special Interests and Hobbies**: carpentry, architecture, engineering, construction, writing poetry, and singing hymns

- **Scripture**: His tribute to Joseph and Hyrum Smith and official announcement of their martyrdom became Section 135 of the Doctrine and Covenants

- **Appearance, Personality, and Qualities**: He was five-feet, eleven inches tall, weighed 180 pounds, wore a beard, was affable, and used correct language. He was polite and dignified in demeanor and fastidious in dress; he was gracious, reserved, cultivated, a man of integrity and self-confidence. He enjoyed telling stories, had a keen sense of humor, and had a hearty laugh that shook his entire body. His vigorous opposition to the tyranny of persecution in Nauvoo gained him the title "Champion of Liberty." He was called "Defender of the Faith" and became known as a living martyr.

- **Died**: July 25, 1887, probably of kidney failure while living in seclusion in Kaysville, Utah; eulogized as a "double martyr" for his near-fatal wounds in Carthage Jail and for his refusal to compromise his religious principles (age 78).

- **1887**: Members: 173,029   Stakes: 31
  Missions: 12   Temples: 2
  Missionaries: 282
  General Authorities: 28

Biographical Highlights

Devoutly religious, John Taylor experienced spiritual manifestations as a youth. He joined the Methodists, left England, and emigrated to Canada at age twenty-four, where he was converted to the gospel in 1836. He moved to Kirtland, Ohio, then to Missouri, and finally to Nauvoo.

When John Taylor left for his mission to England in 1839, he left his family in desperate circumstances, and he was sick for eleven weeks en route. However, with Brigham Young, Wilford Woodruff, and others, he saw almost six thousand people join the Church.

He became an American citizen in 1849. He was an ingenious mechanic; he built and worked one of the first saw mills in Utah, and he also learned how to make furniture. While serving a mission in France, he learned the beet sugar process, which he later introduced to Utah. He served as an associate judge of the provisional State of Deseret and as a member of the Utah territorial legislature for twenty years. For five successive sessions, President Taylor was Speaker of the House. In 1876, he was elected territorial superintendent of schools. He was the first President of the Church to have a significant formal education and is the only one born outside the United States.

John Taylor directed much of his administration while in exile, seeking to avoid arrest due to the U.S. government's persecution of the Saints because of their stand on plural marriage. He instructed polygamous Saints to establish places of refuge, and they did so in Mexico and Canada. President Taylor experienced many adversities as a messenger of the Lord. His response was:

"So far as I am concerned, I say, let everything come as God has ordained it. I do not desire trials. I do not desire affliction. I would pray to God to 'lead me not in[to] temptation, and deliver me from evil; for thine is the kingdom, the power, and the glory.' But if the earthquake bellows, the lightnings flash, the thunders roll, and the powers of darkness are let loose, and the spirit of evil is permitted to rage, and an evil influence is brought to bear on the Saints, and my life, with theirs is put to the test, let it come, for we are the Saints of the most High God, and all is well, all is peace, all is right, and will be, both in time and in eternity." (*GK*, pp. 332-33.)

As President of the Twelve, John Taylor organized the Primary in 1878. During the Jubilee celebration of the Church that same year, he saw that many who owed the Perpetual Emigrating Fund were forgiven of their debts. (The Perpetual Emigrating Fund Company was organized in 1849 to help members of the Church in the United States and Europe travel to Utah.) The Pearl of Great Price was canonized in 1880. Weekly priesthood and bishopric meetings were begun in 1881, and stake presidents were asked to hold monthly priesthood meetings. Quarterly stake conferences were also started. He set the precedent of having the quorums of the priesthood sustain the new First Presidency separately in a Solemn Assembly. During his presidency, settlements were established in Colorado, Wyoming, and Arizona. To encourage the Saints' economic independence, President Taylor established Zion's Central Board of Trade, a coordinating agency that encouraged cooperative economic activity in the stakes of the Church.

"Steadfast to and immovable in the truth, few men have ever lived who have manifested such integrity and such unflinching moral and physical courage as our beloved President who has just gone from us. He never knew the feeling of fear connected with the work of God. But in the face of angry mobs, and at other times when in imminent danger of personal violence from those who threatened his life, and upon occasions when the people were menaced with a public peril, he never blenched—his knees never trembled, his hand never shook. . . .

"Undaunted courage and unyielding firmness were among his most prominent characteristics, giving him distinction among men who were distinguished for the same qualities. With these was combined an intense love of freedom and hatred of oppression. He was a man whom all could trust, and throughout his life he enjoyed, to an extent surpassed by none, the implicit confidence of the Prophets Joseph, Hyrum and Brigham and all the leading men and members of the Church." (Roberts, *Life of John Taylor*, pp. 410-11.)

President Taylor has a lifelong reputation as a powerful speaker. He defended the Church position on plural marriage in a newspaper debate with U.S. vice-president Schuyler Colfax (1869), which historian B. H. Roberts calls one of the most important discussions in the history of the Church. (See *CHC* 5:282-83.) A gifted and prolific writer, he authored many tracts and several larger works that introduced the gospel to new countries. He wrote numerous articles and pamphlets in the United States and Europe defending the Church; he also edited several Church newspapers and wrote many poems, mostly on gospel themes. In addition to a short work entitled *Items on Priesthood* (1881) to help the priesthood serve more effectively, he also wrote *The Government of God* (1852) and *The Mediation and Atonement of Our Lord and Savior Jesus Christ* (1882).

In 1886, President Taylor announced his desire to publish a new hymnbook for the Church. This hymnbook would contain both words and music (all previous hymnbooks had only the words). He called a committee of prominent musicians to produce the book. John Taylor strongly believed that music was an important part of one's religion. Through the subsequent hymnbook that was published, the influence of John Taylor is reflected in the music of the Church today.

Perhaps what is most important, he rallied the Saints to meet the challenge of federal prosecution for plural marriages, one of the most challenging periods in Church history. His life was shortened by his exile to avoid prosecution; he died in hiding.

At John Taylor's funeral, Elder Lorenzo Snow, a man well qualified to judge, said of John Taylor: "The Latter-day Saints feel that they have lost a friend; that we have lost a mighty counselor; that we have lost one of the greatest men who has stood upon the earth since the days of the Son of God—a man whose virtues, whose integrity, whose resolution to pursue the path of righteousness is known, and well known." (*Life of John Taylor*, p. 443.)

Personal Experience

On June 27, 1844, John Taylor was in Carthage Jail with Joseph Smith, Joseph's brother Hyrum and another valiant friend, Willard Richards. Even when offered liberty, John Taylor had loyally refused, choosing to stay by the Prophet's side.

Joseph asked Brother Taylor to sing one of his favorite hymns, "A Poor Wayfaring Man of Grief." John Taylor obliged and later described the song as sounding plaintive and pathetic, "very much in accordance with our feelings at the time for our spirits were all depressed, dull and gloomy and surcharged with indefinite ominous forebodings." (*CHC* 7:101.) Only moments later, a mob charged the jail. A fusillade of shots killed Hyrum and Joseph, and John Taylor was gravely wounded. He survived, however, and sent a letter to Nauvoo counseling the Saints not to retaliate. Although he carried the balls of the gun shots in his body throughout the remainder of his life, he was preserved to lead the Church through one of its darkest hours.

John Taylor's Testimony

"We are engaged in a great work, and in laying the foundation thereof—a work that has been spoken of by all the holy prophets since the world was; namely, the dispensation of the fulness of times, wherein God will gather together all things in one, whether they are things in the earth, or things in the heavens; and for this purpose God revealed Himself, as also the Lord Jesus Christ, unto His servant the Prophet Joseph Smith, when the Father pointed to the Son and said: 'This is my beloved Son, in whom I am well pleased, hear ye Him.' He further restored the everlasting gospel; together with the Aaronic and Melchizedek Priesthoods; both of which are everlasting as God is; and in the interest of humanity sent forth His gospel to the nations of the earth, I am happy to say that I have been a bearer of this gospel to several nations, and have been the means of bringing many to the knowledge of the truth.

"I pray God the Eternal Father that when we have all finished our probation here, we may be presented to the Lord without spot or blemish, as pure and honorable representatives of the Church and kingdom of God on the earth, and then inherit a celestial glory in the kingdom of our God, and enjoy everlasting felicity with the pure and just in the realms of eternal day, through the merits and atonement of the Lord Jesus Christ, our Savior and Redeemer, in worlds without end. Amen." (*Life of John Taylor*, pp. 394, 398.)

Teachings of John Taylor

Agency. There are two things I have always said I would do, and I calculate to carry them out, living or dying. One is to vote for whom I please and the other to worship God as I please. (*JD* 14:338.)

Atonement. From the facts in the case and the testimony presented in the Scriptures, it becomes evident that through the great atonement, the expiatory sacrifice of the Son of God, it is made possible that man can be redeemed, restored, resurrected and exalted to the elevated position designed for him in the creation as a Son of God: that eternal justice and law required the penalty to be paid by man himself, or by the atonement of the Son of God: that Jesus offered Himself as the great expiatory sacrifice; that this offering being in accordance with the demands or requirements of the law, was accepted by the great Lawgiver; that it was prefigured by sacrifices and ultimately fulfilled by Himself according to the eternal covenant. (*Mediation and Atonement*, pp. 170-171.)

Church Discipline (disciplinary councils). What are laws for? What are Bishops' Courts and High Councils for? That when men transgress the laws of God, they shall be tried according to the laws of the Church, and if found guilty, and are worthy of such action, they shall be cast out; that the pure and the righteous may be sustained, and the wicked and corrupt, the ungodly and impure, be dealt with according to the laws of God. This is necessary in order to maintain purity throughout the Church, and to cast off iniquity therefrom. (*JD* 24:171.)

Church Government. Who have we for our ruling power? Where and how did he obtain his authority? . . . . It is by the voice of God and the voice of the people that our present President obtained his authority. . . . He obtains his authority first from God and secondly from the people. . . . Is there a monarch, potentate, or power under the heavens that undergoes a scrutiny as fine as this? No, there is not; and yet this is done twice a year, before all the Saints in the world. You place the power in their hands to govern, dictate, regulate, and put in order the affairs of the kingdom of God. This is, Vox Dei, vox populi. God appoints, the people sustain. (*JD* 1:229-230.)

Citizenship. We are under the United States. But the United States is not the kingdom of God. It does not profess to be under his rule, nor his government, nor his authority. . . .

What is expected of us? That we observe its laws, that we conform to its usages, that we are governed by good and wholesome principles, that we maintain the laws in their integrity and that we sustain the government. . . . We ought to pray. . . for those that are in authority, that they may be led in the right way, that they may be preserved from evil, that they may administer the government in righteousness, and that they may pursue a course that will receive the approbation of heaven. (*JD* 21:68.)

Freedom. We believe in freedom of conscience, we believe that all men should be guaranteed the right to worship God according to the dictates of their conscience. Some may want to worship a God without body, parts or passions; a God that sits on the top of a topless throne; although to me the idea of worshipping such a God would be ridiculous, if other people desire to do it all right, and they should be protected in that right. But while we accord to all men the right to think and the right to worship as they please, we claim the same right for ourselves. (*JD* 24:36-37.)

God the Father. God is our Father; we are his children. He has brought us into his covenant, and it is our privilege to go on from wisdom to wisdom, from intelligence to intelligence, from understanding of one principle to that of another, to go forward and progress in the development of truth until we can comprehend God, for we are his children; we are his sons and daughters; and he is our Father. (*JD* 21:93.)

Gospel. The gospel embraces principles that dive deeper, spread wider, and extend further than anything else that we can conceive. The gospel teaches us in regard to the being and attributes of God; it also teaches us our relationship to that God and the various responsibilities we are under to Him as His offspring; it teaches us the various duties and responsibilities that we are under to our families and friends, to the community, to the living and the dead; it unfolds to us principles pertaining to futurity. In fact, according to the saying of one of the old disciples, it 'brings life and immortality to light,' brings us into a relationship with God, and prepares us for an exaltation in the eternal world. There is something profound and intellectual associated with the principles of the gospel as it is connected with the salvation and exaltation of man. (*JD* 16:389.)

Human Rights. Besides the preaching of the Gospel, we have another mission, namely, the perpetuation of the free agency of man and the maintenance of liberty, freedom and the rights of man. (*JD* 9:340.)

Knowledge. God has restored the gospel for the purpose of bringing life and immortality to light; and without the knowledge of the gospel there is no knowledge of life and immortality; for men cannot comprehend these principles only as they are made known unto them, and they cannot be revealed only through the medium of the gospel and through obedience to the laws of salvation associated therewith. (*JD* 22:218.)

Last Days. This nation and other nations will be overthrown, not because of their virtue, but because of their corruption and iniquity. The time will come, for the prophecies will be fulfilled, when kingdoms will be destroyed, thrones cast down, and the power of the earth shaken, and God's wrath will be kindled against the nations of the earth, and it is for us to maintain correct principles, political, religious, and social, and to feel toward all men as God feels. (*JD* 17:4.)

Law. According to the eternal laws of God and the eternal fitness of things as they exist with him in the eternal worlds and as they exist here upon, all of us are . . . as much obligated to listen to his law and be governed by his counsels and advice . . . [as] we

would be in making a grain of wheat to grow. . . . Being the God and Father of the spirits of all flesh, and having made a world for all flesh to inhabit, and having made provision for the sustenance of that flesh, for their food, clothing, comfort, convenience and happiness, and having given them intelligence and told them to go forth and manipulate the abundance of nature to their use, has he not a right to lead and direct us, to ask obedience to his law? Would not that be a legitimate right, when we reflect upon it? The world says, No, he has no right; I am my own master, etc. Some of the Latter-day Saints almost say the same thing; not quite, but they would like to get near it. "I am a free man; I will be damned if I don't do as I please," etc. Well, I will tell you another part of that story. You will be damned if you do act as you please unless you please to do and to keep the laws of God. We cannot violate his laws with impunity nor trample under foot these eternal principles which exist in all Nature. If all Nature is compelled to be governed by law or suffer loss, why not man? (*JD* 21:113-14.)

Liberty. I was not born a slave! I cannot, will not be a slave. I would not be a slave to God! I'd be His servant, friend, His son. I'd go at His behest; but would not be His slave. I'd rather be extinct than be a slave. His friend I feel I am, and He is mine. . . . I'm God's free man: I will not, cannot be a slave. (*Life of John Taylor*, p. 424.)

Love Others. Now, have I any ill feelings toward these people that persecute and proscribe us? No. I would do them good for evil, give blessings for curses; I would treat them well, treat them honorably. Let us be men of truth, honor and integrity; men that will swear to our own hurt and change not; men whose word will be our everlasting bond. If you see men hungry, feed them, no matter who they are: white, black, or red, Jew, Gentile or Mormon, or anybody else—feed them. If you see men naked, clothe them. If you see men sick, administer to them, and learn to be kind to all men; but partake not of their evil practices. (*JD* 25:312-13.)

Man. Man is an eternal being, composed of body and spirit; his spirit existed before he came here; his body exists with the spirit in time, and after death the spirit exists without the body. In the resurrection, both body and spirit will finally be reunited; and it requires both body and spirit to make a perfect man, whether in time or eternity. . . . The spirit requires a tabernacle to give it power to develop itself and to exalt it in the scale of intelligence, both in time and eternity. (*The Government of God*, pp. 27, 32.)

Mortality. We have learned many things through suffering, we call it suffering; I call it a school of experience. . . . Why is it that good men should be tried? Why is it, in fact, that we should have a devil? Why did not the Lord kill him long ago? Because He could not do without him. He needed the devil and a great many of those who do his bidding just to keep men straight, that we may learn to place our dependence upon God and trust in Him, and to observe His laws and keep His commandments. (*JD* 23:336.)

Parents. You should never say a word or do an act which you would not want your children to copy after. (*JD* 26:112.)

Peace. Peace is the gift of God. Do you want peace? Go to God. Do you want peace in your families? Go to God. Do you want peace to brood over your families? If you do, live your religion, and the very peace of God will dwell and abide with you, for that is where peace comes from, and it doesn't dwell anywhere else. (*JD* 10:56.)

Priesthood. The power manifested by the Priesthood is simply the power of God, for He is the head of the Priesthood, with Jesus as our President and great High Priest; and it is upon this principle that all the works of God have been accomplished, whether on the earth or in the heavens; and any manifestation of power through the Priesthood on the earth is simply a delegated power from the Priesthood in the heavens, and the more the Priesthood on the earth becomes assimilated with and subject to the Priesthood in the heaven the more of this power shall we possess. (*The Mediation and Atonement*, p. 88.)

Revelation. We ought to be a better people than those who make no pretentions to be guided by divine revelation. (*JD* 25:87.)

Satan. Satan has the power to transform himself into an angel of light; he can give visions and revelations as well as spiritual manifestations. (*MS* 19:197.)

Self-Control. Virtue does not consist simply in being prevented from committing evils, but in having temptations presented before us and then governing our passions. (*JD* 22:339.)

Self-Mastery. We have a great mission to perform—we have to try to govern ourselves according to the laws of the kingdom of God, and we find it one of the most difficult tasks we ever undertook, to learn to govern ourselves, our appetites, our dispositions, our habits, our feelings, our lives, our spirits, our judgment, and to bring all our desires into subjection to the law of the kingdom of God and to the spirit of truth. (*JD* 9:12.)

Self-Reliance. I never ask the Lord to do a thing I could do myself. (*JD* 1:27.)

Temples. He [Christ] has told us to . . . build temples. What for? To administer in them. Who for? For the dead who have died without a knowledge of the gospel, that they might participate with us in the blessings which they had not the privilege of enjoying on the earth. . . .We are making preparations for saving the dead, according to the word of God. (*JD* 20:118.)

Trials. I used to think, if I were the Lord, I would not suffer people to be tried as they are. But I have changed my mind on that subject. Now I think I would, if I were the Lord, because it purges out the meanness and corruption that stick around the saints, like flies around molasses. (*JD* 5:115.)

Truth. Wherever we find truth, no matter where, or from what source it may come, it becomes part and parcel of our religious creed, if you please, or our political creed, or our moral creed, or our philosophy, as the case may be, or whatever you may please to term it. (*JD* 14:337.)

Women. When I reflect upon the duties and responsibilities devolving upon our mothers and sisters and the influence they wield, I look upon them as the mainspring and soul of our being here. (*JD* 14:102.)

WILFORD WOODRUFF
1807-1898
Fourth President

- **Born**: March 1, 1807, Farmington, Connecticut

- **Family**: Wilford Woodruff was the son of Aphek and Beulah Thompson Woodruff, the third of nine children. Wilford married Phoebe Whittemore Carter, Mary Ann Jackson, Emma Smoot Smith, Sarah Brown, and Sarah Delight Stocking; had a total of thirty-three children.

- **Baptism**: December 31, 1833, at age 26, in an icy stream near Richland, New York

- **Missions**: Southern States (1834-36); Eastern States and Fox Islands (1837-38); Great Britain (1839-41); Europe (1844-46); the Eastern States (1843, 48-50)

- **Education**: Private schools, School of the Prophets, self-educated

- **Occupation**: Farmer, miller

- **Church Callings:** Missionary, apostle, assistant to and Church historian, first president of St. George Temple, president of YMMIA, general Church recorder

- **Apostle**: Ordained by Brigham Young on April 26, 1839 (served 50 years; age 32-82)

- **President of the Quorum of the Twelve**: October 10, 1880, to April 7, 1889 (served 8½ years)

- **Senior Apostle**: July 25, 1887, to April 7, 1889 (2 years)

- **President of the Church**: April 7, 1889, to September 2, 1898 (served 9½ years; age 82-91)

- **General Authority**: Served 59½ years. Ordained his son, Abraham O. Woodruff, an apostle in 1897.

- **Temples Dedicated**: Two: Manti (1888) and Salt Lake (1893)

- **Favorite Hymn**: "God Moves in a Mysterious Way"

- **Selected Teachings**: *Discourses of Wilford Woodruff*

- **Special Interests and Hobbies**: Hunting, fly fishing, cultivating and improving strains of vegetables, nuts, and fruits.

- **Other Responsibilities While President**: General Superintendent of the Young Men's Mutual Improvement Association and Church Historian

- **Appearance, Personality, and Qualities**: He was five-feet, eight inches tall, weighed 135 pounds, had a stocky build, and wore a beard. He was a tireless missionary, possessed a good sense of humor, and had great zeal. He was a prolific diarist and was designated as "Wilford the Faithful"; many felt that his writing was a spiritual gift. He kept an almost daily journal from 1835 to 1898, and its 7,000 pages provided primary documentation for much of the early history of the Church. It is an important source, for instance, of the sermons of Joseph Smith and Brigham Young and minutes of quorum meetings.

- **Died**: September 2, 1898, of a bladder infection in San Francisco, California (age 91)

- **1898**: Members: 267,251   Stakes: 40
       Missions: 20   Temples: 4
       Missionaries: 1,059
       General Authorities: 26

Biographical Highlights:

Wilford learned early in his youth the value of work, and he labored with his father in the Farmington grist mills. An avid student of the scriptures, he deeply pondered their meaning.

He came close to death many times because of accidents and illnesses. He suffered broken bones in his legs and arms, split his foot with an ax, was bitten by a rabid dog, and was crushed and pinned by falling trees. He nearly lost his life from blood poisoning when he accidentally cut his arm while skinning an ox that had died of poison. He nearly drowned, was almost frozen, was scalded, suffered several severe illnesses, and survived the wreck of a speeding train.

President Woodruff often referred to the fact that Satan wanted to keep him from making his contribution to the building of the kingdom: "The devil has sought to take away my life from the day I was born. . . . I seemed to be a marked victim of the adversary." (Cowley, *Wilford Woodruff*, p. 477.) He believed that the promptings of the Holy Spirit saved his life on several occasions.

Despite these accidents, his health was good. From his youth, he performed hard physical labor and farmed until he was nearly ninety. Curious about scientific advances, he kept abreast of horticulture and irrigation methods.

He joined the Church in 1833. One of the greatest missionaries the Church has ever had, Wilford baptized 1,800 people in England, including 200 ministers.

During his administration, the Salt Lake Temple was completed and dedicated; the value of historical record keeping was reemphasized; the Genealogical Society was organized; the first stakes in Canada and Mexico were organized in 1895; the Saints were encouraged to stay in their homelands instead of emigrating in 1896; weekday religion classes, a precursor to the seminary and Institute of Religion programs, were inaugurated; temple recommends, formerly issued only by the President of the Church, became the responsibility of bishops and stake presidents; fast and testimony meeting, formerly held on the first Thursday of each month, was changed to the first Sunday; the Manifesto (now Official Declaration 1) was announced, withdrawing public support from the performance of new plural marriages in 1890; and a "political manifesto" was drafted in 1896, requiring all general Church officials, before they accepted any political position, to discuss the prospective appointment with presiding Church authorities.

Also while President, Wilford Woodruff served as superintendent of the Young Men's Mutual Improvement Association and was Church Historian. He was a senator in the Provisional State of Deseret and Utah Territory and helped secure statehood for Utah in 1896.

President Woodruff was a great example to his family. It was easy for his children to understand what they should do by what they saw him do. He believed that if children were taught correct principles and if children saw those principles exemplified in the home, "ninety-nine out of every hundred children will observe them through life."

"He was not immune from the heartaches and frailties of domestic life. His marriage to Mary Ann Jackson ended in divorce, and another wife and thirteen children preceded him in death. His philosophy of family living is reflected in an 1894 letter to [his] daughter Blanche: 'We are all expecting to live together forever after death. I think we all as parents and children ought to take all the pains we can to make each other happy as long as we live that we may have nothing to regret'" (Letter to Blanche Woodruff, Sept. 16, 1894. Dean Jessee, "Wilford Woodruff," *EnM* 4:1582.)

Personal Experience

As president of the St. George Temple in 1877, Wilford Woodruff received a remarkable manifestation: "Every one of those men who signed the Declaration of Independence with George Washington called upon me as an Apostle of the Lord Jesus Christ, in the temple at St. George two consecutive nights, and demanded at my hands that I should go forth and attend to the ordinances of the house of God for them. . . . I straightway went into the baptismal font and called upon Brother McAllister to baptize me for the signers of the Declaration of Independence, and fifty other eminent men, making one hundred in all, including John Wesley, Columbus, and others; I then baptized him for every President of the United States except three. When their cause is just, somebody will do the work for them." (*JD* 19:229.) (Note: The work has since been done for Presidents Martin Van Buren, James Buchanan and Ulysses S. Grant.) Heber J. Grant was President of the Church when President Woodruff made this statement.

Wilford Woodruff's Testimony

"I bear my testimony that Joseph Smith was a true prophet of God, ordained of God to lay the foundation of his church and kingdom in the last dispensation and fulness of times. I bear my testimony that in the early spring of 1844 in Nauvoo, the Prophet Joseph Smith called the Twelve Apostles together, and he delivered unto them the ordinances of the Church and kingdom of God, and all of the keys and powers that God had bestowed upon him, he sealed upon our heads. He told us we must round our shoulders and bear off this kingdom or we would be damned. I am the only man now living in the flesh who heard that testimony from his mouth, and I know it is true by the power of God manifest through him. At that meeting he began to speak about three hours upon the subject of the kingdom. His face was as clear as amber, and he was covered with a power that I had never seen in the flesh before. In all his testimony to us, the power of God was visibly manifest in the Prophet Joseph Smith.

"This is my testimony spoken by myself into a talking machine on this the nineteenth day of March 1897, in the ninety-first year of my age." ("President Wilford Woodruff," *The New Era*, Jan. 1972, p. 66 [Record Transcription].)

Teachings of Wilford Woodruff

Agency. Because God himself grants this right [free agency] to every human being upon the earth irrespective of race or color; it is part of the divine economy not to force any man to heaven, not to coerce the mind but to leave it free to act for itself.

He lays before His creature man the everlasting Gospel, the principles of life and salvation, and then leaves him to choose for himself or to reject for himself, with the definite understanding that he becomes responsible to Him for the results of his acts. (*JD* 23:77.)

Baptism for the Dead. We have a great work before us in the redemption of our dead. . . . Those persons may receive their testimony, but they cannot be baptized in the spirit world, for somebody on the earth must perform this ordinance for them in the flesh, before they can receive part in the first resurrection, and be worthy of eternal life. It takes as much to save a dead man as a living one . . . . Have we any time to spend in trying to get rich and in neglecting our dead? I tell you no. (*JD* 22:235.)

Freedom. Those men who laid the foundation of this American government and signed the Declaration of Independence were the best spirits the God of heaven could find on the face of the earth. They were choice spirits . . . noble spirits before God. (*CR*, April 1898, p. 89.)

God the Father. We know that we are created in the image of God, both male and female; and whoever goes back into the presence of God our Eternal Father, will find that he is a noble man, a noble God, tabernacled in a form similar to ours, for we are created after his own image; they will also learn that he has placed us here that we may pass through a state of probation and experience, the same as he himself did in his day of mortality. (*JD* 18:32.)

Holy Ghost. Now, if you have the Holy Ghost with you . . . I can say unto you that there is no greater gift, there is no greater blessing, there is no greater testimony given to any man on earth. You may have administration of angels, you may see many miracles, you see many wonders in the earth; but I claim that the gift of the Holy Ghost is the greatest gift that can be bestowed upon man. (*DWW* 38:451.)

Journals. Men should write down the things which God has made known to them. Whether things are important or not, often depends upon God's purposes; but the testimony of the goodness of God and the things he has wrought in the lives of men will always be important as a testimony. (Cowley, *Wilford Woodruff*, p. 355.)

Last Days. The wickedness committed today in the Christian world in twenty-four hours is greater than would have been committed in a hundred years at the ratio of fifty years ago. And the spirit of wickedness is increasing, so that I no longer wonder that God the Almighty will turn rivers into blood; I do not wonder that He will open the seals and pour out the plagues and sink great Babylon, as the angel saw, like a millstone cast into the sea, to rise no more for ever. I can see that it requires just such plagues and judgments to cleanse the earth, that it may cause to groan under the wickedness and abomination in which the Christian world welters today. (*JD* 14:3.)

Law. The God of heaven, who created this earth and placed his children upon it, gave unto them a law whereby they might be exalted and saved in a kingdom of glory. For there is a law given unto all kingdoms, and all things are governed by law throughout the whole universe. Whatever law anyone keeps, he is preserved by that law, and he receives whatever reward that law guarantees unto him. It is the will of God that all his children should obey the highest law that they may receive the highest glory that is ordained for all immortal beings. But God has given all his children an agency, to choose what law they will keep. (*DWW*, p. 10.)

Missionary Work. The whole secret of our success as far as making converts is concerned is, that we preach the same Gospel in all its simplicity and plainness that Jesus preached, and that the Holy Ghost rests upon those who receive it, filling their hearts with joy and gladness unspeakable, and making them as one; they then know of the doctrine for themselves whether it is of God or man. (*JD* 23:129.)

Motherhood. Upon the shoulders of you mothers rests, in a great measure, the responsibility of correctly developing the mental and moral powers of the rising generation, whether in infancy, childhood, or still riper years. (*JD* 15:12.)

Obedience. The salvation of this people does not depend upon the great amount of teaching, instruction, or revelation that is given unto them but . . . upon obeying the commandments of God. (*JD* 4:190.)

Prayer. I fear, as a people, we do not pray enough, in faith. We should call upon the Lord in mighty prayer and make all our wants known unto him, for if he does not protect and deliver us and save us, no other power will. (*MS* 48:806.)

Priesthood. He [Joseph Smith] lived until he received every key, ordinance and law ever given to any man on the earth, from Father Adam down, touching this dispensation. . . . He received under the hand of John the Baptist the Aaronic Priesthood, with all its keys and powers, and every other key and power belonging to this dispensation, and I am not ashamed to say that he was a Prophet of God, and he laid the foundation of the greatest work and dispensation that has ever been established on the earth. (*JD* 16:267.)

Prophets. The Lord never did bring judgment upon any people of any generation until he raised up prophets to warn them of the impending danger. (*JD* 23:82.)

Repentance. And what is repentance? The forsaking of sin. The man who repents, if he be a swearer, swears no more, or a thief, steals no more; he turns away from all former sins and commits them no more. It is not repentance to say, I repent today, and then steal tomorrow; that is the repentance of the world, which is displeasing in the sight of God. (*JD* 23:127.)

Revelation. The Lord never had—and never will have to the end of time—a Church on the earth without Prophets, Apostles, and inspired men. Whenever the Lord had a people on the earth that He acknowledged as such, that people were led by revelation. (*JD* 24:240.)

Salvation. No man ever did or ever will obtain salvation only through the ordinances of the gospel and through the name of Jesus. There can be no change in the gospel; all men that are saved from Adam to infinitum are saved by the one system of salvation. The Lord may give many laws and many commandments to suit the varied circumstances and conditions of his children throughout the world, such as giving a law of carnal commandment to Israel, but the laws and principles of the gospel do not change. (*JD* 10:217.)

Satan. The enemy of God and man, called the devil, the "Son of the Morning," who dwells here on earth, is a personage of great power; he has great influence and knowledge. He understands that if this kingdom, which he rebelled against in heaven, prevails on the earth, there will be no dominion here for him. He has great influence over the children of men; he labors continually to destroy works of heaven, and he had to be cast out. . . . He is here, mighty among the children of men. There is a vast number of fallen spirits, cast out with him, here on the earth. They do not die and disappear; they have not bodies only as they enter the tabernacles of men. They have not organized bodies, and are not to be seen with the sight of the eye. But there are many evil spirits amongst us, and they labor to overthrow the church and kingdom of God. There never was a prophet in any age of the world but what the devil was continually at his elbow. (*DWW*, pp. 237-38.)

Succession to the Presidency. In answer to the question "Do you know of any reason in case of the death of the President of the Church why the Twelve Apostles should not choose some other person than the President of the Twelve to be President of the Church?" Wilford Woodruff wrote:

"I know several reasons why they should not. First, at the death of the President of the Church the Twelve Apostles become the presiding authority of the Church, and the president of the Twelve is really the President of the Church by virtue of his office as much while presiding over the Twelve Apostles as while presiding over his two counselors. . . .

"Second, in case of the death of the President of the Church it takes a majority of the Twelve to appoint the President of the Church, and it is very unreasonable to suppose that the majority of that quorum could be converted to depart from the course marked out by inspiration and followed by the Apostles at the death of Christ and by the Twelve Apostles at the death of Joseph Smith." (Cowley, *Wilford Woodruff*, p. 561.)

Testimony. It is necessary that all the members of the Church should exercise their powers of reason and reflection and thoroughly understand why they take the course which God points out. Intelligent obedience on the part of His Saints is desired by our Father in heaven. He has given us our agency to think and act for ourselves, on our own volition, to obtain a testimony for ourselves from Him concerning the truth of the principles which He teaches, and then be firm and unshaken in the performance of all which is necessary for salvation. (Clark, *Messages of the First Presidency*, 3:137.)

Trust. We are trying to abide the celestial law of God; we are preaching the gospel of Jesus Christ, and endeavoring to carry out its principles. Now the question is, will it pay us to do so? Will it pay us to be faithful? Will it pay us to pass through whatever trials or afflictions, or persecutions, or even death itself, for the kingdom of God, for salvation and eternal life, the greatest of all gifts which God can bestow on the children of men? I say it will, and I hope that the Latter-day Saints, that all men in authority—that we will all be faithful before the Lord, that we will remember our prayers, labor for the Holy Spirit, labor to know the mind and will of God, that we may know the path to walk in, that we may obtain the spirit of the Lord and the Holy Ghost, and that we may overcome the world and magnify our calling till we get through this probation. (*DWW*, p. 129.)

Women. Oh! Ye Latter-day Saints, you talk about revelation, and wonder if there is any revelation. Why bless your souls, say nothing about the Apostles and elders around me, these mountains contain thousands upon thousands of devoted women, holy women, righteous women, virtuous women, who are filled with the inspiration of Almighty God. Yes, these women have brought forth an army of sons and daughters in these mountains, by the power of God, and these sons and daughters partake of the inspiration of their mothers, as well as of their fathers. (*DWW*, p. 61.)

Youth. I feel to exhort and counsel you my young friends, to listen, to listen to the voice of God and obey it while young, as Samuel did, that you may be great, good, and useful, and the beloved of the Lord and your parents. . . .Your eternal destiny for time and eternity, will in a great measure depend upon the foundation which you lay in the days of your youth. (*DWW*, pp. 265-66.)

LORENZO SNOW
1814-1901
Fifth President

- **Born**: April 3, 1814, in Mantua, Ohio

- **Family**: Lorenzo Snow was the son of Oliver and Rosetta Pettibone Snow, the fifth of seven children. Lorenzo married Charlotte Squires, Mary Adaline Goddard, Sarah Ann Prichard, Harriet Amelia Squires, Eleanor Houtz, Caroline Horton, Mary Elizabeth Houtz, Phoebe Amelia Woodruff, and Sarah Minnie Jensen; had forty-two children.

- **Baptism**: June 19, 1836, at age 22 in the Chagrin River, which runs through Kirtland, Ohio

- **Missions**: Ohio (1837); Southern States (1838-39); Great Britain (1840-43); Europe (1849-52); Hawaii (1864); the Lamanites (1885)

- **Education**: Private schools; one term at Oberlin College, School of the Prophets, self-educated

- **Occupation**: Educator, farmer, businessman

- **Church Callings:** Missionary, stake president, apostle, temple president, additional counselor (1873-74) and Assistant Counselor to the First Presidency (1874-77)

- **Apostle**: Ordained by Heber C. Kimball on February 12, 1849 (served 49½ years; age 34-84).

- **President of the Quorum of the Twelve**: April 7, 1889, to September 13, 1898 (served 9½ years)

- **Senior Apostle**: September 2 to 13, 1898 (11 days)

- **President of the Church**: September 13, 1898, to October 10, 1901 (served 3 years, age 84-87). Previously, there had been lengthy apostolic administrations. For the first time, the new president was selected in just a few days after the death of the former president.

- **General Authority**: Served 52½ years

- **Temples Dedicated:** None

- **Favorite Hymns:** "O My Father" and "For the Strength of the Hills"

- **Selected Teachings**: *Teachings of Lorenzo Snow*, and *Biography and Family Records of Lorenzo Snow*

- **Special Interests & Hobbies**: reading poetry, attending and promoting all forms of high class entertainment, learning in a wide variety of subjects, playing checkers, interest in the arts and humanities, special interest in music. He had a beautiful singing voice.

- **Significant Contribution to the Doctrine of the Church:** "As man now is, God once was: As God now is, man may be." (Romney, *The Life of Lorenzo Snow*, p. 46.)

- **Other Responsibilities While President**: General Superintendent of the Sunday School and also of the Young Men's Mutual Improvement Association

- **Appearance, Personality, and Qualities**: He stood five-feet, six inches tall, weighed 140 pounds, had a slender build, wore a full beard, and had white hair in his later years. Gentle and dignified, he had a heavenly countenance, was cultured, and displayed elegant manners. He was persuasive but not forceful; he could say and do the hardest things in the gentlest, quietest manner possible. Despite his frail appearance, he was strong and robust and could endure great hardships and prolonged mental exertion. He possessed a keen business instinct. Tolerant, broad-minded, and sympathetic, he would always bear kind feelings for the opposing view.

- **Died**: October 10, 1901, of pneumonia in Salt Lake City (age 87)

- **1901**: Members: 292,931 Stakes: 50
  Temples: 4; Missions: 21
  Missionaries: 796
  General Authorities: 26

Biographical Highlights:

Although he worked hard on the family farm, Lorenzo Snow found time for extensive reading and studying. As a youth, he preferred academic study to an apprenticeship. Education was important to him, and he studied at Oberlin College for one term, but his intense desire to preach the gospel led him to sacrifice some of his educational goals. He studied Hebrew and theology, which led to his conversion.

After his baptism in 1836, he traveled across the ocean under miserable conditions to preach the gospel abroad. In 1864, Elder Snow accompanied four other missionaries on a short-term mission to the Sandwich (Hawaiian) Islands. He had apparently drowned when their small boat capsized in Lahaina Harbor, but was restored to life when his friends were impressed to perform mouth-to-mouth resuscitation, a procedure unknown at that time.

He reemphasized missionary work to all the world. Japan, for example, was opened to the missionaries in 1901.

When he became President, the Church was in serious financial difficulty resulting from years of persecution. President Snow promised the Saints that the honest payment of tithing would solve the Church's financial needs as well as their own.

While President, he also served as General Superintendent of the Young Men (1898-1901) and as General Superintendent of the Sunday School

(May-October 1901) and organized the Polysophical Society to promote cultural refinement for the community. He served in the Utah legislature with distinction for twenty-nine years, ten of them as President of the Legislative Council. When called to preside over a settlement at Box Elder, he changed the name to Brigham City to honor Brigham Young.

In 1885, after his return from a short mission, he was tried and imprisoned for violation of the 1882 Edmunds Act, which prohibited the practice of polygamy. He remained in prison for eleven months before being released under the mandate of the U.S. Supreme Court.

A keen businessman, he managed many financial and business enterprises, including a successful cooperative in Brigham City. As President of the Church, he reemphasized the law of tithing and improved the financial strength of the Church. He emphasized the worldwide administration of the Council of the Twelve.

As God Is, Man May Be

About four years after his baptism, during which time he had labored very hard as a missionary in several states, Lorenzo returned to Nauvoo. He had received a call to serve a mission to England and left in a few days. He had accepted an invitation to spend an evening in the home of his friend Henry G. Sherwood, and while listening to Brother Sherwood's explanation of the parable of the husbandman in Matthew 22, he later recalled that "the Spirit of the Lord rested mightily upon me—the eyes of my understanding were opened, and I saw as clearly as the sun at noonday, with wonder and astonishment, the pathway of God and man. I formed the following couplet which expresses the revelation, as it was shown to me, and explains Father Smith's dark saying to me at a blessing meeting in the Kirtland temple, prior to my baptism, as previously mentioned in my first interview with the Patriarch:

As man now is, God once was:
As God now is, man may be.

"Felt this to be sacred communication which I related to no one except my sister Eliza, until I reached England, when in a confidential, private conversation with President Brigham Young, in Manchester, I related to him this extraordinary manifestation." (LeRoi C. Snow, "Devotion to a Divine Inspiration," *IE*, June 1919, p. 656.)

"Elder Snow was startled by this revelation and amazed at the magnitude of the doctrine involved. Until then he had never heard the Prophet or others high in the councils of the Church advance such a doctrine, yet when he began to reason on this matter, it seemed perfectly logical, and in his innermost soul he felt it was true. He reasoned that if God is the literal Father of the spirit of man, it is within the realm of probability that man in the process of time may ultimately achieve Godhood. And in the same line of reasoning, it is not inconsistent to believe that if man, formed in the image of God and endowed with Godlike attributes, can ascend to the plane of Deity, God should have ascended the scale in a similar manner." (Romney, *The Life of Lorenzo Snow*, pp. 46-47.)

Three years later, Lorenzo Snow talked with the Prophet Joseph about this revelation. The Prophet assured him: "Brother Snow, that is true doctrine, and it is a revelation from God to you." (*IE*, June 1919, p. 656.)

Personal Experience

At age eighty-four, Lorenzo Snow was sustained as the fifth President of the Church. Worried about his advanced age, the immense burdens of administration, and the Church's financial debt, he pleaded for three days for a manifestation of divine will. He received no answers to his prayer and was in the process of leaving the temple when a glorious manifestation was given. He related it to his granddaughter, Allie Young Paul, when they were together in the temple, saying he had seen the Savior: "It was right here that the Lord Jesus Christ appeared to me at the time of the death of President Woodruff. . . . He stood right here, about three feet above the floor. It looked as though he stood on a plate of solid gold."

She said: "Grandpa told me what a glorious personage the Savior is and described his hands, feet, countenance, and beautiful white robes, all of which were of such a glory of whiteness and brightness that he could hardly gaze upon Him. Then Grandpa came another step nearer to me and put his right hand on my head and said, 'Now, granddaughter, I want you to remember that this is the testimony of your grandfather, that he told you with his own lips that he actually saw the Savior here in the temple and talked with him face to face.'" (LeRoi Snow, *IE*, Sept. 1933, p. 677.)

The Lord affirmed that President Snow should serve and that he should immediately reorganize the First Presidency. The reorganization took place without the lengthy interval that had followed the death of the first four presidents of the Church and established a tradition of immediate succession.

Lorenzo Snow's Testimony

"I will close . . . by bearing my testimony to the knowledge of God that I have received in relation to this work. It is true. I received a knowledge of the truth of this work by a physical administration of the blessing of God. And when receiving the baptism of the Holy Ghost I knew I was immersed in a divine principle that filled my whole system with inexpressible joy and from that day to the present has blessed my labors. . . .

"This was the testimony fifty years ago of a certain individual who stood forth and claimed that God had authorized him to baptize people for the remission of sins, and lay hands upon them for the reception of the Holy Ghost, which should impart unto them a knowledge from the eternal worlds that he had this authority.

"This person was Joseph Smith and he conferred this authority, which was given unto him by holy angels, upon others who were sent to bear testimony to the world that those who would receive these holy ordinances, should receive the testimony from the Almighty that they were thus authorized to so administer. . . . This is my testimony before this people and before the world.

"And may God bless us, may he pour out his Spirit upon the Latter-day Saints. And may we be faithful in all of our labors, having the motto indelibly stamped upon our hearts, 'The Kingdom of God or nothing.'" (*CR*, April 1880, pp. 81-82.)

Teachings of Lorenzo Snow

Discouragement. We have been sent into the world to do good to others; and in doing good to others we do good to ourselves. . . . When you find yourselves a little gloomy, look around you and find somebody that is in a worse plight than yourself, go to him and find out what the trouble is, then try to remove it with the wisdom which the Lord bestows upon you; and the first thing you know, your gloom is gone, you feel right, the Spirit of the Lord is upon you, and everything seems illuminated. (*CR*, April 1899, pp. 2-3.)

Exaltation. The ultimatum of our travel in this path of exaltation will bring to us the fulness of our Lord Jesus Christ, to stand in the presence of our Father, to receive of His fulness, to have the pleasure of increasing in our posterity worlds without end, to enjoy those pleasant associations that we have had in this life, to have our sons and daughters, our husbands and our wives, surround us with all the enjoyment that heaven can bestow, our bodies glorified like unto the Savior's, free from disease and all the ills of life, and free from the disappointments and vexations and the unpleasant sacrifices that we are making here. (*MS* 61:350.)

Fathers. The men ought to be more fatherly at home, possessing finer feelings in reference to their wives and children . . . more kindly and godlike. When I go into a family I do admire to see the head of that family administering to it as a man of God, kind and gently, filled with the Holy Ghost and with the wisdom and understanding of heaven. (*JD* 12:148.)

Forgiveness. The Lord requires that men should forgive one another, even seventy times seven. And even if the party does not ask forgiveness, we are to forgive for a certain number of times. He that forgives not his brother, we are told, there remaineth in him the greater sin—that is, he is a greater sinner than the person that offended him. (*CR*, April 1898, p. 63.)

Goodness. The idea is not to do good because of the praise of men, but to do good because in doing good we develop godliness within us; we shall become allied to godliness, which will in time become part and portion of our being. (*JD* 23:192.)

Gospel. Mormonism, a nickname for the real religion of the Latter-day Saints, does not profess to be a new thing, except to this generation. It proclaims itself as the original plan of salvation, instituted in the heavens before the world was, and revealed from God to man in different ages. That Adam, Enoch, Noah, Abraham, Moses, and other ancient worthies had this religion successively, in a series of dispensations, we, as a people, verily believe. To us, the gospel taught by the Redeemer in the meridian of time was a restored gospel, of which, however, He was the author, in His pre-existent state. Mormonism, in short, is the primitive Christian faith restored, the ancient gospel brought back again—this time to usher in the last dispensation, and wind up the work of redemption as pertaining to this planet. (*MS* 64:1.)

Individuality. We believe that we are the offspring of our Father in heaven, and that we possess in our spiritual organizations the same capabilities, powers and faculties that our Father possesses, although in an infantile state, requiring to pass through a certain course or ordeal by which they will be developed and improved according to the heed we give to the principles we have received. (*JD* 14:300.)

Love God. The god of the world is gold and silver. The world worships this god. It is all-powerful to them, though they might not be willing to acknowledge it. . . . Latter-day Saints should show whether they have so far advanced in the knowledge, in the wisdom and in the power of God that they cannot be overcome by the god of the world. . . . We have got to love God more than we love the world, more than we love gold or silver, and love our neighbor as ourselves. (*TLS*, p. 310.)

Marriage (benefits of temple marriage). When two Latter-day Saints are united together in marriage, promises are made to them concerning their offspring that reach from eternity to eternity. They are promised that they shall have the power and the right to govern and control and administer salvation and exaltation and glory to their offspring worlds without end. And what offspring they do not have here, undoubtedly there will be opportunities to have them hereafter. What else could man wish? A man and a woman in the other life, having celestial bodies, free from sickness and disease, glorified and beautified beyond description, standing in the midst of their posterity, governing and controlling them, administering life, exaltation and glory, worlds without end. (*DNW* 54:481.)

Mortality. The Lord designs to bring us up into the celestial kingdom. He has made known through direct revelation that we are his offspring, begotten in the eternal worlds, that we have come to this earth for the special purpose of preparing ourselves to receive a fulness of our Father's glory, when we shall return into his presence. Therefore, we must seek the ability to keep this law, to sanctify our motives, desires, feelings and affections, that they may be pure and holy, and our will in all things be subservient to the will of God, and have no will of our own except to do the will of our Father. . . . One of the chief difficulties that many suffer from is that we are too apt to forget the great object of life, the motive of our Heavenly Father in sending us here to put on mortality, as well as the holy calling with which we have been called; and hence, instead of rising above the little transitory things of time, we too often allow ourselves to come down to the level of the world without availing ourselves of the divine help which God has instituted, which alone can enable us to overcome them. We are no better than the rest of the world if we do not cultivate the feeling to be perfect, even as our Father in heaven is perfect. (*JD* 20:189, 191.)

Parents. I would plead with you, my young brethren and sisters, to honor your fathers and your mothers, that your days may be long in the land which the Lord hath given to them and to you. Be obedient and loving to them; and after they have climbed to the summit of the hill of life, perhaps through many a hard-fought struggle, and begin to descend, try to do all in your power to make the road smooth and pleasant for them. By their devotion to you and to your welfare they have proved themselves worthy of your affection, and God expects you to be loyal to them. He has honored them in the past, and will yet honor them more abundantly; but their joy will not be fully complete if their children disregard their wishes and are untrue to them and to God. observe this commandment which God has given, to honor your fathers and your mothers. (*TLS*, p. 137.)

Resurrection. We know that in the future, after we have passed through this life, we will then have our wives and our children with us. We will have our bodies glorified, made free from every sickness and distress, and rendered most beautiful. There is nothing more beautiful to look upon than a resurrected man or woman. There is nothing grander that I can imagine that a man can possess than a resurrected body. (*CR*, Oct. 1900, p. 4.)

Revelation. God established the Church of Jesus Christ of Latter-day Saints by direct revelation: this is a FACT, clearly and distinctly revealed to thousands. The so-called "Mormon" people, in these valleys, are the acknowledged people of God, and are here, not by their own choice, but by immediate command of God. (*JD* 26:367.)

Revelation. There is a way by which persons can keep their consciences clear before God and man, and that to preserve within them the Spirit of God, which is the spirit of revelation to every man and woman. It will reveal to them, even the simplest of matters, what they shall do, by making suggestions to them. We should try to learn the nature of this spirit, that we may understand its suggestions, and then we will be able to do right. This is the grand privilege of every Latter-day Saint. We know that it is our right to have the manifestations of the Spirit every day of our lives. (*TLS*, p. 112.)

Suffering. We are here that we may be educated in a school of suffering and of fiery trials, which school was necessary for Jesus our Elder Brother, who, the Scriptures tell us, was made perfect through suffering. It is necessary we suffer in all things that we may be qualified and worthy to rule and govern all things, even as our Father in heaven and His Elder Son Jesus. (*MS* 13:363.)

Tithing. The time has now come for every Latter-day Saint, who calculates to be prepared for the future and to hold his feet strong upon a proper foundation, to do the will of the Lord and to pay his tithing in full. (*MS* 61:533.)

Women. You sisters, I suppose, have read that poem which my sister composed years ago, and which is sung quite frequently now in our meetings ["O My Father"]. It tells us that we not only have a Father in "that high and glorious place," but that we have a Mother too; and you will become as great as your Mother, if you are faithful. (*TLS*, pp. 7-8.)

JOSEPH F. SMITH
1838-1918
Sixth President

- **Born:** November 13, 1838, in Far West, Missouri

- **Family**: Joseph Fielding Smith was the son of Hyrum and Mary Fielding Smith, the oldest of two children. Joseph F. married Levira Annett Clark Smith, Julina Lambson, Sarah Ellen Richards, Edna Lambson, Alice Ann Kimball, and Mary Taylor Schwartz; had forty-eight children, including five adopted.

- **Missions**: Hawaii (1854-57); Great Britain (1860-63); Hawaii (1864); European Mission President (1873-75, 1877); Eastern States (1878)

- **Education**: Ward schools, self-educated

- **Occupation**: Church worker, farmer, civic official

- **Church Callings:** Missionary, high councilor, historian, apostle, mission president, stake president (1875); additional counselor in the First Presidency (1866-77); Second Counselor in the First Presidency 1880-87, 1889-1901

- **Apostle**: Ordained by Brigham Young on July 1, 1866 (served 35 years; age 27-62)

- **President of the Quorum of the Twelve**: No record

- **Senior Apostle**: October 10 to October 17, 1901 (7 days)

- **President of the Church**: October 17, 1901, to November 19, 1918 (served 17 years; age 62-80)

- **General Authority**: Served 52½ years. He ordained two sons, Hyrum Mack Smith (1901) and Joseph Fielding Smith (1910) as apostles; David Asael Smith served as Second and First Counselor to the Presiding Bishop

- **Temples Dedicated:** None

- **Favorite Hymns**: "Uphold the Right" and "I Know That My Redeemer Lives"

- **Selected Teachings**: *Gospel Doctrine*

- **Special Interests and Hobbies**: Long car rides, golfing, attending plays and concerts, enjoying music, playing checkers, and riding horses.

- **Vision**: "The Redemption of the Dead," which became Doctrine & Covenants Section 138 in 1979.

- **Other Responsibilities While President**: President of Salt Lake Temple (1899-1911); General Superintendent of the Sunday School; General President of the Young Men's Mutual Improvement Association

- **Appearance, Personality, and Qualities**: He stood five-feet, eleven inches tall, weighed 185-195 pounds, wore a full beard and glasses. He was kind, humorous, loyal, charitable (despite attacks on his character by the national press), and was always clean and orderly in his personal habits. He was known as "a preacher of righteousness."

- **Died**: November 19, 1918, of bronchopneumonia in Salt Lake City, Utah (age 80).

- **1918**: Members: 495,962 Stakes: 75
  Missions: 22 Temples: 4
  Missionaries: 1,015
  General Authorities: 26

Biographical Highlights

He goes by Joseph F. The "F." in his name stands for "Fielding," but he is traditionally referred to by the initial only to reduce confusion with his son, Joseph Fielding Smith, also a Church President.

When he was only two months old, Joseph nearly suffocated when a mob broke into his father's house, ransacked it, and overturned a mattress on top of him.

His father, Hyrum Smith, and his uncle, the Prophet Joseph Smith, were martyred on June 27, 1844.

When Joseph F. was a young boy, he learned well the importance of honesty, responsibility, and hard work. At the age of eight, he drove an ox team over two hundred miles from Nauvoo to Winter Quarters. He cared for the animals, chopped wood, and hauled water from streams, doing the work of a man while still such a young boy.

Joseph helped his mother, Mary Fielding Smith, maintain a cabin in Salt Lake City until her death in 1852, when he was thirteen. She was a great example of faith and courage to him.

At the age of fifteen, Joseph F. began a life of service to the Church by accepting a mission call to the Sandwich Islands (now Hawaii).

As a missionary, Joseph F. experienced illness, poverty, and discouragement, but he received a spiritual reinvigoration through a dream. He dreamed that he was on a journey where he was greeted by his parents, President Brigham Young, and the Prophet Joseph Smith. To him, it was not a dream but "a reality." He said: "There could not be anything more real to me. I felt the hand of Joseph Smith. I felt the warmth of his stomach, when I put my hand against him. I saw the smile upon his *face. . . . I know* that was a reality, to show me my duty, to teach me something, to impress upon me something that I cannot forget." The effect of this manifestation was life-changing: "When I awoke

that morning I was a man, although only a boy. There was not anything in the world that I feared. I could meet any man or woman or child and look them in the face, feeling in my soul I was a man every whit." He summarized simply: "That vision, that manifestation and witness that I enjoyed at that time has made me what I am, if I am anything that is good, or clean, or upright before the Lord if there is anything good in me. That has helped me out in every trial and through every difficulty." (Smith, *Life of Joseph F. Smith*, pp. 445-46.)

President Smith's first wife divorced him but his other five wives remained loving and devoted. His son Joseph Fielding said: "His love for his wives and children was boundless in its magnitude and purity. The world did not know—could not possibly know—the depths of his love for them. The wicked and the depraved have ridiculed and maligned him; but the true condition of his family life and wonderful love for his family is beyond comprehension. O how he prayed his children would always be true." (Smith, *Life of Joseph F. Smith*, p. 4.)

President Smith and his growing family lived most frugally. Often they had only the means for the bare necessities. One Christmas he wept openly as he saw the abundance in store windows downtown, knowing he lacked the money to buy even the most meager gifts for his family. He was a very affectionate husband and father and always kissed and embraced his wife and children, regardless of the time or place. He had missed this affection in his own life after the death of his parents.

As Second Counselor in the First Presidency, Joseph had spent time in hiding during the polygamy crisis. He also had to cope with the financial chaos and the negative public sentiment left in its wake. Part of the battle took place on the national scene. Reed Smoot, an apostle and elected senator, was denied his seat in the U.S. Congress on the grounds that he was a practicing polygamist, although he was not. During the Senate hearings to unseat him, which began in January 1904 and lasted for the next thirty months, it became apparent that the Church itself was on trial. [See United States Senate Reed Smoot Hearings (1904) 4:181-84.] President Smith responded by issuing an official statement on April 5, 1904, upholding the provisions of the 1890 Manifesto. He ordered the Manifesto to be added to the Doctrine and Covenants, satisfying critics who pointed out that the LDS scriptures contained the revelation authorizing plural marriage but no revelation terminating it. Along with other Church leaders, President Smith himself was called to testify. He took advantage of the opportunity to make influential contacts and to meet newsmen. It was the beginning of a new public image for the Church.

He brought the Church members to a better appreciation of early Church history while ushering the Church into the twentieth century. He clarified important doctrines, directed the construction of a new headquarters building, issued an official statement on the origin of humankind (1909), and urged members to hold regular home evenings. He published his addresses in 1918 in a book titled *Gospel Doctrine*.

During President Smith's administration, an information center opened on Temple Square, and the Church acquired historical sites and began building visitors centers. The Church also became completely free of debt (1906), began publication of *The Children's Friend* magazine (later called *The Friend* in 1970), inaugurated the home evening program in 1915, and created a committee that reformed and systematized priesthood work and instituted specific ages for Aaronic Priesthood ordinations (1908). The seminary program was instituted in 1912. In addition to his many religious duties, President Smith served in the Territorial Legislature of Utah from 1865 to 1874.

He was the first President to be born to LDS parents, to drive an automobile, to be photographed in motion pictures, to occupy the Church Office Building (1917), and to visit Europe. He was the only President to be orphaned (age 13).

Vision of the Redemption of the Dead

On October 3, 1918, while reading First Peter in the Bible, President Smith received a magnificent vision, wherein he saw Jesus Christ during the time the Savior's body lay in the tomb for three days following his crucifixion. The Savior was visiting the spirits of those who had already died. President Smith said at the October conference, "I have not lived alone these five months. I have dwelt in the

spirit of prayer, of supplication, of faith and of determination; and I have had my communication with the Spirit of the Lord continuously."

"The eyes of my understanding were opened, and the Spirit of the Lord rested upon me, and I saw the hosts of the dead small and great." He reported seeing the Lord visit the spirits of the dead and saw that righteous spirits were appointed to minister to them as well. Among the "faithful" who were teaching others were his own father Hyrum, the Prophet Joseph Smith, John Taylor, Wilford Woodruff, and other choice spirits. "The dead who repent will be redeemed through obedience to the ordinances of the house of God, and after they have paid the penalty of their transgressions, and are washed clean, shall receive a reward according to their works, for they are heirs of salvation."

"Thus was the vision of the redemption of the dead revealed to me, and I bear record, and I know that this record is true through the blessing of our Lord and Savior, Jesus Christ, even so. Amen." (*Life of Joseph F. Smith*, pp. 468-71; see also D&C 138.)

This vision was presented to the counselors in the First Presidency, Quorum of the Twelve Apostles, and the Patriarch on October 31, 1918, and was accepted as a revelation from God. It was published in the *Improvement Era* in December 1918, and in 1981 it was canonized and published as Section 138 of the Doctrine and Covenants.

Joseph F. Smith's Testimony

"I desire to bear my testimony to you for I have received an assurance which has taken possession of my whole being. It has sunk deep into my heart; it fills every fiber of my soul; so that I feel to say before this people, and would be pleased to have the privilege of saying it before the whole world, that God has revealed unto me that Jesus is the Christ, the Son of the living God, the Redeemer of the world; that Joseph Smith is, was, and always will be a prophet of God, ordained and chosen to stand at the head of the dispensation of the fulness of times, the keys which were given to him, and he will hold them until the winding up scene. . . . I know that this is the kingdom of God, and that God is at the helm. He presides over his people. He presides over the president of this Church. . . .

"It is by his power that [the Church] has grown and continued, and has become what it is, and it will continue to grow and spread, until it shall fill the earth with glory, and with the knowledge of the Father and of the Son, whom to know is life eternal. This is my testimony to you, my brethren and sisters, and I bear witness of it in the name of the Lord Jesus Christ. Amen." (*GD*, pp. 501-502.)

Teachings of Joseph F. Smith

Adversity. Sometimes we are prone to charge God with causing our afflictions and our troubles; but if we could see as God sees, if we could understand as he understands, if we could trace the effects back to the cause, and that truly, by the spirit of correct understanding, we would unquestionably discover that our troubles, or suffering, or affliction are the result of our own indiscretion or lack of knowledge, or of wisdom. It was not the hand of God that put affliction and trouble upon us. (*IE* 20:821.)

Book of Mormon. The Book of Mormon . . . cannot be disproved, for it is true. There is not a word or doctrine, of admonition, of instruction within its lids [leaves], but what agrees in sentiment and veracity with those of Christ and His Apostles, as contained in the Bible. Neither is there a word of counsel, of admonition or reproof within its lids, but what is calculated to make a bad man a good man, and a good man a better man, if he will hearken to it. It bears the mark of inspiration from beginning to end, and carries conviction to every honest-hearted soul. (*JD* 25:99-100.)

Courage. After we have done all we could do for the cause of truth, and withstood the evil that men have brought upon us, and we have been overwhelmed by their wrongs, it is still our duty to stand. We cannot give up; we must not lie down. Great causes are not won in a single generation. To stand firm in the face of overwhelming opposition, when you have done all you can, is the courage of faith.

The courage of faith is the courage of progress. Men who possess that divine quality go on; they are not permitted to stand still if they would. They are not simply the creatures of their own power and wisdom; they are instrumentalities of a higher law and a divine purpose. (*GD*, p. 119.)

Dangers. There are at least three dangers that threaten the Church within, and the authorities need to awaken to the fact that the people should be warned unceasingly against them. As I see these, they are flattery of prominent men in the world, false educational ideas, and sexual impurity.

But the third subject mentioned—personal purity, is perhaps of greater importance than either of the other two. We believe in one standard of morality for men and women. If purity of life is neglected, all other dangers set in upon us like the rivers of waters when the flood gates are opened. (*GD*, pp. 312-13.)

Death. The spirits of all men, as soon as they depart from this mortal body, whether they are good or evil, we are told in the Book of Mormon, are taken home to that God who gave them life, where there is a separation, a partial judgment, and the spirits of those who are righteous are received into a state of happiness which is called paradise, a state of rest, a state of peace, where they expand in wisdom, where they have respite from all their troubles, and where care and sorrow do not annoy.

The wicked on the contrary, have no part nor portion in the Spirit of the Lord, and they are cast into outer darkness, being led captive, because of their own iniquity by the evil one. And in this space between death and the resurrection of the body, the two classes of souls remain, in happiness or in misery, until the time which is appointed of God that the dead shall come forth and be reunited both spirit and body, and be brought to stand before God and be judged according to their works. This is the final judgment. (*GD*, p. 448.)

Endurance. If you fail, never mind. Go right on; try again, try it somewhere else. Never say quit. Do not say it cannot be done. . . . The word "fail" ought to be expunged from our language and our thoughts. . . . If we continue to try, failing, as it were, or missing one mark, should not discourage us; but we should fly to another, keep on in the work, keep on doing, patiently, determinedly doing our duty, seeking to accomplish the purpose we have in view. (*GD*, p. 132.)

Fasting. The law to the Latter-day Saints, as understood by the authorities of the Church, is that food and drink are not to be taken for twenty-four hours, "from even to even," and that the Saints are to refrain from all bodily gratification and indulgences. Fast day being on the Sabbath, it follows, of course, that all labor is to be abstained from. . . .

Now, while the church requires the Saints in all the world to fast from "even to even," and to abstain both from food and drink, it can easily be seen from the Scriptures and especially from the words of Jesus, that it is more important to obtain the true spirit of love for God and man, "purity of heart and simplicity of intention," than it is to carry out the cold letter of the law. . . .

Many are subject to weakness, others are delicate in health, and others have nursing babies; of such it should not be required to fast. Neither should parents compel their little children to fast. . . . Teach them the principle, and let them observe it when they are old enough to choose intelligently, than to compel them.

It is evident that the acceptable fast is that which carries with it the true spirit of love for God and man; and that the aim in fasting is to secure perfect purity of heart and simplicity of intention—fasting unto God in the fullest and deepest sense—or such a fast would be a cure for every practical and intellectual error; vanity would disappear, love for our fellows would take its place, and we would gladly assist the poor and the needy." (*IE*, Dec. 1902, pp. 147-49.)

Forgiveness. Our plain duty—so plain that none should misunderstand it, none can misunderstand it unless they allow their prejudices and human weaknesses to prevail over their better judgment; our plain duty is to live in the spirit of forgiveness, in the spirit of humility before the Lord, in the love of the truth more than the love of ourselves and our personal interests. (*CR*, April 1909, p. 4.)

Knowledge/Intelligence. There is a difference between knowledge and pure intelligence. Satan possesses knowledge, far more than we have, but he has no intelligence or he would render obedience to the principles of truth and right. I know men who have knowledge who understand the principles of the gospel, perhaps as well as you do, who are brilliant, but who lack the essential qualification of

pure intelligence. They will not accept and render obedience thereto. Pure intelligence comprises not only knowledge, but also the power to properly apply that knowledge. (*GD*, p. 58.)

Love God. Why should we not love him with all our heart and mind and strength, since he has given us life, since he has formed us in his own likeness and image, since he has placed us here that we may become like unto his Only Begotten Son and to inherit the glory, exaltation and reward provided for God's own children? (*CR*, Oct. 1914, p. 6.)

Marriage. Marriage constitutes the most sacred relationship existing between man and woman. It is of heavenly origin, and is founded upon eternal principles. As a part and portion of the great plan of salvation . . . it is destined to continue not only while time shall last but throughout all eternity. Indeed it is an exigency upon which man's happiness, the perpetuity of his earthly existence, and his future dominion, glory and exaltation depend, and which, in the wisdom of God, must of necessity continue as the seal of the natural, legitimate, and inevitable domestic union of the sexes forever. (*MS*, May 19, 1874, p. 312.)

Mother's Love. I learned in my childhood . . . that no love in all the worlds can equal the love of a true mother. . . . [My mother's love] was life to me; it was strength; it was encouragement; it was love that begat love or liking in myself. I knew she loved me with all her heart. She loved her children with all her soul. She would toil and labor and sacrifice herself day and night, for the temporal comforts and blessings, to her children. There was no sacrifice of self—of her own time, of her leisure or pleasure, or opportunities for rest—that was considered for a moment, when it was compared with her duty and her love to her children. . . .

I have learned to place a high estimate upon the love of a mother. I have often said, and will repeat it, that the love of a true mother comes nearer [to] being like the love of God than any other kind of love. (*GD*, pp. 314-15.)

Obedience. Obedience is a requirement of heaven and is therefore a principle of the gospel. (*JD* 19:193.)

Priesthood Keys. The priesthood in general is the authority given to man to act for God. Every man ordained to any degree of the priesthood, has this authority delegated to him.

But it is necessary that every act performed under this authority shall be done at the proper time and place, in the proper way, and after the proper order. The power of directing these labors constitutes the keys of the priesthood. In their fulness, the keys are held by only one person at a time, the prophet and President of the Church. He may delegate any portion of this power to another, in which case that person holds the keys of that particular labor.

Thus, the president of a temple, the president of a stake, the bishop of a ward, the president of a mission, the president of a quorum, each holds the keys of the labors performed in that particular body or locality. His priesthood is not increased by this special appointment, for a seventy who presides over a mission has no more priesthood than a seventy who labors under his direction; and the president of an elder's quorum for example, has no more priesthood than any member of the quorum. But he holds the power of directing the official labors performed in the mission or the quorum, or in other words, the keys of that division of that work. So it is throughout all the ramifications of the priesthood—a distinction must be carefully made between the general authority, and the directing of the labors performed by that authority. (*IE* 4:230.)

Profanity. We should stamp out profanity, and vulgarity, and everything of that character that exists among us; for all such things are incompatible with the gospel and inconsistent with the people of God. (*GD*, p. 241.)

Prophet. I have the right to bless, I hold the keys of the Melchizedek Priesthood and of the office and power of patriarch. It is my right to bless; for all the keys and authority and power pertaining to the government of the Church and to the Melchizedek and Aaronic Priesthood are centered in the presiding officers of the Church. There is no business, nor any office, within the Church that the President of the Church may not fill, and may not do, if it is necessary, or if it is required of him to do it. He holds the office of patriarch; he holds the office of high priest and of apostle, of seventy, of elder, of bishop, and of priest, teacher and deacon in the Church; all these belong to the Presidency of the Church of Jesus Christ of Latter-day Saints, and they can officiate in any and in all of these callings when the occasion requires. (*CR*, Oct. 1915, p. 7.)

Repentance. True repentance is not only sorrow for sins and humble penitence and contrition before God, but it involves the necessity of turning away from [our sins,] a discontinuance of all evil practices and deeds, a thorough reformation of life, a vital change from evil to good, from vice to virtue, from darkness to light. Not only so, but to make restitution, so far as it is possible, for all the wrongs we have done, to pay our debts, and restore to God and man their rights—that which is due them from us. This is true repentance, and the exercise of the will and all the powers of body and mind is demanded to complete this glorious work of repentance; then God will accept it. (*JD* 19:190.)

Resurrection. I cannot express the joy I feel at the thought of meeting my father, and my precious mother, who gave me birth in the midst of persecution and poverty. . . . The thought of meeting my children who have preceded me beyond the veil, and meeting my kindred and my friends, what happiness it affords! For I know I shall meet them there. God has shown me that this is true. He has made it clear to me, in answer to my prayer and devotion, as he has made it clear to the understanding of all men who have sought diligently to know him. (*GD*, p. 429.)

Revelation. It is the right and the privilege of every man, every woman, and every child who has reached the years of accountability to enjoy the spirit of revelation and to be possessed of the spirit of inspiration in the discharge of their duties as members of the Church. (*CR*, April 1912, p. 5.)

Sabbath Day. The Sabbath is appointed unto you to rest from your labors. The Sabbath is a special day for you to worship, to pray and to show zeal and ardor in your religious faith and duty—to pay devotions to the Most High.

The Sabbath is a day when you are required to offer your time and attention in worship of the Lord; whether in meeting, in the home, or wherever you may be—that is the thought that should occupy your mind. The Sabbath day is a day when, with your brothers and sisters, you should attend the meetings of the Saints prepared to partake of the Sacrament of the Lord's Supper; having first confessed your sins before the Lord and your brethren and sisters and forgiven your fellows as you expect the Lord to forgive you. (*IE*, July 1910, pp. 842-43.)

Satan. Let it not be forgotten that the evil one has great power in the earth, and that by every possible means he seeks to darken the minds of men and then offers them falsehood and deception in guise of truth.

Satan is a skillful imitator, and as genuine gospel truth is given the world in ever increasing abundance, so he spreads the counterfeit coin of false doctrine. Beware of his spurious currency, it will purchase for you nothing but disappointment, misery and spiritual death. The "Father of Lies" he has been called, and such an adept has he become through the ages of practice in his nefarious work, that were it possible he would deceive the very elect. (*JI*, Sept. 1902, p. 562.)

Satan/Witchcraft. The gifts of the Spirit and the powers of the holy priesthood are of God, they are given for the blessing of the people, for their encouragement, and for the strengthening of their faith. This Satan knows full well; therefore he seeks by imitation miracles to blind and deceive the children of God. Remember what the magicians of Egypt accomplished in their efforts to deceive Pharaoh as to the divinity of the mission of Moses and Aaron. . . .

The danger and power for evil in witchcraft is not so much in the witchcraft itself as in the foolish credulence that superstitious people give to the claims made in its behalf.

It is outrageous to believe that the devil can hurt or injure an innocent man or woman, especially if they are members of the Church of Christ—unless that man or woman has faith that he or she can be harmed by such an influence and by such means. If they entertain such an idea, they are liable to succumb to their own superstitions. There is no power in witchcraft itself, only as it is believed in and accepted. . . .

No man or woman who enjoys the Spirit of God and the influence and power of the holy Priesthood can believe in these superstitious notions, and those who do, will lose, indeed have lost, the influence of the Spirit of God and of the Priesthood, and have become subject to the witchery of Satan, who is constantly striving to draw away the Saints from the true way, if not by the dissemination of such nonsense, then by other insidious methods. (*GD*, pp. 376-77.)

Self-Control. Our first enemy we will find within ourselves. It is a good thing to overcome that enemy first and bring ourselves into subjection to the will of the Father, and into strict obedience to the principles of life and salvation which he has given to the world for the salvation of men. When we shall have conquered ourselves, it will be well for us to wage our war without, against false teachings, false doctrines, false customs, habits and ways against error, unbelief, the follies of the world that are so prevalent, and against infidelity, and false science, under the name of science, and every other thing that strikes at the foundations of the principles set forth in the doctrine of Christ for the redemption of men and the salvation of their souls. (*CR*, Oct. 1914, p. 128.)

Smith, Joseph. I was acquainted with the Prophet Joseph Smith in my youth. I was familiar in his house, with his boys and with his family. I have sat on his knee. I have heard him preach. I distinctly remember being present in the council with my father and the Prophet Joseph Smith and others. From my childhood to youth I believed him to be a prophet of God. From my youth until the present I have not only believed that he was a prophet, for I have known that he was. (Quoted in Nibley, *TPC*, p. 205.)

Testimony. If you have that spirit toward God and his work in these latter days, you will build steadily and slowly, it may be, but surely, upon a foundation that will endure throughout the countless ages of eternity. And if you do not get any great manifestations, you need not worry about it. You will get the testimony of Jesus Christ in your hearts, and you will know God and Jesus whom he has sent, whom to know is life eternal, just as well as those who receive visions. (*CR*, April 1940, p. 42.)

HEBER J. GRANT
1856-1945
Seventh President

- **Born**: November 22, 1856, in Salt Lake City

- **Family**: Heber Jeddy Grant was the only child of Jedediah Morgan and Rachel Ivins Grant. At age 20, he married Lucy Stringham on November 1, 1877 (she died on January 3, 1893; had six children); at age 27, he married Hulda Augusta Winters on May 26, 1884 (she died on June 1, 1952; had one child); at age 27, he married Emily J. Harris Wells on May 27, 1884 (she died on May 25, 1908; had five children). He had a total of twelve children; his two sons died at ages five and seven.

- **Missions**: The Indians (Colorado, New Mexico, Southeastern Utah) (1883-1884); opened and presided over the Japanese Mission (1901-1903); President of British and European Missions (1904-1906).

- **Education**: Private schools; self-educated

- **Occupation**: Businessman

- **Church Callings**: Secretary of general YMMIA, ward MIA superintendent, stake president, apostle, mission president (twice), business manager of the *Improvement Era*, which he helped to establish

- **Apostle**: Ordained by George Q. Cannon on October 16, 1882 (served 36 years; age 25-62)

- **President of the Council of the Twelve**: November 23, 1916, to November 23, 1918 (served 2 years)

- **Senior Apostle**: November 19 to November 23, 1918 (4 days)

- **President of the Church**: November 23, 1918, to May 14, 1945 (served 26½ years; age 62-88)

- **General Authority**: Served 62½ years

- **Temples Dedicated**: Three: Hawaii (1919), Alberta (1923), Arizona (1927)

- **Favorite Hymns**: "Come, Come Ye Saints," "Should You Feel Inclined to Censure," and "Let Each Man Learn to Know Himself." (He liked the message in the last stanza: "So first improve yourself today and then improve your friends tomorrow" and sang this hymn throughout the Church.)

- **Selected Teachings**: *Gospel Standards*

- **Special Interests and Hobbies**: Baseball, volleyball, golfing, exercising each morning, taking long car rides, singing, penmanship, attending the theater and movies, reading, and attending sports events. When he found an inspirational literary work that pleased him, he would buy it in quantity and distribute copies to his family and friends.

- **Legacy of Letters**: President Grant was very close to his family, but constant travel took him away from his home. He was a prodigious letter writer. More than 50,000 of his letters are preserved in the Church Archives, many of them to his family.

- **Appearance, Personality, and Qualities**: He stood six feet tall, weighed 175-180 pounds, had a slender build, wore a beard and glasses. He was good humored and optimistic. He looked upon problems as a means of testing his endurance, was persistent in achieving goals and overcoming obstacles, had keen business instincts, inspired confidence in others. He was very generous and often paid bills for widows and supported missionaries. He suffered from boils and insomnia, and in 1940, suffered partial paralysis.

- **Motto:** He adopted as his motto a statement by Ralph Waldo Emerson, nineteenth-century American philosopher and essayist: "That which we persist in doing becomes easier for us to do, not that the nature of the thing itself has changed, but that our power to do it is increased." (Ralph Waldo Emerson, *Focus on American Literature*, edited by Philip McFarland, p. 132.)

- **Died**: May 14, 1945, of heart failure in Salt Lake City, Utah (age 88)

- **1945:** Members: 954,004 Stakes: 149
  Missions: 38 Temples: 7
  Missionaries: 1,313
  General Authorities: 31

Biographical Highlights

Early in his youth, Heber developed a spirit of independence and determination that later made him outstanding among his associates. His father died when Heber was nine days old. His mother greatly influenced his life and taught him courage, self-confidence, self-control, and perseverance. As a boy, he became an expert marble player, then hired other boys to do his chores, paying them in marbles. He was an inspiration to many through his willingness to persevere until he achieved his goals, adding to his strong will an unwavering faith that God would turn his weaknesses to strengths. One goal he set was to become a competent baseball player; ultimately, his team won territorial championships in Utah, California, Colorado, and Wyoming.

Heber worked very hard as a child, often foregoing boyhood activities to help his widowed mother with household chores. He had expected a mission call at the April 1876 general conference but did not receive one. The brethren felt he was already performing "a very splendid mission" in providing for his widowed mother.

After he was teased for his poor handwriting, he vowed to be a good penman and spent many hours practicing. He earned first prize for his penmanship at the state fair and later taught handwriting at the University of Deseret.

Later, President Grant had a great desire to sing the beloved hymns of the Church. As a young boy he had taken singing lessons but had been unable to carry a tune. His music instructor had told him he could sing, but added, "I would like to be a least forty miles away when you are doing it." (*GS*, p. 351.) Nevertheless, Heber was persistent and kept on singing though he lacked musical talent.

As another example of his persistence, he faithfully kept a journal. "I sometimes feel almost like stopping the writing of a journal," he wrote on January 9, 1884, "as my grammar is so poor, also my spelling that I dislike to leave such a record as I have to make under the circumstances, but I am of the opinion that it is almost a matter of duty that I keep a journal and this is the main reason that I am willing to do so." (Gibbons, *Heber J. Grant*, p. viii.)

President Grant's determination came in part from his mother. He often said she was "all to me." She set an example of courage, love, and honor that he acknowledged and followed. He said that one reason he was President of the Church was because he followed the advice and counsel and the burning testimony of God that came to him from his mother. She taught him he would be a success if he would always do what was right.

When he was preparing for marriage, his friends tried to talk him into getting married by the local bishop and later being sealed when the Salt Lake Temple was completed. But he ignored them, and made the long journey to the St. George Temple to be "married properly to start out with."

Church leaders had foretold President Grant's apostleship from his childhood. At the age of twenty-three, he was called as President of the Tooele Stake. Two years later, he became the first Apostle to be born in Utah. He felt unworthy to be an Apostle and questioned the Lord about the call. His prayers were answered in a marvelous vision that confirmed his call and put an end to his self-doubts.

"During Heber J. Grant's early service as an apostle,

he concluded that wealth and moneymaking were honorable when dedicated to the common good, by which he meant two things: almsgiving and the establishing of businesses to aid the Church and community. During his years as a young Apostle, he did both. His gifts to friends and worthy purposes often took one-third of his income. At a time when Apostles commonly engaged in private activities, he was tireless in establishing and developing 'home institutions' to benefit the community. The enterprises included a Utah retail and wholesale business, a livery stable, two 'home' insurance companies, a bank, a Salt Lake newspaper, the famed Salt Lake Theater, the Utah Sugar Company, and a series of less prominent enterprises." (Ronald W. Walker, "Heber J. Grant," *EnM* 2:566.)

He was instrumental in preserving the reputation of the Church and its financial credit during the Panic of 1893 but lost his personal fortune and never fully recovered it. Nationally known as a businessman, President Grant dealt extensively with non-Mormons nationwide and brought sophisticated business management methods to Church administration. He helped the Church acquire many valuable financial assets and helped change the image of the Church to that of a progressive, mainstream American religion. In 1922, he became the first President to speak on the radio.

In his talks, he emphasized home industry, tithing, financial support of the Church, the Word of Wisdom, and temple work. He had the unenviable task of guiding the Saints through the difficulties of the Great Depression and World War II. He placed great importance on music, which is reflected in the 1920 creation of the General Music Committee.

During his administration, the Institute of Religion program was established (1926); the Church Security Program, now called the Welfare Program, was established (1936), to which he donated a large dry farm in western Utah, worth more than eighty thousand dollars; and the first Assistants to the Quorum of the Twelve were called (1941).

Personal Experience

When President Grant's first wife, Lucy Stringham Grant, was dying, President Grant tried to explain to his five little daughters and son that she would not recover. The oldest daughter could not understand why he could not heal her by priesthood administration. President Grant prayed that his daughter would not lose her faith in the power of the priesthood but would instead gain a willingness that the Lord's will be done. Sister Grant died, and not one hour later President Grant heard his oldest daughter comforting her little brother with these words: "Do not weep, do not cry, Heber; since we went out of this room the voice of the Lord from Heaven has said to me, 'In the death of your Mamma the will of the Lord shall be done.'" (*IE*, June 1940, p. 330.)

Heber J. Grant's Testimony

"I bear witness to you today that God lives, that I know that Jesus is the Christ, the Savior of the world, the Redeemer of mankind; that I know that Joseph Smith was and is a prophet of the true and living God. . . .

"I do not have the language at my command to express the gratitude to God for this knowledge that I possess; and time and time again my heart has melted, my eyes have wept tears of gratitude for the knowledge that he lives and that this gospel called 'Mormonism' is in very deed the plan of life and salvation, that it is the only true gospel upon the face of the earth, that it is in every deed the gospel of the Lord Jesus Christ." (*CR*, Oct. 1918, pp. 24-25.)

Teachings of Heber J. Grant

Death. Death seems a most terrible thing, as near as I can judge by attending the funerals of people where the surviving relatives do not know the truth, but to a Latter-day Saint, while death brings sorrow into our homes and our hearts, that sorrow is more or less of the same nature that we feel when we are temporarily called to part with our dear ones who are going out into the mission field or who are moving away for some time. That awful anguish that I have seen exhibited by those who know not the truth, I believe never comes into the heart of a true Latter-day Saint. It has fallen to my lot to part with two wives, to part with a beloved mother, to bury both of my sons, one daughter, and most of my lifelong friends, and yet I do not believe that I have suffered at all in comparison to what I have seen others suffer who know not the truth. (*IE* 42:521.)

Duty. There is but one path of safety to the Latter-day Saints, and that is the path of duty. It is not testimony, it is not marvelous manifestations, it is not knowing that the gospel of Jesus Christ is true. . . . It is not actually knowing that the Savior is the Redeemer, and that Joseph Smith was His prophet, that will save you and me, but it is the keeping of the commandments of God, the living the life of a Latter-day Saint. (*GS*, p. 200.)

Education. I have seen nothing and read nothing but what has confirmed in me in the conviction that the mere development and improvement of the body and the intellect by education, without developing the spirit, does not accomplish what education ought to do for a person. (*GD*, p. 160.)

Enduring to the End. This life is a school, and commencement day to us will be when the battle of this life is o'er and we commence anew to travel on forever. Then if we can pass an examination, we are welcomed back into the presence of our Heavenly Father, because we have been true and faithful. (*CR*, Oct. 1914, pp. 77-78.)

Enthusiasm. I do not believe we accomplish very much in life unless we are enthusiastic, unless we are earnest, and unless we practice what we preach. (*CR*, Apr. 1910, p. 40.)

Example. I wish in my heart that all the members of the Church would have the loyalty in their souls, not only to believe the word of the Lord, but to put it into practice. (*GS,* p. 38.)

Fast Offering Donations. I am converted to the fact that if the Latter-day Saints as a people would actually do without two or three meals once a month, as prescribed, on fast days, and give the full equivalent to the bishop, thus benefiting their own individual health and that of their families—if they conscientiously paid a full day donation, each and every person giving the equivalent of two or three meals one Sunday in each month—it would fully take care of those who are in distressed circumstances. (*GS*, pp. 122-23.)

Giving. The Lord loves a generous giver. No man living upon the earth can pay donations for the poor, can pay for building meetinghouses and temples. . . . can take of his means and send his boys and girls out to proclaim this gospel, without removing selfishness from his soul. (*IE* 42:713.)

God the Father. We believe absolutely that God is a personal being. We believe in the Scripture which states that we were made in the image of God—"created He him, male, and female created He them." Therefore, the God that all Latter-day Saints believe in and worship is a God of individuality. Nothing can be made in your image that does not have all the parts that we have. We do not believe that God is a mere congeries of laws floating in the universe—but we believe that we are the children of God, made in His image. (*MS* 84:1.)

Gospel. It is conceded by all who have taken the time to study in any degree whatsoever, the plan of life and salvation and the principles of the gospel of Jesus Christ, on which life and salvation are based, that their object is to develop man so that he will become sufficiently perfected to be worthy to dwell in the presence of our Father in heaven. . . . Every principle of the gospel has been revealed to us for individual advancement and for our individual perfection. (*MS* 66:168-69.)

Human Rights. Every faithful Latter-day Saint believes, beyond a shadow of doubt, that to each individual the free exercise of conscience, the right and control of property, and the protection of life are inherent rights of which he should never be deprived. (*GS*, pp. 133-34.)

Humility. Next to the committing of sin there is no more fruitful cause of apostasy among the Latter-day Saints than when we put our trust in the arm of flesh. I firmly believe that no man who honestly bows down every day of his life and supplicates God in sincerity for the light of his Holy Spirit to guide him will ever become proud and haughty. On the contrary, his heart will become filled with meekness, humility and childlike simplicity. (*GS* p. 31.)

Missionary Work. I feel sorry for the man or woman who has never experienced the sweet joy which comes to the missionary who proclaims the gospel of Jesus Christ, who brings honest souls to a knowledge of the truth, and who hears the expressions of gratitude and thanksgiving that come from the hearts of those who have been brought by his [or her] labor to a comprehension of life eternal. (*CR*, Oct. 1907, p. 23.)

Missionary Work. If we labor all the days of our life and save but one person, great shall be our joy with that person in the life to come. And if that one person is only our dear self, that is the thing that counts. (*GS*, p. 41.)

Mother. There seems to be a power which the mother possesses in shaping the life of the child that is far superior, in my judgment, to the power of the father, and this almost without exception. I have talked with a great many highly educated men and women who have usually been willing to credit their mothers for their success in life more than the fathers. As the daily vocations in life take father away from home, they do not have the opportunity to get as close to the hearts of their children as do the mothers. After all it is by love, genuine love of our fellows, that we accomplish the most. A mother's love seems to be the most perfect and the most sincere, the strongest of any love we know anything about. I, for one, rejoice in it because of its wonderful example to me. (*RS* 20:299-300.)

Music. The singing of our sacred hymns, written by the servants of God, has a powerful effect in converting people to the principles of the gospel and in promoting peace and spiritual growth. Singing is a prayer to the Lord. . . . Sing with the Spirit of God. Love the words that you sing. I love the songs of Zion. I am confident that the hymns of Zion, when sung with the proper spirit, bring a peaceful and heavenly influence into our homes, and also aid in preaching the gospel of Jesus Christ. (*GS*, pp. 168-70.)

Music. I recommend to the youth of Zion, that they go to work with determination and learn to sing . . . because, next to familiarity with the scriptures, the ability to sing will assist them when they are called to the nations of the earth to preach the gospel. (*GS*, p. 171.)

Opposition. There are two spirits with all men— one telling them what to do that is right, and one telling them what to do that will please themselves, that will gratify their own pride and ambition. If we

live as we ought to live, we will always follow that spirit that teaches us to do that which is right. (*CR*, April 1938, p. 12.)

Persistence. If you have ambitions, dream of what you wish to accomplish and then put your shoulder to the wheel and work. Day-dreams without work do not amount to anything; it is the actual work that counts. . . . I believe in the people that have both the faith and the works and are determined to do things. (*GS*, p. 357.)

Prayer. The prayerful and humble man will always realize and feel that he is dependent upon the Lord for every blessing that he enjoys, and in praying to God he will not only pray for the light and the inspiration of His Holy Spirit to guide him, but he will feel to thank Him for the blessings that he receives, realizing that life, that health, that strength, and that all the intelligence which he possesses come from God, who is the Author of his existence. (*IE*, Dec. 1942, p. 779.)

Selfishness. I have been impressed with the fact that there is a spirit growing in the world today to avoid giving service, an unwillingness to give value received, to try to see how little we can do and how much we can get for doing it. This is all wrong. Our spirit and aim should be to do all we possibly can, in a given length of time, for the benefit of those who employ us and for the benefit of those with whom we are associated. The other spirit—to get all we can, and give as little as possible in return—is contrary to the gospel of the Lord Jesus Christ. It is not right to desire something for which we do not give service or value received. That idea is all wrong, and it is only a question of time when the sheep and the goats will be separated. (*GS*, pp. 183-84.)

Self-Improvement. I do not believe that any man lives up to his ideals, but if we are striving, if we are working, if we are trying, to the best of our ability, to improve day by day, then we are in the line of our duty. If we are working to remedy our own defects, if we are so living that we can ask God for light, for knowledge, for intelligence, and above all, for his Spirit, that we may overcome our weaknesses, then I can tell you, we are in the straight and narrow path that leads to life eternal. Then we need have no fear. I am not afraid of any individual ever injuring me, but I am afraid that perchance I may fail to be as faithful and diligent as I ought to be; I am afraid I may fail to use all the talents God has given me, in the way I ought to use them. (*CR*, April 1909, p. 111.)

Sincerity. The fundamental thing for a Latter-day Saint is to be honest. The fundamental thing for a Latter-day Saint is to value his word as faithfully as his bond; to make up his mind that under no circumstances, no matter how hard it may be, by and with the help of the Lord, he will dedicate his life and his best energies to making good his promise. (*GS*, p. 30.)

Success. The trouble with a great many people is, they are not willing to pay the price; they are not willing to make the fight for success in the battle of life. (*CR*, Oct. 1910, p. 5.)

Teaching. Teaching by precept without example is mighty poor teaching. (*CR*, April 1911, p. 24.)

Temple Work. I believe that if I could find the time to go to the temple and do temple work once a week, there is hardly a man in the entire Church of Jesus Christ of Latter-day Saints but who can find the same time if he wishes to plan his work accordingly. The trouble with so many people is they do not have the desire. (I am speaking of people who live where there is a temple.) If you get into your heart and soul that this is one of the most important things you as Latter-day Saints can do, you will find a way to do it. (*GS*, p. 257.)

Testimony. Wherever the gospel of Christ has gone, men and women by the hundreds and thousands have embraced it and been able to bear individual testimony that they received a witness of the divinity of the work in which we as Latter-day Saints are engaged after supplicating God for a testimony. This testimony has not come through their own study, nor through the natural intelligence with which God has endowed them, but in answer to earnest and sincere prayer, uttered in the name of Jesus Christ our Redeemer, for light and knowledge regarding the divinity of this work. (*GS*, p. 26.)

Thrift. If there is any one thing that will bring

peace and contentment into the human heart, and into the family, it is to live within our means, and if there is any one thing that is grinding, and discouraging and disheartening it is to have debts and obligations that one cannot meet. (*GS*, p. 111.)

Tithing. I want to repeat to the Latter-day Saints my firm belief that God our Heavenly Father prospers and blesses and gives wisdom to those men and to those women who are strictly honest with Him in the payment of their tithing. I believe that when a man is in financial difficulty, the best way to get out of that difficulty (and I speak from personal experience, because I believe that more than once in my life I have been in the financial mud as deep as almost anybody) is to be absolutely honest with the Lord and never allow a dollar to come into our hands without the Lord receiving ten per cent of it. (*CR*, April 1912, p. 30.)

Welfare Plan. Our primary purpose was to set up, in so far as it might be possible, a system under which the curse of idleness would be done away with, the evils of a dole abolished, and independence, industry, thrift, and self-respect be once more established amongst our people. The aim of the Church is to help the people to help themselves. Work is to be re-enthroned as the ruling principle of the lives of our Church membership. (*CR*, Oct. 1936, p. 3.)

Women. Talk about sacrifice! Why the sacrifice of the women of this Church and their devotion to it are beyond the power of pen and tongue to pay tribute. (*CR*, April 1934, p. 17.)

Word of Wisdom. We are promised that if we obey the Word of Wisdom it will give us physical strength, whereby the destroying angel shall pass us by as he did the children of Israel. And we are promised that we shall have hidden treasures of knowledge if we live in accordance with the Word of Wisdom. (*CR*, April 1930, p. 188.)

Work. I assert with confidence that the law of success, here and hereafter, is to have a humble and prayerful heart, and to work, work, WORK. (*GS*, p. 182.)

GEORGE ALBERT SMITH
1870-1951
Eighth President

- **Born**: April 4, 1870, in Salt Lake City, Utah

- **Family**: George Albert Smith was the son of John Henry and Sarah Farr Smith, the second of eleven children. At age 22, George Albert married Lucy Emily Woodruff on May 25, 1892 (she died on November 5, 1937); they had three children. He was the only president who was a widower.

- **Missions**: Southern Utah (1891); Southern States—Lucy joined in the work (1892-94); European Mission President (1919-21)

- **Education**: Ward school, Brigham Young Academy, one year at the University of Utah

- **Occupation**: Businessman

- **Church Callings:** Apostle, General President of YMMIA, YMMIA General Board member, ward Sunday School superintendent, stake MIA superintendent, missionary

- **Apostle**: Ordained by Joseph F. Smith on October 8, 1903 (served 42 years; age 33-75)

- **President of the Twelve**: July 1, 1943, to May 21, 1945 (served 2 years)

- **Senior Apostle**: May 14 to May 21, 1945, (7 days)

- **President of the Church**: May 21, 1945, to April 4, 1951 (served 6 years, age 75-81)

- **General Authority**: Served 47½ years

- **Temple Dedicated**: One: Idaho Falls (1945)

- **Favorite Hymns**: "Let Us Oft Speak Kind Words" and "Nay, Speak No Ill"

- **Selected Teachings**: *Teachings of George Albert Smith* and *Sharing the Gospel with Others*

- **Special Interests and Hobbies**: Marking pioneer sites and trails; outdoor activities (swimming, hunting, fishing, camping); loved horses, playing the harmonica, banjo, and guitar; enjoyed visiting the Indians, collecting objects of art, scouting, and singing, especially humorous songs (learned as a boy) and the songs of Zion. He was a promoter of air transportation.

- **Favorite Phrase**: "We are all our Father's children" (appears on his gravestone).

- **Other Important Responsibilities**: Appointed U.S. Government Receiver and Disbursing Agent for Utah by U.S. President William McKinley (1898); elected President of the International Irrigation Congress (1916); elected President of the International Dry Farm Congress (1917); elected Vice-President of the National Society of the Sons of the American Revolution (1922); elected a member of National Executive Board of Boy Scouts of America (1931).

- **Appearance, Personality, and Qualities**: He was six feet tall, weighed 160 pounds, was slender, had white hair, a thin face, a goatee, and wore glasses. He was universally kind and considerate, made friends easily, and had a very patient manner. He had a remarkable sense of humor and was known as the "Apostle of Love." He gave the gift of hope to others.

- **Died**: April 4, 1951, of respiratory infection in Salt Lake City, Utah (age 81).

- **1951**: Members: 1,111,314   Stakes: 184
  Missions: 43   Temples: 8
  Missionaries: 5,800
  General Authorities: 31

Biographical Highlights

George Albert received his patriarchal blessing at age 14, which foretold his future calling to the Quorum of the Twelve. It said: "Thou shalt become a mighty apostle in the church and kingdom of God upon the earth, for none of thy father's family shall have more power with God than thou shall have for none shall excel thee." (*TGAS*, p. xix.)

George was the fourth generation of his family to serve as a General Authority. His father, John Henry Smith, grandfather, George A. Smith, and great grandfather, John Smith, had been counselors to Church Presidents. He and his father were the only father and son to be members of the Council of the Twelve at the same time.

He was poor and worked tirelessly from his earliest years to improve his financial position, obtaining employment in the Federal Land Office of Utah. Despite continuing bouts of ill health and impaired eyesight, he had a distinguished career as a Church leader and national figure. He suffered from lupus erythematosus for many years (a rare disease that affects all the tissues of the body and produces chronic weakness).

His personal creed declared in part, "I would be a friend to the friendless and find joy in ministering to the needs of the poor." He was known for his efforts to help the troubled and friendless, to settle disagreements, to further human rights, and to reduce prejudice. The major theme of his life was service to humankind. His chief legacy is an example of Christlike love.

His administration was a time of reaching out and lifting people after World War II, when the Church provided welfare assistance to Europe. He helped revitalize the missionary program, and the number of missionaries rose to more than 5,000. There was a general feeling of hatred, distrust, and despair that prevailed throughout the world, and George Albert Smith had the personality and character to cope with these problems. He acquired several historical sites for the Church, promoted missionary efforts in Great Britain, and developed the Lamanite Foster Placement Program. He became the first General Authority to fly in an airplane (1920). He served in the general presidency of the YMMIA, appeared on the cover of *Time* magazine in conjunction with the pioneer centennial in Utah 1947, and was the first president to be televised at general conference (1949). An honorary chief among many Indian tribes, he headed a delegation to the nation's capital to initiate plans to help Native Americans, and he was instrumental in bringing the Scouting program into the Church in 1912. He served on both Church and National Scouting committees and was awarded Scouting's highest honors, the silver beaver and buffalo. He was active in promoting the cause of the blind in Utah. He became founding president of the Utah Trails and Landmarks Association in 1930, and he organized a drive to build more than 100 monuments and markers for historic trails and landmarks.

President Smith loved missionary work. When he traveled by train, he would sit by someone who was alone, begin a conversation, explain Mormonism, leave a tract, and continue in this way until he had proselyted nearly everyone in the train car. Years later, he did the same when traveling by plane.

President Smith prophesied of the marvelous success that would come through the worldwide missionary work of the Church. He encouraged the Church's use of technology. Telecasts of general conference began in 1949 during his administration. He said: "We must preach the gospel to the South American countries . . . to every African section we haven't been in yet . . . to Asia . . . in all parts of the world where we have not yet been permitted to go. I look upon Russia as one of the most fruitful fields for the teaching of the gospel of Jesus Christ." (*CR*, Oct. 1945, p. 119.)

Humanitarian for the Church

He believed that the Church needed more friends among non-Mormons who would offer a good word about Mormonism when the opportunity arose. He made a point of cultivating people of prominence who could befriend the Church, and he made hundreds of nonmember friends.

He felt that his special mission was to break down prejudice toward the Church and its people. He never lost an opportunity to show others that he loved them, regardless of their station in life. He would point out their virtues and then, using tact and wisdom, would point out additional truths of the restored gospel. Two sections of his personal creed apply to this aspect of his life: First, "I would teach the truth to the understanding and blessing of all mankind," and second, "I would not seek to force people to live up to my ideals but rather love them into doing the thing that is right."

While Ezra Taft Benson was mission president in Europe, immediately after World War II, President Smith visited Flora Benson and her children several times, once blessing a very sick daughter with complete recovery. He sought opportunities to help, particularly those who were sick.

Personal Experience of Living Righteously

President Smith's life was not without suffering, physically and emotionally. Yet he always looked for the positive during those trials. Some of his most sacred experiences occurred during his times of greatest distress. In 1900, while an apostle, he became very ill and was close to death. He dreamed that in a wooded countryside, he met his grandfather, George A. Smith, for whom he had been named. The grandfather stopped, looked his grandson in the eye and said, "I would like to know what you have done with my name." President Smith related: "Everything I had ever done passed before me as though it were a flying picture on a screen. . . . My whole life passed before me. I smiled and looked at my grandfather and said: 'I have never done anything with your name of which you need be ashamed.' He stepped forward and took me in his arms, and as he did so, I became conscious again of my earthly surroundings. My pillow was . . . wet with tears of gratitude that I could answer unashamed." (*SGO*, p. 112.)

President Smith's Testimony Inspires Others

As a college student, I had a personal experience with President Smith. I was working at Temple Square part-time. One day I heard President Smith bear his testimony to some visitors in the tabernacle. Later he came over to me, put his arms around me, looked me in the eye, and said, "The Lord and I want you to prepare for a mission." I told President Smith that serving a mission had been a personal goal of mine for many years. I shall never forget the beautiful feeling I had that day that I knew President Smith was the Lord's prophet. I expressed in silent prayer my thanks to my Heavenly Father for this witness. (Personal experience of the author, Emerson R. West.)

Example of Love for Others

Once while President Smith's car was parked in downtown Salt Lake City, his auto robe (lap robe) was stolen. He fretted over the incident and said, "If I had thought the man who took it really needed it, I would have presented it to him and he would not have become a thief." (Pusey, *Builders of the Kingdom*, p. 242.)

Example of Forgiveness and Putting the Kingdom of God First

On Monday, May 21, 1945, fourteen apostles were assembled in the Salt Lake Temple to reorganize the First Presidency. George Albert Smith had been selected and ordained by the brethren to be the new President. President Smith occupied one of the three chairs on the far side of the altar. The two vacant chairs were waiting for the men he would select as his counselors. Under President Grant, the counselors had been J. Reuben Clark, Jr., and David O. McKay. President Smith had been deeply hurt when Elder McKay had insisted that Emily Smith Stewart, George Albert Smith's daughter, be released from the Primary General Board. (She and the Primary general president, May Anderson, had irreconcilable differences over the management of the Primary Children's Hospital.) Although Elder McKay had tried hard to make the parting free of acrimony, he felt strongly that this solution was best. George Albert Smith had taken his daughter's part and had appealed to both the First Presidency and the Quorum of the Twelve but to no avail. He had yielded only when President Grant admonished him to accept the recommendation of the Brethren. Now George Albert Smith was President of the Church.

Up to this point, the course of the ceremony could have been foreseen, for it followed the customary pattern. The question arose over the choice of counselors, which is the prerogative solely of the President. Some assumed that he would not ask David O. McKay to continue as second counselor because of their differences in the Primary board controversy. George Albert was not in a position to pass over one who, in his opinion, had dealt unjustly with his daughter and denied his own requests for redress of his family grievances. Would he use his new authority to right what he believed to be old wrongs?

It is clear that continuation of these experienced and dedicated brethren in the positions they had occupied would be best for the Church. George Albert put aside personal feelings and animosity and rose to a decision befitting a man of God.

The triumph of love and duty over wounds of the past brought a general release of goodwill and fraternal affection. All the Brethren were aware of the hurdle George Albert had cleared. Once more he had demonstrated that his admonition to "seek ye first the kingdom of God and righteousness" was not just a slogan but the rule of his life. (*Builders of the Kingdom*, pp. 314-15.)

George Albert Smith's Testimony

"I learned when I was a boy that this is the work of the Lord. I learned that there were prophets living upon the earth. I learned that the inspiration of the Almighty would influence those who lived to enjoy it.

"I do not know of any man in all the world who has more reason to be grateful than I. I am thankful for my birthright, thankful for parents who taught me the gospel of Jesus Christ and set the example in their home. . . .

"I do not have an enemy that I know of, and there is no one in the world that I have any enmity towards. All men and all women are my Father's children, and I have sought during my life to observe the wise direction of the Redeemer of mankind—to love my neighbor as myself.

"I am grateful to my Heavenly Father that I was born in this land of the free, in this great nation, in

this valley, among the people who have dwelt here. I am grateful for the preservation of my life. Several times when I have been apparently ready to go to the other side, I have been kept here for some other work to be done. When I think of what a weak, frail, individual I am, to be called to be the leader of this church. . . .

"I have lived a long time, as compared with the average of human beings, and I have had a happy life. It will not be many years, in the natural course of events, until the summons to the other side will reach me. I look forward to that time with pleasant anticipation. And after eighty years in mortality, traveling in many parts of the world, associating with many great and good men and women I witness to you, that I know today better than I ever knew before that God lives; that Jesus is the Christ; that Joseph Smith was a prophet of the living God; and that the Church that he organized under the direction of our Heavenly Father, the Church of Jesus Christ of Latter-day Saints—the Church that was driven into the wilderness—is operating under the power and authority of the same priesthood that was conferred by Peter, James, and John upon Joseph Smith and Oliver Cowdery.

"I know this, as I know that I live, and I realize that to bear this testimony to you is a very serious matter and that I shall be held accountable by my Heavenly Father for this and all other things that I have taught in his name. Realizing this and knowing that if I were to mislead you that I would be held accountable for it, with love and kindness in my heart for all, I bear this witness in the name of Jesus Christ our Lord. " (*IE*, April 1950, p. 264.)

Teachings of George Albert Smith

Creed. I would be a friend to the friendless and find joy in ministering to the needs of the poor. I would visit the sick and afflicted and inspire in them a desire for faith to be healed. I would teach the truth to the understanding and blessing of all mankind. I would seek out the erring one and try to win him back to a righteous and happy life. I would not seek to force people to live up to my ideals but rather love them into doing the thing that is right. I would live with the masses and help solve their problems that their earth life may be happy. I would avoid the publicity of high positions and discourage the flattery of thoughtless friends. I would not knowingly wound the feelings of any, not even one who may have wronged me, but would seek to do him good and make him my friend. I would overcome the tendency to selfishness and jealousy and rejoice in the successes of all the children of my Heavenly Father. I would not be an enemy to any living soul. Knowing that the Redeemer of mankind has offered to the world the only plan that will fully develop us and make us really happy here and hereafter I feel it is not only a duty but also a blessed privilege to disseminate this truth. (*IE*, Mar. 1932, p. 295.)

Equality. All the people of the earth are our Father's children. . . . Regardless of race, creed, or color, all men [and women] are our brothers [and sisters]. (*CR*, April 1947, p. 42.)

Exaltation. One of the beautiful things to me in the gospel of Jesus Christ is that it brings us all to a common level. It is not necessary for a man to be a president of a stake, or a member of the Quorum of the Twelve, in order to attain a high place in the celestial kingdom. The humblest member of the Church, if he keeps the commandments of God, will obtain an exaltation just as much as any other man. In as far as we observe to keep the laws of the Church, we have equal opportunities for exaltation. (*CR*, Oct. 1933, p. 25.)

Faith. Faith is a gift of God; it is the fruitage of righteous living. It does not come to us by our command, but is the result of doing the will of our Heavenly Father. (*CR*, Oct. 1913, p. 103.)

God the Father. The Lord has blessed us with a knowledge that he lives, and has a body, and that we are created in his image. We do not believe that he is some kind of essence or that he is incomprehensible. If you have received the witness that has come to me [you] and know as I know that our Heavenly Father has revealed himself to the children of men, that he is a personal God, that we are created in his image, that our spirits were begotten by him, that he has given us an opportunity to dwell upon the earth to receive a physical tabernacle, in order that we may be prepared to return into his presence and live eternally with him. (*CR*, Oct. 1921, p. 38.)

Gospel. The gospel of Jesus Christ is not just for

us. It is for the people of the world, all our Father's children, and at the present time we have over 5800 missionaries out in the world, from this little Church. What for? To go to all these people and say, "Keep all the good things that you have, keep all that God has given you that enriches your life, and then let us share something with you that will add to your happiness and increase your satisfaction." That is the spirit of the gospel of Jesus Christ. Our happiness is conditioned upon our loving our fellow men, all of whom are children of our Heavenly Father. (*CR*, Oct. 1950, p. 9.)

Happiness. Our eternal happiness will be in proportion to the way that we devote ourselves to helping others. (*CR*, Oct. 1936, p. 71.)

Home. If our houses are not in order, let us set them in order. Let us renew our determination to honor God and keep his commandments, to love one another, to make our homes the abiding place of peace. Each of us can contribute to that in the homes in which we live. (*CR*, Apr. 1950, p. 169.)

Judgment. We are living eternal life, and our position hereafter will be the result of our lives here. Every man will be judged according to his works, and he will receive only that degree of glory that he has earned. (*CR*, April 1945, p. 139.)

Love. Love is the great power to influence this world, and if we do not find more love in the world soon, if people do not get together better than they are, then, as you have already been told, the predictions that are in the scriptures will be fulfilled. (*CR*, April 1950, p. 169.)

Love. Men [and women] cannot approach the likeness of God except by the practice of love to their fellow men. Only by love can peace and joy be made to cover the earth. (*CR*, Oct. 1948, p. 23.)

Love Others. We should keep His commandments and love one another. Then our love should pass beyond the border lines of the Church and reach out after the children of men. (*IE*, Dec. 1945, p. 747.)

Marriage, Temple. Grateful should we be for a knowledge of the eternity of the marriage covenant. If in this life only had we hope, we should indeed be of all men most miserable. The assurance that our relationship here as parents and children, as husbands and wives will continue in heaven and that this is but the beginning of a great and glorious kingdom that our Father has destined we shall inherit on the other side fills us with hope and joy. One of the greatest evidences to me of the divinity of this work is that it teaches there is eternal life on the other side and that there will be a reunion there of the loved ones who have known each other here. Consequently, as parents, we may well be patient and loving toward our children, for they will eternally abide with us on the other side, if we and they are faithful. The few years that we live here may be regarded as a time in which we become acquainted, but, when we mingle in the other side, we will know each other better than we have here. (*CR,* Oct. 1905, p. 29.)

Missionary Work. As we go forward, each of us, each having an influence with our neighbors and friends, let us not be too timid. We do not need to annoy people, but let us make them feel and understand that we are interested, not in making them members for membership, but in bringing them into the Church that they may enjoy the same blessings that we enjoy. (*CR,* Apr. 1948, p. 162.)

Mortality. Today is the beginning of eternal happiness or eternal disappointment for you. (*CR,* Oct. 1944, p. 94.)

Music. I am grateful for a Church that teaches the joy and encourages the sweet influence that comes from music. So important are the hymns of the Church, that our Heavenly Father appointed the Prophet's wife Emma to select hymns that were appropriate for sacred services. We do have excellent hymns in this Church. Even our Primary children, beginning in their tender years, are taught not only to sing the songs of the world, but they are taught to sing the praises of our Heavenly Father and to give thanksgiving in the music that is prepared. What a comforting, uplifting influence there is in music. (*CN,* Feb. 16, 1946, p. 3.)

People of Other Faiths. In all these churches there are good men and good women. It is the good that is in these various denominations that holds them together. It has been my privilege to be with people in many parts of the world and to be in the homes of many people of the various denominations of the world, both Christian and Jew. I have been with the Mohammedans; I have been with those who believe in Confucius; and I might mention a good many others. I have found wonderful people in all these organizations, and I have the tremendous responsibility wherever I go among them, that I shall not offend them, not hurt their feelings, not criticize them, because they do not understand the truth. (*CR,* Oct. 1945, p. 168.)

Prayer. Reference has been made in this conference to the importance of seeking the Lord in prayer. And we should know that our prayers will not avail us much unless we repent of our sins. Faith, repentance, baptism by immersion for the remission of sins, laying on of hands for the gift of the Holy Ghost are the fundamental teachings of our Heavenly Father to us, and have been the groundwork of the Church since it was organized. (*CR,* Oct. 1944, p. 95.)

Requirements in Christ's Church. Faith, repentance, baptism by immersion (for that was the form of baptism that our Master received), laying on of hands for the gift of the Holy Ghost, as taught by him are the requirements in his Church that all men must subscribe to if they would obtain celestial glory. (*CR,* Oct. 1922, p. 99.)

Righteousness. There are two influences ever present in the world. One is constructive and elevating and comes from our Heavenly Father; the other is destructive and debasing and comes from Lucifer. We have our agency and make our own choice in life subject to those unseen powers. There is a division line well defined that separates the Lord's territory from Lucifer's. If we live on the Lord's side of the line, Lucifer cannot come there to influence us, but if we cross the line into his territory, we are in his power. By keeping the commandments of the Lord we are safe on His side of the line, but if we disobey His teachings, we voluntarily cross into the zone of temptation and invite the destruction that is ever present there. Knowing this, how anxious we should always be to live on the Lord's side of the line. (*IE* 38:278.)

Sabbath. There was no happiness. . . which resulted from violating the Sabbath day in the time of Moses . . . there is no happiness for us now, when we violate the Sabbath day. (*CR,* April 1944, p. 28.)

Scriptures. [The scriptures] have been referred to . . . as letters from our heavenly Father. They may be so received, at least they are his advice and his counsel to all the children of men given to them that they may know how to take advantage of their opportunities, that their lives may not be spent in vain. (*CR*, Oct. 1923, p. 70.)

Self-Control. We should not lose our tempers and abuse one another. I want to say that nobody ever abused anybody else when he had the spirit of the Lord. It is always when we have some other spirit. (*CR*, Oct. 1950, p. 8.)

Service. Every kind act that we perform for one of our Father's children is but a permanent investment made by us that will bear eternal dividends. (*CR*, April 1914, p. 13.)

Sharing the Gospel. My understanding is that the most important mission that I have in this life is: first, to keep the commandments of God, as they have been taught to me; and next, to teach them to my Father's children who do not understand them. (*CR*, Oct. 1916, p. 50.)

Testimony. No matter how gifted we may be, or how choice our language, it is the spirit of our Father that reaches the heart and brings conviction of the divinity of this work. (*CR*, Oct. 1904, p. 66.)

Tithing. The Lord has given us the privilege of contributing one-tenth of our interest for His Church, for the development of His work in the world. (*CR*, April 1941, p. 25.)

Thoughts. You will be held accountable for your thoughts, because when your life is completed in mortality, it will be the sum of your thoughts. (*SGO*, p. 63.)

Wives. Brethren, be kind to your wives. I hope that there is no man here who has married one of the daughters of God—and He loves them, they are His daughters—who is not willing to do by her as he knows the Lord would have him do. Do not make her just a convenience in the home to do the slavery and to gratify his appetites—that is not what women were given to men, as wives, for—and I want to say to you that it is your duty and your privilege, as men who hold the Priesthood, to honor your wives and your children if you expect them to honor you. Unless you honor them, God will not be pleased with you. Live in such a way, in love and kindness, that peace and prayer and thanksgiving will be in your homes together. (*CR*, April 1948, p. 183.)

Women. I am proud to belong to a church which was first to extend the franchise to women. It was the Prophet Joseph Smith who first turned the key for the emancipation of women of this world, and it was your organization in whose interest it was turned, and I am sure you are grateful for that. It was not a whim of his, it was an inspiration from the Lord. . . . He didn't intend that womankind should be in slavery to man. . . . The Lord has not said that woman should not be her husband's equal in all good things, and in the blessings that would flow to the sexes. And so, my sisters, you have been given not only your franchise in the Church, but you have been given your franchise in the country, in the Union in which you live. The Lord has given you these privileges. Your vote counts just as much as the vote or your husband or your brother, and it should be just as intelligently used. (*RSM*, Jan. 12, 1925, pp. 10-11.)

Word of Wisdom. I want to say to you that the use of tobacco, a little thing as it seems to some men, has been the means of destroying their spiritual life, has been the means of driving from them the companionship of the Spirit of our Father, has alienated them from the society of good men and women, and has brought upon them the disregard and reproach of the children that have been born to them, and yet the devil will say to a man, Oh, it's only a little thing. (*CR*, April 1918, p. 40.)

Worldliness: I fear that the Latter-day Saints, in many cases, are blinded by . . . their desire to be what the world is; and we have been told in such plain language by our Heavenly Father that we cannot live as the world lives and enjoy His spirit. (*CR*, April 1929, p. 30.)

DAVID O. McKAY
1873-1970
Ninth President

- **Born**: September 8, 1873, in Huntsville, Utah

- **Family**: David Oman McKay was the son of David and Jennette Evans McKay, the third of ten children. At age 27, David married Emma Ray Riggs on January 2, 1901 (she died on November 14, 1970); they had seven children.

- **Missions**: Great Britain (1897-99); Tour of world missions (1920-21); European Mission President (1922-24)

- **Education**: LDS Church Academy (Weber), University of Utah graduate (1897) (president and valedictorian of his class)

- **Occupation**: Educator (faculty member at Weber State Academy)

- **Callings Prior to President**: Missionary, stake Sunday School Board and superintendency, assistant and general superintendent of the Sunday School, Church commissioner of education; mission president, apostle, Second Counselor in the First Presidency (1934-51)

- **Apostle**: Ordained by Joseph F. Smith on April 9, 1906 (served 45 years; age 32-77)

- **President of the Quorum of the Twelve**: September 30, 1950, to April 9, 1951 (served 6 months)

- **Senior Apostle**: April 4 to April 9, 1951 (5 days)

- **President of the Church**: April 9, 1951, to January 18, 1970 (served 19 years; age 77-96)

- **General Authority**: Served 64 years (longer than any other general authority to date)

- **Temples Dedicated**: Five: Swiss (1955), Los Angeles (1956), New Zealand (1958), London (1958), Oakland (1964).

- **Favorite Hymn**: "I Need Thee Every Hour"

- **Selected Teachings**: *Gospel Ideals* and *Cherished Experiences*

- **Special Interests and Hobbies**: Horseback riding, swimming, debate, singing, attending the theater, music, reading English literature, and memorizing poetry. He played the piano for Church meetings and the Huntsville town orchestra.

- **Appearance, Personality, and Qualities**: He was six-feet one-inch tall, weighed 195-200 pounds in his prime, had a kindly humor, was optimistic. He always smiled. He showed a tremendous zest for life, was stately and distinguished in appearance, and was always impeccably dressed. He was a humanitarian, a great teacher, and had a well-stocked and retentive memory. He could quote at will from his literary and inspirational library. He was the first president without a beard since Joseph Smith.

- **Died**: January 18, 1970, of congestive heart failure in Salt Lake City, Utah (age 96)

- **1970**: Members: 2,807,456
  Stakes: 500   Temples: 13
  Missions: 88   Missionaries: 14,387
  General Authorities: 40

Biographical Highlights

At the age of eight, David Oman McKay learned the value of work when he became "the man of the house" when his father was called on a mission. He did the household chores, milked the cows, and fed the livestock. In the summers he delivered by horseback the daily newspaper to a nearby mining town. On these trips he spent much of his time reading and memorizing passages from the world's great literature. Additionally, he helped his mother care for the three younger children. With all this responsibility, he still had time to play second base for the town baseball team. His home was the schoolroom for a lifetime of valiant service to the Lord. His parents' example of willingness to endure sacrifices for the gospel's sake influenced the children to do likewise.

In his youth, David desired to know that the Church was truly restored in its purity. Once, as his saddle horse stood by his side, he knelt by a berry bush and prayed. At the completion of his prayer, he recalled, no change came. He said, "I must say I am just the same 'old boy' that I was before I prayed." (Middlemiss, *Cherished Experiences,* p. 9.) He would later tell the important lesson he learned from that experience: that testimony comes not by simple request, but by combining seeking with obedience, service, and sacrifice.

He loved the scriptures, the works of Shakespeare, and other literary masterpieces. He had an amazing memory and could readily quote from that which he had read. In his writings and speeches, he attacked pertinent issues with precision and force.

He was the first Church President to have been a deacon because few boys received the Aaronic Priesthood before the 1870s.

He was the first Church President to have been married in the Salt Lake Temple, the first to travel by jet to stake conferences, and the first to complete a formal college degree.

David attended Weber State Academy in Ogden, graduating in 1893. He taught for one year in Huntsvil] le, then continued his education at the University of Utah. He played the piano in the dance band, played right guard on the football team, and was president of his class, all the while making such high grades that he graduated as valedictorian of his class. It was at the University of Utah that he he met his sweetheart, Emma Ray Robbins Riggs. After graduation, he was called on a mission to Great Britain. When he returned, he married Emma Ray and accepted a job as a teacher at Weber Academy, where he later served as principal.

"He was a very popular and effective teacher. He believed that teachers must lead students to stretch their minds into the world of ideas. He also believed that teachers must develop in students the moral and ethical values that lead to responsible citizenship. 'Teaching is the noblest profession in the world,' he proclaimed, for 'upon the proper education of youth depend the permanency and purity of the home, the safety and perpetuity of the nation.' Teachers must be the exemplars, and he scolded the nation for not recognizing the need to pay for outstanding teachers in the classroom." (James B. Allen, "David O. McKay," *EnM* 2:871.)

As the general Sunday School superintendent, he emphasized teacher training. He stressed "every member a missionary," authorized the Language Training Mission, and approved a standard plan for teaching the gospel to investigators. He appointed Regional Representatives of the Twelve, presided over the first general conference transmitted by satellite, and authorized the Church correlation program, the Family Home Evening program, and a worldwide chapel-building program.

As Church President, he sponsored the founding of Church colleges, seminaries, Institutes of Religion, and the expansion of Brigham Young University. During his administration, the Church grew from 1.1 million members to 2.8 million members, most of them outside of the United States.

In 1961, he authorized the ordination of members of the First Council of the Seventy to the office of high priest, which gave them the authority to preside at stake conferences, thereby easing the growing administrative burdens of the Quorum of the Twelve.

He was the most widely traveled Church President to that date (having traveled about one million miles). He visited all of the missions in Europe and was the first President to visit missions in South Africa, South America, the Pacific Isles, New Zealand, and Australia while in office. Stakes staffed with local leadership were organized throughout the world. He emphasized the value of family life and education, denounced communism, encouraged civic participation, and authorized a strong statement in 1969 affirming civil rights for all races.

In 1916, President McKay suffered severe injuries in an automobile accident, his face so badly lacerated that many felt he would be permanently disfigured for life. Heber J. Grant blessed him that he would be completely healed, and he was.

President McKay became a personal friend of several U.S. presidents and international statesmen, meeting with top government leaders, expressing the true mission of the Church, correcting misconceptions, and leaving a spirit of friendship. John Foster Dulles, U.S. Secretary of State, called him the best goodwill ambassador the United States had.

One day, when President McKay was in his early nineties, he was climbing a hill to inspect a site for a new chapel. Two local church leaders thought to assist him, one on either arm. Partway up the hill President McKay stopped and said, "Brethren, I don't mind helping one of you climb this hill, but I can't carry you both." (Stewart, *Remembering the McKays*, p. 34.)

President and Sister McKay's marriage became a model of mutual love, courtesy, respect, and security. Throughout their married life, he enjoyed opening the car door for her, offering his arm, or holding her coat. He called her "the sweetest, most helpful wife that ever inspired a man to noble endeavor." When they were both confined to their wheelchairs, they would, with good-humor, challenge each other to a race to the elevator.

President McKay remembered: "My home life from babyhood to the present time has been the greatest factor in giving me moral and spiritual standards and in shaping the course of my life. Sincerity, courtesy, consistency in word and deed exemplified in the lives of my parents and others have proved a safeguard and guidance." (Schluter, *A Convert's Tribute to President David O. McKay*, p. 27.)

Personal Experience

While on a mission tour in 1920, and touring the islands of the South Pacific, David McKay received a vision of the Savior and the life hereafter, about which he wrote:

"[After falling asleep] I beheld in vision . . . a beautiful city. . . . I then saw a great concourse of people approaching the city. . . . Instantly my attention seemed centered upon their Leader; and though I could see only the profile of his features and his body, I recognized him at once as my Savior! The tint and radiance of his countenance were glorious to behold! There was a peace about him which seemed sublime—it was divine! The city, I understood, was his. It was the City Eternal, and the people following him were to abide in peace and eternal happiness. But who were they?

"As if the Savior read my thoughts, he answered by pointing to a semicircle that then appeared above them, and on which were written in gold the words: 'These are they who have overcome the world who have truly been born again!'

"When I awoke, it was breaking day over Apia Harbor." (Middlemiss, *Cherished Experiences from the Writings of President David O. McKay*, p. 102.)

David O. McKay's Testimony

"I bear you my testimony that the head of this Church is our Lord and Savior, Jesus Christ. I know the reality of his existence, of his willingness to guide and direct all who serve him. I know he restored, with his Father, to the Prophet Joseph Smith the gospel of Jesus Christ in its fulness. I know that these brethren whom you have sustained today are men of God. I love them. Don't you think anything else. God's will has been done. May we have increased power to be true to the responsibilities that the Lord and you have placed upon us, I pray in the name of Jesus Christ. Amen." (*IE*, June 1951, p. 407.)

Teachings of David O. McKay

Agency. Next to the bestowal of life itself, the right to direct that life is God's greatest gift to man. . . . Freedom of choice is more to be treasured than any possession earth can give. It is inherent in the spirit of man. It is a divine gift to every normal being. Whether born in abject poverty or shackled at birth by inherited riches, everyone has this most precious of all life's endowments—the gift of free agency, man's inherited and inalienable right. (*CR*, April 1950, p. 32.)

Character. A man's reaction to his appetites and impulses when they are aroused gives the measure of that man's character. (*GI*, p. 349.)

Chastity. No one can transgress the law of chastity and find peace. (*CR*, Oct. 1920, p. 44.)

Children. There are three fundamental things to which every child is entitled. First, a respected name; second, a sense of security; third, opportunities for development. (*CR*, April 1935, p. 113.)

Conscience. That man is not at peace who is untrue to the whisperings of Christ—the promptings of his conscience. (*CR*, Oct. 1965, p. 10.)

Constitution (U.S.). Next to being one in worshipping God there is nothing in this world upon which this Church should be more united than in upholding and defending the Constitution of the United States. (*CR*, Oct. 1939, p. 105.)

Courage. Moral courage springs from sincerity, the unassuming, most substantial virtue of the human soul. Everyone experiences a thrill at a feat involving physical courage; but the greatest heroes have won their laurels in manifestations of moral courage. Take for example John the Baptist denouncing the sensual Herod; Peter before the Sanhedrin; Paul in a Roman dungeon; Luther at the Diet of Worms; Joseph Smith facing Carthage and martyrdom; and Christ before Pilate and on the Cross. (*IE*, July 1940, p. 395.)

Death. Death cannot touch the spirit of man. . . . Life is full of partings. Parents are saying good-bye to boys drafted into the army. Missionary farewells are being held weekly. We say good-bye to our boys and girls who go back to college. Nearly every parting is associated with sadness. The suddenness of parting intensifies the sadness, but in all these temporary partings there is the hope of a reuniting, which, to an extent, alleviates sorrow

caused by separation. The point I wish to make is that this parting, caused by death, though sudden and somewhat extended, is no less free from the realization of another meeting—the hope of a mother to meet her soldier boy on his return; the hope of a mother to meet her missionary son when he comes back with an honorable release; the hope of parents to meet their son after he has perhaps completed a college course. . . . .Death may have power over the body, for we are, in this life, open to accident and disease, and death may take advantage of these conditions, but there its power ends. Death cannot touch the spirit. If there is any truth that is taught through the gospel of Jesus Christ, it is the truth of the immortality of the soul. (*GI*, p. 55.)

Education. True education seeks . . . to make men and women not only good mathematicians, proficient linguists, profound scientists, or brilliant literary lights, but also honest men, combined with virtue, temperance, and brotherly love—men and women who prize truth, justice, wisdom, benevolence, and self-control as the choicest acquisitions of a successful life. (*GI*, p. 441.)

Example. When we talk to the world about the need of applying religion, our first duty is to apply it in our lives. (*CR*, Oct. 1914, p. 89.)

Friendship. Christ should be your best friend. (*CR*, Oct. 1929, p. 13.)

God the Father. There is a tendency, it seems to me, among Christian nations to move toward a conception of God very much similar to the conception of the Buddhist who say: "There is no personal God-Creator on whose mercy and good will the universe is dependent. Everything owes its origin and development to its own inherent vitalism, or, what comes to the same, to its own will to live. Human ignorance it is which alone invented a personal God-Creator." The Buddhist utterly rejects the belief in a personal God. So do many in the Christian world. In opposition to this false conception of God, I wish to declare that today I feel as I have never felt before in all my life that God is my Father. He is not just an intangible power, a moral force in the world, but a personal God with creative powers, the Governor of the world, the Director of our souls. I should like to have the young men of Israel feel so close to him that they will approach him daily, not in public alone, but in private. (*GI*, p. 554.)

Gospel. The mission of the gospel of Jesus Christ [is] to make evil-minded men and women good, and make good men and women better: in other words, to change men's lives, to change human nature. (*CR*, Oct. 1958, p. 94.)

Gratitude. Thankfulness is measured by the number of words; gratitude is measured by the nature of our actions. (CR, Oct. 1955, p. 4.)

Happiness. (Ten Rules of Happiness)
1. Develop yourself by self-discipline.
2. Joy comes through creation—sorrow through destruction. Every living thing can grow: Use the world wisely to realize soul growth.
3. Do things which are hard to do.
4. Entertain upbuilding thoughts. What you think about when you do not have to think shows what you really are.
5. Do your best this hour, and you will do better the next.
6. Be true to those who trust you.
7. Pray for wisdom, courage, and a kind heart.
8. Give heed to God's messages through inspiration. If self-indulgence, jealousy, avarice, or worry have deadened your response, pray to the Lord to wipe out these impediments.
9. True friends enrich life. If you would have friends, be one.
10. Faith is the foundation of all things— including happiness. (*IE*, June 1951, p. 401.)

Home. No other success can compensate for failure in the home. (*CR*, April 1964, p. 5.)

Humor. A person without a sense of humor misses much of the joy of living. (James B. Allen, "David O. McKay," *TPC*, p. 293.)

Immortality. In what, then, does true immortality consist? It consists in the persistence of personality after death. The Savior's heartbeats were silenced, his body placed in the tomb; but his personality, the eternal part, lived and moved and had its being in the eternal beyond to which his persecutors were unresponsive and dead. I believe with all my soul in the persistence of personality after death. I cannot believe otherwise. *(GI*, p. 54.)

Love Others. Christianity is love in action. There is no better way to manifest love for God, than to show an unselfish love for your fellowmen. (*GI*, p. 129.)

Marriage. Let us instruct young people who come to us, first, to young men through the Church, to know that a woman should be queen of her own body. The marriage covenant does not give the man the right to enslave her or to abuse her or to use her merely for the gratification of his passion. Your marriage ceremony does not give you that right.

Second, let them remember that gentleness and consideration after the ceremony [are] just as appropriate and necessary and beautiful as gentleness and consideration before the wedding.

Third, let us realize that manhood is not undermined by the practicing of continence, not withstanding what some psychiatrists claim. Chastity is the crown of beautiful womanhood, and self-control is the source of true manhood, if you will know it, not indulgence. . . .

Let us teach our young men to enter into matrimony with the idea that each will be just as courteous and considerate of a wife after the ceremony as during courtship. (*CR*, Apr. 1952, pp. 86-87.)

Missionary. Every member a missionary. (*CR*, April 1959, p. 122.)

Motherhood. Motherhood is the one thing in all the world which most truly exemplifies the God-given virtues of creating and sacrificing. Though it carries the woman close to the brink of death, motherhood also leads her into the very realm of the fountains of life and makes her co-partner with the Creator in bestowing upon eternal spirits mortal life. . . .

Motherhood is just another name for sacrifice. From the moment the wee, helpless babe is laid on the pillow beside her, Mother daily, hourly, gives of her life to her loved one. . . . No language can express the power and beauty and heroism of a mother's love. To each mother's son or daughter, we would say: you need no suggestions on how to make your mother happy on Mother's Day as on every day in the year. If you keep the spotless character and purity of soul she has given you, she will rejoice as the most blessed of mothers. (*GI*, pp. 456-57.)

Obedience. Every world problem may be solved by obedience to the principles of the gospel of Jesus Christ. (*CR*, April 1920, p. 116.)

Personal Philosophy: "Whate'er Thou Art, Act Well Thy Part." [As a young man, David O. McKay found this as an inscription on a stone arch of a home in Stirling, Scotland. He was later to refer to that moment of commitment as a major source of strength throughout his life. (*CR*, Oct. 1954, p. 83.)]

Religion. True religion has three manifestations; first, the thought, the feeling, the mental and spiritual attitude of the individual toward his God; second, worship; and third, service to one's fellows. (*CR*, April 1929, p. 98.)

Resurrection. If Christ lived after death, so shall men, each one taking the place in the next world for which he is best fitted. Since love is as eternal as life; the message of the resurrection is the most glorifying ever given to man; for when death takes a loved one from us, we can look with assurance into the open grave and say, "He is not here," and "He will arise again." (*GI*, p. 63.)

Reverence. Akin to the respect for law and a contributing factor toward it is reverence for sacred things. It has been truly said that reverence is the noblest state in which a man can live in the world. . . . The true expression of reverence is found in the Savior's admonition to love the Lord thy God with all thy might, mind, and strength, and thy neighbor as thyself. (See Matt. 22:37-39.). . . . The principle of self-control lies at the basis of reverence. (*GI*, p. 225.)

Self-control. Let us resolve that we shall practice more self-control in our homes, control our tempers and our tongues, and control our feelings, that they may now not wander beyond the bounds of right and purity. (*GI*, p. 160.)

Stewardship. Let me assure you, Brethren, that some day you will have a personal Priesthood interview with the Savior Himself. If you are interested, I will tell you the order in which He will ask you to account for your earthly responsibilities.

First, He will request an accountability report about *your relationship with your wife*. Have you actively been engaged in *making her happy* and ensuring that *her needs* have been met as an individual?

Second, He will want an accountability report about *each of your children* individually. He will not attempt to have this for simply a family stewardship, but will request information about your relationship to *each and every child*.

Third, He will want to know what you personally have done with the *talents* you were given in the pre-existence.

Fourth, He will want a *summary of your activity in your church assignments*. He will not be necessarily interested in what assignments you have had, for in His eyes the home teacher and a mission president are probably equals, but He will request a summary of how you have been of service to your fellowmen in your church assignments.

Fifth, He will have *no* interest in how you earned your living, but if you were honest in all your dealings.

Sixth, He will ask for an accountability on what you have done to contribute in a positive manner to your community, state, country, and the world. (*Address to employees of the Physical Facilities Dept. of the Church, Hotel Utah*, June 1965.)

Teacher. No greater responsibility can rest upon any man [or woman] than to be a teacher of God's children. (*CR*, Oct. 1916, p. 57.)

Testimony. There is nothing a man can possess in this world which will bring more comfort, more hope and faith, than a testimony of the existence of a Heavenly Father who loves us, or of the reality of Jesus Christ, his Only Begotten Son, that those two heavenly personages appeared to the Prophet Joseph Smith and established the Church of Jesus Christ, and that men are officially authorized to represent Deity. (Middlemiss, *Man May Know for Himself*, p. 12.)

Trust. To be trusted is a greater compliment than to be loved. (*CR*, Oct. 1934, p. 91.)

JOSEPH FIELDING SMITH
1876-1972
Tenth President

- **Born**: July 19, 1876, in Salt Lake City

- **Family**: Joseph Fielding Smith was the son of Joseph Fielding and Julina Lambson Smith, the fourth of thirteen children. At age 21, he married Louie E. Shurtliff on April 26, 1898 (she died on March 30, 1908; had two children); at age 32, he married Ethel G. Reynolds on November 2, 1908 (she died on Aug. 26, 1937; had nine children); and at age 61, he married Jessie Ella Evans on April 12, 1938 (she died on August 3, 1971.)

- **Mission**: Great Britain (1899-1902)

- **Education**: Public and ward schools, LDS Business College

- **Occupation**: Genealogist, historian, and writer (author of 25 books and numerous articles)

- **Church Callings**: Missionary, YMMIA General Board, high councilor, apostle, assistant and Church historian, president of Genealogical Society, temple president, Counselor in the First Presidency, 1965-70

- **Apostle**: Ordained by Joseph F. Smith on April 7, 1910 (served 60 years; age 33-93)

- **President of the Quorum of the Twelve**: April 9, 1951, to January 23, 1970 (served 19 years)

- **Senior Apostle**: January 18 to January 23, 1970 (5 days)

- **President of the Church**: January 23, 1970, to July 2, 1972 (served 2½ years; age 93-95). At age 93, he was the oldest man to become president.

- **General Authority**: Served 62 years

- **Temples Dedicated**: Two: Ogden and Provo (1972)

- **Favorite Hymns**: " I Know That My Redeemer Lives"; he wrote, "Does the Journey Seem Long?"

- **Selected Teachings**: *Doctrines of Salvation, Answers to Gospel Questions, Seek Ye Earnestly,* and *Take Heed to Yourselves*

- **Special Interests and Hobbies**: Baking pies, playing handball, swimming, researching, writing, playing the piano for wife Jessie, and flying. (A friend in the National Guard would often take him flying in a jet fighter.) He typed his own conference addresses and some of his books, a skill unusual among men of his generation.

- **Appearance, Personality, and Qualities**: He stood five-feet, nine inches tall, weighed 165 pounds, had a medium build, and wore glasses. He possessed a great sense of humor, exhibited a dignified decorum in public, was modest, kind, and showed love and benevolence. He was optimistic, had tender feelings, demonstrated a strong sense of duty, showed fairness and justice tempered with mercy. He was a theologian, gospel scholar, and a preacher of righteousness. He honored his name and never allowed himself to be called by the nickname "Joe."

- **Died**: July 2, 1972, of a heart attack in Salt Lake City (age 95)

• **1972**: Members: 3,218,908 Stakes: 581
Missions: 102 Temples: 15
Missionaries: 16,357
General Authorities: 41

Biographical Highlights

From childhood, Joseph Fielding Smith was an early riser, a characteristic that lasted throughout his life and was his formula for getting things done. He was up every morning before six o'clock and put in a heavy day's work. "People die in bed," he cautioned, "and so does ambition." One of his sons recalled, "Somehow it seemed immoral to Dad for us to lie in bed after six o'clock. Of course I only tried it once. Father saw to that." Responding to the question, "How do you get so much done?" President Smith said, "It's in the bag," meaning that he was a brown-bagger, and that by not having to go out for lunch, he saved three hundred hours a year. (Joseph Fielding McConkie, *TPC*, pp. 336-37.)

Joseph began assisting his mother in her professional duties as a licensed midwife when he was ten years old. Whenever a call came for his mother's services, it was Joseph's job to hitch the horse to the buggy and drive his mother to the home of the expectant mother. He would wait until the baby was delivered—sometimes nearly freezing to death. "He fervently wished that mothers might time things a little bit better." (Smith and Stewart, *Life of Joseph Fielding Smith*, pp. 52-53.)

President Smith's daughter, Amelia Smith McConkie, said: "His birth was in fulfillment of his mother's earnest prayers for a son as Hannah had raised Samuel and would dedicate his life to serving the Lord. Both his mother and father became Joseph's teachers. He was an apt student for he loved the scriptures and the history of the Church. Because of the hardships and privations he experienced growing up, life itself taught him many lessons. These lessons included lengthy separations from his father and sometimes his mother as well." (*CN*, Oct. 30, 1993, p. 8.)

He spent his life in Church service from the age of twenty-three until his death, nearly seventy-five years later. He served as a missionary, Church historian for sixty-four years, president of the Genealogical Society and of the Salt Lake Temple,

an apostle, a counselor in the First Presidency and Church President.

In 1899, he left to serve a mission to England, where missionary work was difficult because of persecution against the Church. He was often insulted, had doors shut abruptly in his face, and was a target for mud, rocks, and other debris. He was a faithful missionary, but few were willing to listen, and he baptized no one. It was very discouraging. However, some families in the Church today, with British ancestry, claim family stories that reflect his influence on their families.

He was called the "most prolific writer the Church had known" and "greatest doctrinal teacher of his generation." His twenty-five books and many articles helped educate generations of Church members about the history and doctrine of the Kingdom.

His favorite sayings were "study the scriptures" and "keep the commandments." He had a great love for Christ and the scriptures. He delighted Church audiences in his later years by singing duets with his third wife, Jessie, who was a Tabernacle Choir soloist. Most often he accompanied her while she sang.

He wrote the words to several hymns, including "The Best Is Not Too Good for Me," "Come, Come, My Brother, Wake! Awake!", "Does the Journey Seem Long?" and "We Are Watchmen on the Tower of Zion."

During his administration, Mondays were set aside for family home evenings (1970). Three new Church publications, *The Ensign*, *The New Era*, and *The Friend*, superseded all former general and auxiliary magazines (1971). The first health services missionaries were called (1971). The first area conference was held in Manchester, England (1971). The prospective elders program replaced the Aaronic Priesthood adult program (1972). He appointed mission representatives of the Twelve, instituted the Welfare Services Missionary program, and authorized churchwide use of the Teacher Development Program.

He was the only Church President whose father also served as President, and he was the only President who served on the Quorum of the Twelve with a brother, Hyrum Mack Smith.

Known among his family, friends, and associates as a kind and merciful person, President Smith advised new bishops: "If you ever make any mistakes in judgment, make them on the side of mercy."

Herbert B. Maw, former Utah governor and twenty years younger than Joseph Fielding, shared this interesting insight about a handball game with Elder Smith: "I thought I would just take it easy on the old gentleman and not beat him too far. Imagine my chagrin when he gave me the trouncing of my life! I thought that I was a good handball player, but I was no competition for him at all." (Smith and Stewart, *Life of Joseph Fielding Smith*, p. 15.)

President Smith was interested and curious about all facets of modern life, especially flying, and his attention was especially drawn to military jets. On June 9, 1954, he took his first flight in a fighter: "Colonel Alma Winn invited me to take a ride with him in a jet plane. . . . It was a wonderful experience," and a few days later he flew with Colonel Winn again. (Gibbons, *Joseph Fielding Smith*, pp. 399-400.) He was the only Church president to have unofficially piloted a military jet.

"President Smith liked pie and he liked children, he liked good books, and he loved to hear Jessie sing. . . . He constantly taught his family that the blessings of the kingdom of heaven were not associated with office or position. His doctrine was that true greatness is found in the family." (McConkie, *TPC*, pp. 339-40.)

Personal Experience

President Smith was kind and exhibited very tender feelings, especially to the young. At one of his last conferences, a little girl left her parents and ran up to him. He picked her up and held her close. Reproved later by her parents who feared she might be lost in the crowd, the child replied, "I wasn't lost; I was in the arms of the Prophet." (*CN*, July 8, 1972, p. 7.)

Priesthood Blessing Bestowed

"An interesting instance of healing by President Smith while touring in Brazil was related in the *Ensign* by Richard D. Proctor, a missionary there at the time. It seems that a certain woman in Canoas had recently joined the Church and was eagerly looking forward to President Smith's visit to nearby Porto Alegre. She got so excited about it she suffered a heart attack and had to be hospitalized. When informed of her condition, and of her keen disappointment in not being able to meet him, President Smith decided personally to visit her and administer to her. When he entered the hospital room, the woman gave a cry of joy, exclaiming, 'Now that he has come, I'm sure to get well!' Then President Smith placed his hands upon her head and commanded the sickness to depart from her. From that time on there were no symptoms of the woman's heart attack. Later she explained that when President Smith placed his hands upon her head and began to speak, the pain immediately left her. The physicians, amazed and uncomprehending, found her medically sound and released her the following day. The sister continued faithful in the gospel, testifying to many of the miraculous healing. It was an added witness to her of the divinity of the gospel of Jesus Christ." (Smith and Stewart, *Life of Joseph Fielding Smith*, pp. 316-17.)

Joseph Fielding Smith's Testimony

Joseph Fielding Smith studied the history of the Church, the gospel, and scriptures from childhood, memorizing scriptures from a young age. He said: "I was born with a testimony of the gospel. . . . I do not remember a time when I did not have full confidence in the mission of the Prophet Joseph Smith and in the teachings and guidance of my parents." (*Ibid.*, p. 56.)

President Smith bore this inspiring testimony shortly before his death:

"As I stand now, in what I might call the twilight of life, with the realization that in a not-far-distant day I shall be called upon to give an account of my mortal stewardship, I bear testimony again of the truth and divinity of this great work.

"I know that God lives and that he sent his beloved Son into the world to atone for our sins."

"I know that the Father and Son appeared to the Prophet Joseph Smith to usher in this final dispensation.

"I know that Joseph Smith was and is a prophet; moreover, that this is the Lord's church, and that the gospel cause shall roll forward until the knowledge of the Lord covers the earth as the waters cover the sea.

"I am sure that we all love the Lord. I know that he lives, and I look forward to that day when I shall see His face, and I hope to hear his voice say unto me: 'Come, ye blessed of my Father, inherit the kingdom prepared for you from the foundation of the world.' (Matt. 25:34)." (*Ensign*, Dec. 1971, p. 136.)

Teachings of Joseph Fielding Smith

Covenant. (New and everlasting) What is the new and everlasting covenant? . . . Some members of the Church who are misled and misinformed in regard to what the new and everlasting covenant really is. The new and everlasting covenant is the sum total of all gospel covenants and obligations. (*DS* 1:156.)

God the Father. God is our Father; he is the being in whose image man is created. He has a body of flesh and bones as tangible as man's (D&C 130:22), and he is the literal and personal father of the spirits of all men. He is omnipotent and omniscient; he has all power and all wisdom; and his perfections consist in the possession of all knowledge, all faith or power, all justice, all judgment, all mercy, all truth, and the fulness of all godly attributes. . . . We must believe in God as the possessor of the fulness of these characteristics and attributes. I say also that he is an infinite and eternal being. . . . I am grateful that we know he is an infinite and eternal being who knows all things and has all power and whose progression consists not in gaining more knowledge or power, not in further perfecting his godly attributes, but in the increase and multiplying of his kingdoms. (*Ensign,* May 1971, p. 3.)

Gospel. There is no cure for the ills of the world except the gospel of Jesus Christ. . . . And so we invite all of our Father's children, everywhere, to believe in Christ, to receive him as he is revealed by living prophets, and to join The Church of Jesus Christ of Latter-day Saints. . . . To the honest in heart in all nations we say: The Lord loves you. He wants you to receive the full blessings of the gospel. (*Ensign*, July 1972, p. 27.)

Holy Ghost (Gift of Holy Ghost). What is the gift of the Holy Ghost? Nothing more nor less than the right to the companionship of the Holy Ghost. . . . Every man can receive a manifestation of the Holy Ghost, even when he is out of the Church, if he is earnestly seeking for the light and for the truth. The Holy Ghost will come and give the man the testimony he is seeking, and then withdraw; and the man does not have a claim upon another visit or constant visits and manifestations from him. He may have the constant guidance of that other Spirit, the Spirit of Christ. Every man may receive a manifestation from the Holy Ghost when he is seeking for the truth, but not the power to call upon the Holy Ghost whenever he feels he needs the help, as a man does who is a member of the Church. . . .

Every member of the Church has had hands laid upon his [or her] head for the gift of the Holy Ghost. He has a right to receive the revelations that are expedient and necessary for his guidance individually; not for the Church, but for himself. He has a right through his obedience, through his humility, to receive light and truth as it shall be revealed through the Spirit of Truth, and he who will hearken to that Spirit and seek for the gift of the Spirit in humility and faith shall not be deceived. (*DS* 1:40, 42-44.)

Holy Spirit of Promise. The Holy Spirit of Promise is the Holy Ghost who places the stamp of approval upon every ordinance: baptism, confirmation, ordination, marriage. The promise is that the blessings will be received through faithfulness.

If a person violates a covenant, whether it be of baptism, ordination, marriage or anything else, the Spirit withdraws the stamp of approval, and the blessings will not be received.

Every ordinance is sealed with a promise of a reward based upon faithfulness. The Holy Spirit withdraws the stamp of approval where covenants are broken. (*DS* 1:45.)

Light of Christ (conscience and inspiration). The Lord has not left men (when they are born into this world) helpless, groping to find the light and truth, but every man that is born into the world is born with the right to receive the guidance, the instruction, the counsel of the Spirit of Christ, or Light of Truth, sometimes called the Spirit of the Lord. . . . Often spoken of as conscience—every man has a conscience and knows more or less when he does wrong, and the Spirit guides him if he will hearken to its whisperings. . . . It is through this Spirit that the inspiration comes to those who are members of the Church. This Spirit has been poured out and is the active agency by which the great discoveries in these modern times have been accomplished. (*DS* pp. 51-53.)

Music. Music is truth. Good music is gracious praise of the Lord. It is delightsome to the ear, and it is one of our most acceptable methods of worshipping. . . . My soul is always lifted up, and my spirit cheered and comforted, when I hear good music. (*CR*, Oct. 1969, p. 110.)

Priesthood. Every man who is ordained to the priesthood has authority to officiate in some capacity in the Church. Without priesthood there could be no church, and if there were no priesthood, no official act could be performed in the name of the Lord. Men would be left in darkness without an understanding of the truth, for the power of God could not be made manifest. . . .

This Holy Priesthood, which is eternal, is the authority which prevails in all the universe. The ordinances of the gospel are made valid through its power, and without it the knowledge of God could not be made manifest. It is by this authority and through the ordinances that man is able to know of God. Without the priesthood it would be impossible for man to gain the knowledge which would bring him into the presence of the Father. (*IE*, June 1967, p. 93.)

Priesthood. Do not think because somebody has a higher office in this Church than you have that you are barred from blessings, because you can go into the temple of the Lord and get all the blessings there are that have been revealed, if you are faithful; you can have them sealed upon you as an elder in this Church, and then you have all that any man can get. There have to be offices in the Church, and we are not all called to the same calling, but you get the fulness of the priesthood in the temple of the Lord by obeying this which I have read to you. . . .

There is no exaltation in the kingdom of God without the fulness of priesthood. How could a man be an heir in that kingdom with the priesthood? While the sisters do not hold the priesthood, they share in the fulness of its blessings in the celestial kingdom with their husbands.

To obtain the fulness of the priesthood does not mean that a man must become President of the Church. Every man who is faithful and will receive these ordinances and blessings obtains a fulness of the priesthood, and the Lord has said that "he makes them equal in power, and in might and in dominion." (D&C 76:95.) Only one man at a time on the earth holds the keys of the priesthood, only one man at a time has the power to receive revelations for the Church; but the Lord has made it possible for every man in the Church through his obedience, to receive the fulness of the priesthood through the ordinances of the temple of the Lord. This cannot be received anywhere else. (*DS* 3:132-33.)

Repentance. Repentance is one of the most comforting and glorious principles taught in the gospel. In this principle the mercy of our Heavenly Father and his Only Begotten Son, Jesus Christ, is made manifest perhaps more strongly than in any other principle. What a dreadful thing it would be if there were no forgiveness of sin and no means for the remission of sin for those who are humbly repentant! We can only imagine in part the horror that would overtake us, if we had to endure the punishment of our transgressions forever and ever without the hope of any relief. . . . If the Father had not sent Jesus Christ into the world, then there could have been no remission of sins and there could have been no relief from sin through repentance. (*The Restoration of All Things,* pp. 196-97.)

Restoration. If Joseph Smith was verily a prophet, and if he told the truth when he said that he stood in the presence of angels sent from the Lord, and obtained keys of authority, and the commandment to organize the Church of Jesus Christ once again on the earth, then this knowledge is of the most vital importance to the entire world. No man can reject that testimony without incurring the most dreadful consequences, for he cannot enter the kingdom of God. It is, therefore, the duty of every man to investigate that he may weigh this matter carefully and know the truth. (*DS* 1:189-190.)

Sacrament. We take upon ourselves obligations to do certain definite things. We are placed under covenant, to do what? To take upon us the name of Jesus Christ, to always remember Him, to keep His commandments which He has given us. These three things we covenant to do every time we eat that bread, every time we drink that water which has been dedicated, consecrated to that very purpose. (*CR*, April 1944, p. 51.)

Scripture. I know of no time in the history of the Church, of no time in the history of the world, when it has been more important or necessary for the people to know the will of God, and to make themselves acquainted with that which he has revealed. (*CR*, Oct. 1934, p. 63.)

Smith, Joseph and Hyrum. "Death of Two Testators Required." He had to die. Why? Because we read in the scriptures that the testimony is not of force without the death of the testator—that is, in his particular case, and in the case of Christ. It was just as necessary that Hyrum Smith lay down his life a martyr for this cause as a witness for God as it was for Joseph Smith, so the Lord permitted them both to be taken in that way and both sealed their testimony with their blood. Both of them held the keys of the dispensation of the fulness of times jointly, and they will through all the ages of eternity. Then naturally the Council of the Twelve came into its place, and by right Brigham Young became President of the Church. (*DS* 1:221.)

Temple. If we go into the temple, we raise our hands and covenant that we will serve the Lord and observe his commandments and keep ourselves unspotted from the world. If we realize what we are doing, then the endowment will be a protection to us all our lives—a protection which a man who does not go to the temple does not have. I have heard my father say that in the hours of temptation,

he would think of the promises, the covenants that he made in the House of the Lord, and they were a protection to him. . . . This protection is what these ceremonies are for, in part. They save us now and exalt us hereafter, if we will honor them. I know that this protection is given, for I, too, have realized it, as have thousands of others who have remembered their obligations. (*Utah Genealogical and Historical Magazine*, 21:104.)

Testimony. A testimony of the gospel is a convincing knowledge given by revelation to the individual who humbly seeks the truth. Its convincing power is so great that there can be no doubt left in the mind when the Spirit has spoken. It is the only way a person can truly know that Jesus is the Christ and his gospel is true. There are millions of people on the earth who believe that Jesus lived and died and that his work was for the salvation of souls; but unless they have complied with his commandments and have accepted his truth as it has been restored, they do not know and cannot know the significance of his mission and its benefits to mankind. Only through humble repentance and submission to the plan of salvation can this be made known. The way is open to all if they will receive his truth and accept his ordinances and abide faithfully in them. (*AGQ* 3:31.)

Women. There is nothing in the teachings of the gospel which declares that men are superior to women. The Lord has given unto men the power of priesthood and sent them forth to labor in his service. A woman's calling is in a different direction. The most noble, exalting calling of all is that which has been given to women as the mothers of men. Women do not hold the priesthood, but if they are faithful and true, they will become priestesses and queens in the kingdom of God, and that implies that they will be given authority. (*DS* 3:178.)

Youth. The Lord bless you and keep you, which most assuredly will be so as you learn his laws and live in harmony with them. Be true to every trust. Honor thy father and thy mother. Dwell together in love and conformity. Be modest in your dress. Overcome the world, and do not be led astray by the fashions and practices of those whose interests are centered upon the things of the world. (*Ensign*, July 1972, p. 28.)

HAROLD B. LEE
1899-1973
Eleventh President

- **Born**: March 28, 1899, in Clifton, Idaho

- **Family**: Harold Bingham Lee was the son of Samuel Marion and Louisa Bingham Lee, the second of six children. At age 24, he married Fern Lucinda Tanner on November 14, 1923 (she died on September 24, 1962; they had two daughters); at age 64, he married Freda Joan Jensen on June 17, 1963 (she died on July 1, 1981).

- **Mission**: Western States (1920-1922)

- **Education**: Oneida Stake Academy; Albion (Idaho) State Normal School; University of Utah (teacher's certificate)

- **Occupation**: Educator, sales manager, Salt Lake City commissioner

- **Church Callings:** Missionary, ward superintendent of the Sunday School, high councilor, stake president, managing director of the Church welfare program, apostle, First Counselor in the First Presidency, 1970-72

- **Apostle**: Ordained by Heber J. Grant on April 10, 1941 (served 31 years; age 42-73)

- **President of the Quorum of the Twelve**: January 23, 1970, to July 7, 1972 (served 2½ years)

- **Senior Apostle**: July 2 to July 7, 1973 (5 days)

- **President of the Church**: July 7, 1972, to December 26, 1973 (served 1½ years; age 73-74)

- **General Authority**: Served 32½ years

- **Temples Dedicated:** None

- **Favorite Hymns**: "I Need Thee Every Hour" and the third verse of "How Firm A Foundation"

- **Selected Teachings**: *Teachings of Harold B. Lee*, *Stand Ye in Holy Places*, and *Ye Are the Light of the World*

- **Special Interests and Hobbies**: Gardening, playing the piano, fishing, watching football and basketball games, and making home repairs.

- **Appearance, Personality, and Qualities**: He was five-feet, nine inches tall, weighed 175-180 pounds, and had a medium build. He was spiritually sensitive and had a strong but controlled sense of humor. He was compassionate, gracious, gentlemanly, and always impeccably dressed. He was a builder of confidence and a resolver of problems. He seldom forgot people's names and could recall where he had met them.

- **Died**: December 26, 1973, from cardiac and lung failure in Salt Lake City, Utah (age 74)

- **1974**: Members: 3,306,658   Stakes: 630
Missions: 110   Temples: 15
Missionaries: 17,258
General Authorities: 44

Biographical Highlights

Harold B. Lee's life began on a small farm in Clifton, Idaho, where he learned the meaning of work. He often remarked that he had everything money could not buy. He worked hard to develop careers in education, business, and government, enhancing a lifelong interest in civic affairs. He served two terms on the Salt Lake City Commission and sat on the Board of Directors of the Union Pacific Railroad from 1957 until his death. He was also elected to the board of the Equitable Life Assurance Company of New York.

As president of the Salt Lake Pioneer Stake during the Great Depression, he initiated programs of self-help and relief that ultimately led to his appointment by the First Presidency in 1935 to organize a welfare program for the entire Church. After his call to the Quorum of the Twelve in 1941, he continued to work with the welfare program, later organizing the Welfare Services Department.

Elder Lee served as chairman of the executive committee of the Church correlation program, which initiated sweeping organizational changes to accommodate the Church's rapid international expansion. This program emphasized the family and the home, the connection of auxiliary organizations with priesthood structure, simplification of the curriculum, using scriptures as foundational teaching documents, and restructuring Church magazines to focus on age groups (children, youth, and adults) rather than organizations. He initiated a program for single members, and oversaw the reorganization of the youth program. He played the organ or piano for the Quorum of the Twelve at their weekly meetings in the temple and served on the Church Music Committee.

President Lee was the youngest president in forty years. In August 1972, one month after his ordination, he spoke at the Church's second area conference in Mexico City. The 17,000 devoted Saints in attendance made up the largest indoor conference ever held in the Church, some of whom had come from as far away as Panama, Honduras, and Costa Rica and had traveled up to fifty-three hours "to see the living prophet." (Goates, *Harold B. Lee,* p. 472.)

He was the first President of the Church to visit Israel, a trip he made in 1972. Elder Gordon B. Hinckley, who traveled with him, said that he "felt something of heaven when President Lee bore his testimony at the Garden Tomb. I saw that night President Harold B. Lee . . . standing in the stature of a prophet who bore witness of the living reality of the Lord Jesus Christ." (*Ibid,* p. 601.) President Lee organized the first branch of the Church in the Holy Land. David B. Galbraith, the first branch president, commented: "President Lee's visit . . . will be regarded as a landmark of the restoration of the Gospel. It was . . . the first visit made by a living prophet of the Lord in two thousand years." (*Ibid.,* p. 491.)

President Lee related the following experience about cutting a mission tour short because of a stomach ulcer:

"On the way across the country, we were sitting in the forward section of the airplane. Some of our Church members were in the next section. As we approached a certain point en route, someone laid his hand upon my head. I looked up; I could see no one. That happened again before we arrived home, again with the same experience. Who it was, by what means or what medium, I may never know, except I knew that I was receiving a blessing that I came a few hours later to know I needed most desperately.

"As soon as we arrived home, my wife very anxiously called the doctor. It was now about 11 o'clock at night. He called me to come to the telephone, and he asked me how I was, and I said, 'Well, I am very tired, I think I will be all right.' But shortly thereafter, there came massive hemorrhages which, had they occurred while we were in flight, I wouldn't be here today talking about it. I know that there are powers divine that reach out when all other help is not available." (*CR,* April 1973, p. 179.)

Harold B. Lee was sensitive to the needs and problems of others. As a peacemaker, he enriched, blessed, and healed innumerable lives. A persuader of people and a guardian of moral integrity, he had unusual spiritual insight and great understanding.

For someone who loved and appreciated family life as he did, the bitterest tests came with the death of his wife in 1962. He met this trial faithfully, testifying, "I have come to learn that only through heartbreak and a lonely walk through the valley of the shadow of death do we really begin to glimpse the path that Jesus walked. Only then can we come to claim kinship with Him who gave His life that men might be." (*BYU Speeches of the Year,* 1963, p. 11.) He also lost his daughter Maurine in 1965.

After President Lee's death, Elder Gordon B. Hinckley of the Council of the Twelve summarized his life: "President Lee was frequently knocked down by circumstances during his long odyssey from farm to the office of Church President. But he stood up again where he had fallen and then moved on to greater achievement . . . for out of that chastening process there came a refinement, a patience, a polish, an understanding, a grace beautiful to witness and marvelous in its expression." ("Harold B. Lee," *DN,* Dec. 29, 1973, p. 2A.)

Personal Experience

"I have a believing heart that started with a simple testimony that came when I was a child—I think maybe I was around ten or eleven years of age. I was with my father out on a farm away from our home, trying to spend the day busying myself until my father was ready to go home. Over the fence from our place were some tumbledown sheds that would attract a curious boy, and I was adventurous. I started to climb through the fence, and heard a voice as clearly as you are hearing mine, calling me by name and saying, 'Don't go over there!' I turned to look at my father to see if he were talking to me, but he was way up at the other end of the field. There was no person in sight. I realized then, as a child, that there were persons beyond my sight, for I had definitely heard a voice. Since then, when I hear or read stories of the Prophet Joseph Smith, I too have known what it means to hear a voice, because I've had the experience." (Lee, *SYHP,* p. 139.)

Personal Revelation from God or Satan

President Lee taught that we receive personal revelation or answers from the source of power we obey. He felt faith, prayer, and obedience to the commandments were important in communicating with God. He also taught that, through the Holy Spirit, we must learn to distinguish Godly revelation from personal thoughts and desires and from the influence of Satan.

One evening the stake presidency and the high council of the Pioneer Stake in Salt Lake City, where President Lee served as stake president, had met and excommunicated a man for a serious offense. The next day, the man's brother told President Lee that he had prayed and the Lord had told him that the excommunicated man was innocent.

As President Lee talked with him, the man confessed that he himself was an inactive Church member. He informed him that the stake presidency and high council had heard the evidence and prayed about the situation, and his brother had been found guilty. He asked the man for an explanation for the difference in their answers. The man confessed that he must have received the answer from the wrong source. President Lee said: "And you know, that's just as great a truth as we can have. We get our answers from the source of the power we list to obey. If we're keeping the commandments of God, we'll get our answers from God." (*THBL,* pp. 421-23.)

A Special Witness of Jesus Christ

A few days after his call to the apostleship, Elder Lee was asked to give a radio talk on Easter Sunday.

"I locked myself in one of the rooms in the Church Office Building and took out the Bible. I read in the gospels, particularly the scriptures pertaining to the death, crucifixion, and resurrection of the Lord, and as I read, I suddenly became aware that something strange was happening. It wasn't a story I was reading, for it seemed as though the events I was reading about were very real, as though I were actually living these experiences. On Sunday night I delivered my humble message and said, 'And now, I, one of the least of the apostles here on earth today, bear you witness that I too know with all my soul that Jesus is the Savior of the world and he lived and died and was resurrected for us.'

"I knew because of a special kind of witness that had come to me the preceding week. Then someone asked, 'How do you know? Have you seen?' I can say that more powerful than one's sight is the witness that comes by the power of the Holy Ghost bearing testimony to our spirits that Jesus is the Christ, the Savior of the world. To that, I bear testimony." (Lee, *YALW,* pp. 26-27.)

Harold B. Lee's Testimony

"The Lord and Savior, Jesus Christ, is the head of this Church. I happen to be the one who has been called to preside over His Church at the present time here upon the earth. There is no more powerful weapon that can be forged than the powerful teachings of the gospel of Jesus Christ.

"There are two things that, when fully applied, would save the world. The first is to put the full might of the priesthood of the kingdom of God to work, and the second is the powerful teachings of the gospel of Jesus Christ.

"No truly converted Latter-day can be immoral; no truly converted Latter-day Saint can be dishonest, nor lie, nor steal. That means that one may have a testimony as of today, but when he stoops to do things that contradict the law of God, it is because he has lost his testimony, and he has to fight to regain it again. Testimony isn't something that you have today and you keep always. Testimony is either going to grow to a brightness of certainty or it is going to diminish to nothingness, depending on what we do about it. The testimony that we recapture day by day, is the thing that saves us from the pitfalls of the adversary. . . .

"With all sincerity I bear my witness to you that by a witness of the spirit, more powerful than I have ever experienced before, I know that the Savior lives. As I have sought to live as close as I know how, to know His mind and will concerning matters, and to take the first steps during this last change in the presidency of the church, I need your faith and prayers. Pray for me. . . . I plead with you to pray for me." (*CN*, Aug. 19, 1972, pp. 3, 5.)

Teachings of Harold B. Lee

Church Discipline. [Bishops, branch presidents, stake and district presidents] To be a judge requires spiritual guidance, tact, and wisdom, but it takes courage when action is necessary. . . . Stake presidents and bishops must realize that the gospel is designed to change us all, to make us more like the Master. When we let members lead a double and destructive life, instead of doing them a favor as we suppose, we damage them, sometimes, irreparably. . . . The gospel is to save man, not to condemn them, but to save; it is sometimes necessary to confront and to discipline as the Lord has directed us. When individuals are on the wrong path, our task is to redirect them lovingly, and not to watch idly from our vantage point on the straight and narrow path. (*THBL*, p. 117-18.)

Commandments. The greatest message that one in this position could give to the membership of the Church is to keep the commandments of God, for therein lies the safety of the Church and the safety of the individual. Keep the commandments. There could be nothing that I could say that would be a more powerful or important message today. (*Ensign*, Aug. 1972, p. 20.)

Conversion. To become converted, according to the scriptures, meant having a change of heart and the moral character of a person turned from the controlled power of sin into a righteous life. It meant to "wait patiently on the Lord" until one's prayers can be answered. . . .

Conversion must mean more than just being a "card carrying member of the Church" with a tithing receipt, a membership card, a temple recommend, etc. It means to overcome the tendencies to criticize and to strive continually to improve inward weaknesses and not merely the outward appearances. (*Ensign*, June 1971, p. 8.)

Courage. What is courage? Courage is the quality of every virtue acting at its highest testing point. (*THBL*, p. 606.)

Death. Death of a loved one is the most severe test that you will ever face, and if you can rise above your griefs and if you will trust in God, then you will be able to surmount any other difficulty with which you may be faced. (*NE*, Aug. 1971, p. 4.)

Death. Everyone who lives upon this earth was born to die. That may sound a gruesome thing to say, but if in this life only we had hope in Christ, we would be like all men most miserable. Suppose that everyone who became ill would be administered to and he would live and never die. What a tragedy would befall this whole earth, and the whole plan of salvation would fail! The manner of one's passing is not the important thing. But it is: How did he die? Was he prepared to go? Some go by a heart attack; some go by an accident. . . . It isn't the manner of one's passing that is the important thing, but it is the way we prepare ourselves. (*THBL*, p. 50.)

Example. You cannot lift another soul until you are standing on higher ground than he is. You must be sure, if you would rescue the man, that you yourself are setting the example of what you would have him be. You cannot light a fire in another soul unless it is burning in your own soul. You teachers, the testimony that you bear, the spirit with which you teach and with which you lead is one of the most important assets that you can have, as you help to strengthen those who need so much, wherein you have so much to give. (*THBL*, 462.)

Family Home Evening. This "Home Evening" should be devoted to prayer, singing hymns, songs, instrumental music, scripture reading, family topics and specific instructions on the principles of the Gospel, and on the ethical problems of life, as well as on the duties and obligations of children to parents, the home, the Church, society and the nation. (*YALW*, p. 82.)

Forgiveness. If the time comes when you have done all that you can do to repent of your sins, whoever you are, wherever you are . . . then you will want that confirming answer as to whether or not the Lord has accepted you. In your soul-searching, if you seek for and you find that peace of conscience, by that token you may know that the Lord has accepted your repentance. (*Ensign*, July 1973, p. 122.)

God the Father. We only find God by searching for him. You . . . have but to look around you to see evidences of the continual workings of some great Intelligence or power beyond your own. Contemplate man's own body for a moment and consider the stupendous miracle of his existence, his birth, his development, the functioning of life processes and the touch of divinity that seems inherent in him, and with awe you will exclaim at the wonder of it all. "What is man, that thou art mindful of him?" (Psalm 8:4.) Go out into the stillness of the night and observe the myriads of stars that are inlaid in a background of ebony and watch them night after night moving in exact patterns and regularity. . . . All these and more are perpetual evidences of power with purpose. (*THBL*, p. 6.)

Gospel. All the principles of the gospel are but invitations to learning the gospel by the practice of its teachings. No person knows the principle of tithing until he pays tithing. No one knows the principle of the Word of Wisdom until he keeps the Word of Wisdom. Children, or grownups for that matter, are not converted to tithing, the Word of Wisdom, keeping the Sabbath day holy, or prayer by hearing someone talk about these principles. We learn the gospel by living it. (*SYHP*, p. 215.)

Holy Ghost. Baptism by immersion symbolizes the death and burial of the man of sin; and the coming forth out of the water, the resurrection to a newness of spiritual life. After baptism, hands are laid upon the head of the baptized believer, and he is blessed to receive the Holy Ghost. Thus does the one baptized receive the promise or the gift of the Holy Ghost or the privilege of being brought back to the presence of one of the Godhead, by obedience to whom and through his faithfulness one so blessed might receive the guidance and direction of the Holy Ghost in his daily walks and talks, even as Adam walked and talked in the Garden of Eden with God, his Heavenly Father. To receive such guidance and such direction from the Holy Ghost is to be spiritually reborn. (*CR*, Oct. 1947, p. 64.)

Home. The most important of the Lord's work you will ever do will be within the walls of your own home. (*Decisions for Successful Living*, p. 248.)

Home Teaching/Missionary Work. Home teaching then means "watching over the Church" as the scriptures have defined it. Missionary work is but home teaching to those who are not now members of the Church, and home teaching is nothing more or less than missionary work to Church members. (*THBL*, p. 496.)

Obedience. The most important of all the commandments in the gospel to you and to me is that particular commandment which for this moment requires in each of us the greatest soul searching to obey. (*SYHP*, p. 215.)

Parents. I have asked myself if the failure of children to take care of their aging parents, when they come to a day of want and are in need of sustenance, is due to the failure of parents, in the days gone by, to teach those same children to avoid the curse of idleness, and to be responsible in righteousness before our Heavenly Father. Unless we teach our children today correct principles, they, like some children today, will be thankless and without the natural affection necessary to cement this society upon a firm, determined foundation. (*CR*, Apr. 1946, p. 71.)

Priesthood. Priesthood defined is the power of God given to man to act for Him in all things pertaining to the salvation of man—and I should add, within the limitations of each endowment of authority by the laying on of hands. (*SYHP*, p. 266.)

Repentance. Today I could desire with all my heart that all within the sound of this broadcast would likewise thank God for one more day! For what? For the opportunity to take care of some unfinished business. To repent; to right some wrongs; to influence for good some wayward child; to reach out to someone who cries for help—in short, to thank God for one more day to prepare to meet God. (*IE*, Dec. 1970, p. 30.)

Revelation. The Lord has said it is not only important that there be revelation to the Church through His mouthpiece, the one who held the keys, but His church must also be founded on personal revelation, that every member of the Church who has been baptized and has received the Holy Ghost must be admonished so to live that each might receive a personal testimony and a witness of the divine calling of Him who was called to lead as the president of the Church so that he will accept those words and that counsel as if from the mouth of the Lord Himself. Otherwise, the gates of hell would prevail against that individual. (*SYHP*, pp.129-30.)

Revelation from the Lord/General Conference. If you want to know what the Lord has for this people at the present time, I would admonish you to get and read the discourses that have been delivered at this conference, for these brethren have spoken by the power of the Holy Ghost . . . . It is the mind of the Lord, the will of the Lord, the voice of the Lord, and the power of God unto salvation. (*Ensign*, July 1973, p. 74.)

Scriptures. The Lord has given us in the standard works the means by which we should measure truth and untruth. (*THBL*, p. 153.)

Temple. We talk about security in this day, and yet we fail to understand that . . . we have standing the holy temple wherein we may find the symbols by which power might be generated that will save this nation from destruction. Therein may be found the fulness of the blessings of the priesthood. (*THBL*, p. 574.)

Testimony. Testimony isn't something you have today, and you are going to have always. A testimony is fragile. It is as hard to hold as a moonbeam. It is something you have to recapture every day of your life. (*CN*, July 15, 1972, p. 4.)

Trials. We have to be tried and tested by poverty, by sickness, by the death of loved ones, by temptation, sometimes by the betrayal of supposed friends, by affluence and riches, by ease and luxury, by false educational ideas, and by the flattery of the world. . . . So, we must be refined; we must be tested in order to prove the strength and power that are in us. (*SYHP,* pp. 114-15.)

Women. Woman, who has within her the power of creation in company with her legal and lawful husband here, and to whom she is sealed in celestial wedlock, may have eternal increase in the worlds to come. Woman is the homemaker in her own home, and an exemplar to her posterity in the generations that succeed her. Woman is a helpmate to her husband and is to render him more perfect than he otherwise would be. Woman's influence can bless a community or a nation to that extent to which she develops her spiritual powers in harmony with the heaven-sent gifts which she has been by nature endowed. If she does not forfeit her priceless heritage by her own willful negligence, she can be largely instrumental in safeguarding democracy and downing a would-be tyrant. Year in and year out, she may cast the aura of her calming and refining influence to make certain that her posterity will enjoy the opportunities to develop to their fullest potential their spiritual and physical natures. (*RS,* Jan. 1967, p. 12-13.)

Youth. We love the youth of the Church. . . . The future of the Church is secure, but it will be even brighter if our youth in their word and in their conversation show forth the charity and purity that can come only from one who is a believer. (*YALW,* pp. 63-64.)

SPENCER W. KIMBALL
1895-1985
Twelfth President

- **Born**: March 28, 1895, in Salt Lake City

- **Family**: Spencer Woolley Kimball was the son of Andrew and Olive Woolley Kimball, the fifth of eleven children. At age 22, Spencer married Camilla Eyring on November 16, 1917 (she died on September 20, 1987); they had four children.

- **Mission**: Central States (1914-16)

- **Education**: Public schools; one semester at the University of Arizona

- **Occupation**: Insurance and real estate broker

- **Church Callings:** Missionary, stake clerk, second counselor in stake presidency, stake president, and apostle

- **Apostle**: Ordained by Heber J. Grant on October 7, 1943 (served 30 years; age 48-78)

- **President of the Quorum of the Twelve**: July 7, 1972, to December 30, 1973 (served 1½ years)

- **Senior Apostle**: December 26 to December 30, 1973 (5 days)

- **President of the Church**: December 30, 1973, to November 5, 1985 (served 12 years; age 78 to 90)

- **General Authority**: Served 42 years

- **Temples**: **Rededicated:** Five: Arizona, St. George (1975); Laie (1978); Logan (1979); Manti (1985). **Dedicated**: Twenty-one: Washington (1974); São Paulo (1978); Tokyo, Seattle (1980); Jordan River (1981); Atlanta Georgia, Apia Samoa, Nuku'alofa Tonga, Santiago Chile, Papeete Tahiti, Mexico City (1983); Boise Idaho, Sydney Australia, Manila Philippines, Dallas Texas, Taipei Taiwan, Guatemala City (1984); Freiberg Germany, Stockholm Sweden, Chicago Illinois, Johannesburg South Africa (1985). In addition, while serving in the First Presidency, President Hinckley rededicated or dedicated 17 temples during President Kimball's tenure.

- **Mottos**: (1) "Let us lengthen our stride." (2) "Do It!" (3) "Keep a journal."

- **Favorite Hymn**: "I Need Thee Every Hour"

- **Selected Teachings**: *The Miracle of Forgiveness, Faith Precedes the Miracle*, and *Teachings of Spencer W. Kimball*

- **Special Interests and Hobbies**: Displaying mementos from Indian friends, journal-keeping, sports (in his younger years), especially basketball and handball, singing solos and in quartets, and playing the piano.

- **Appearance, Personality, and Qualities**: He stood five-feet, six and one-half inches tall, weighed 165 pounds, had a medium build, ruddy complexion, white hair, and wore glasses. He had a good sense of humor and a quick wit. He suffered many health problems, enduring open heart surgery and throat cancer. The removal of most of his vocal cords left him with a distinctive weak, raspy voice, but he still pursued his duties energetically. He had great enthusiasm, was a powerful innovator, loved to be among the people, and was a forceful, frank, and persuasive speaker. He preached vigorously against racial prejudice. He demonstrated a legendary capacity for hard work and an equally well-known ability to love and serve all races and nationalities.

- **Died**: November 5, 1985, of heart failure in Salt Lake City (age 90)

- **1985**: Members: 5,920,000   Stakes: 1,570
  Missions: 195   Temples: 37
  Missionaries: 29,265
  General Authorities: 78

Biographical Highlights

As a boy, Spencer demanded much of himself. He excelled in school and church activities and filled many leadership positions throughout his growing-up years. He systematically memorized scriptures and hymns, and at age fourteen he read the Bible from cover to cover.

Spencer W. Kimball is a great example of persistence. Health problems afflicted him continually. When he was seven, he nearly drowned; at ten he suffered a facial paralysis; his mother died when he was eleven, and at twelve he had typhoid fever. In adulthood he had smallpox, scores of boils, a major heart attack, and throat cancer. He had repeated surgery on his heart, throat, and brain and several lesser surgeries. He responded with stronger faith in, and greater closeness to, his Heavenly Father. He was called a "modern miracle" and a modern "Job."

As an apostle, Elder Kimball traveled all over the world and served on many committees. For a quarter-century, he chaired the Lamanite Program after receiving a special assignment from President George Albert Smith to look after the Indians. President Kimball initiated the Indian Student Placement Program and had a special love for Native Americans and other ethnic groups.

He set a remarkable pace in building temples, expanding the scope of missionary activities, and ministering to members worldwide. He led the Church with unusual spiritual power and energetic determination during a period of dramatic vitality and growth. He emphasized the importance of simple basics and defined the three-fold mission of the Church: (1) to preach the gospel, (2) to redeem the dead, and (3) to perfect the Saints. He encour-

aged planting gardens, cleaning up yards, maintaining personal journals, writing family histories, and improving family life. "Lengthen Your Stride" and "Do It" became mottos for the worldwide Church.

President Kimball has been admired for his powerful and persuasive speaking and writing. His book, *The Miracle of Forgiveness*, published in 1969, is widely used by leaders to counsel Church members regarding moral transgression. He was candid about the dangers of sexual sins, including homosexuality and pornography. He "put into writing his feelings about how people could and should become reconciled to the Lord after making mistakes. The book grew out of long experience and deep personal concern and knowing that even active Latter-day Saints needed his message.

"A woman came to [President Kimball] in the temple and asked, 'Do you remember me?' Embarrassed, he admitted he did not. Relief lighted her face. 'You worked and prayed with my husband and me until three o'clock in the morning. If after these nineteen years of repentance you do not remember me or my sins, perhaps the Lord will also remember them no more. Thank you.'" (Edward L. Kimball, "Spencer W. Kimball, *TPC*, 1986 pp. 406-407.)

During his administration, the LDS scriptural canon was expanded (1976) with the addition to the Doctrine and Covenants of two visions, one received by Joseph Smith and the other by Joseph F. Smith. The First Quorum of the Seventy was reconstituted and the genealogy name extraction program was inaugurated (1975). A revelation was announced extending priesthood and temple blessings to all worthy male members (1978). The first all-Church women's fireside was held, and the Missionary Training Center was established in Provo, Utah (1978). Women leaders began to speak in general conference. The Ancestral File concept was added to the four-generation program (1979); various church meetings were consolidated into the three-hour schedule (1980); a network initially consisting of 500 satellite dishes for stake centers outside of Utah was created (1981); major changes were made in the financing of meetinghouse buildings and maintenance (1981). A new edition of the scriptures with LDS chapter headings and an extensive cross-reference system was published—the Bible in 1979 and Triple Combination in 1981.

Area presidencies were established (1984), and a new LDS hymnbook was published (1985).

Other accomplishments: General conferences were shortened from three days to two and stake conferences were scheduled semiannually instead of quarterly. Stake presidents, rather than General Authorities, were permitted to ordain and set apart bishops; stake presidents, when specifically authorized by the Twelve, were allowed to ordain patriarchs. Women were authorized to give prayers in sacrament meetings; nonmembers were permitted to attend priesthood meetings. Emeritus status was initiated for ailing and aged General Authorities. Members of the Second Quorum of the Seventy were designated to serve for periods of three to five years (1984). A major thrust was given to missionary work around the globe, and a new subtitle, "Another Testament of Jesus Christ," was given to the *Book of Mormon*. Twenty-one new temples were dedicated and five temples were rededicated in various areas of the world, including the Orient, South and Central America, Europe, Africa, Australia, the South Pacific, and several cities in the United States.

President Kimball was the first president to call a Lamanite to be a General Authority. He also called General Authorities from Germany, England, Japan, Brazil, Canada, Switzerland, Belgium, Argentina, and the Netherlands. He was the first president to visit the Orient and to make a visit behind the Iron Curtain while in office. His tenure proved to be one of the most active periods in twentieth-century Church history.

Priesthood Revelation for All Worthy Men

Continuing revelation was manifested in the Salt Lake Temple on June 1, 1978, as the First Presidency and the Quorum of the Twelve met in an upper room. They were engaged in mighty prayer, with President Kimball being voice. The subject had been discussed by President Kimball with his counselors and the Quorum of the Twelve, as a whole and individually, for several months. Following the revelation, those present were assured that it was the Lord's will that priesthood and temple blessings be extended to every worthy male member, regardless of race or color. Within a few days, worthy black male members began to be ordained

to the Melchizedek Priesthood. This revelation was added to the Doctrine and Covenants as Official Declaration 2.

Challenge to Women of the Church

President Kimball helped to enlarge the role of women in the Church. He appreciated the intellectual achievements and also the homemaking skills of his wife, Camilla, a former school teacher and an avid reader and learner. He was anxious to change the narrow view some men had of the roles of their wives and daughters. While he affirmed the importance of motherhood, he encouraged women not to lose sight of their own identity and well-being. He spoke on some of these ideas at the general women's fireside held in September 1978. (See *Ensign*, Nov. 1978, p. 104; also *Teachings of Spencer W. Kimball* in this chapter.)

Goodwill, Humility, and Humor

Francis M. Gibbons, former secretary to the First Presidency, relates: "During the years of his presidency, except at the end, when he seldom left his apartment, President Kimball often walked around the Church Administration Building, often into offices unannounced. It was one way to exercise. Regardless of the number of times we might plead with him just to call and let us go to him instead of his coming to see us, he never complied. One never knew when the door would open to reveal the prophet of the Lord standing there. And usually, he would bestow a hug and a kiss on the cheek before taking up the business he had in mind. Who could fail to reciprocate that love? And who could fail to try to measure up to the high standard of achievement he set, to lengthen our stride, to quicken our pace, to extend our reach, to 'do it'?" (Gibbons, *Spencer W. Kimball*, p. xiv.)

President Kimball had a wonderful sense of humor. "He once boarded the elevator at Church headquarters carrying a briefcase bulging with correspondence. There stood a colleague with a small, thin, leather folder under his arm. Looking at his friend, then at the folder, President Kimball asked mischievously, 'Are we overworking you?'" (*Ibid.*, p. xiii.)

President Kimball admonished the members to lengthen their stride by developing greater faith, obedience, and diligence; by preparing their children for missions and temple marriage; by becoming active in civic and political affairs; and by reaching out to share the gospel with neighbors and friends.

At the end of one general conference, he said, "I have made up my mind that when I go home from this conference this night there are many, many areas in my life that I can perfect. I have made a mental list of them, and I expect to go to work as soon as we get through with conference." (*CR*, Oct. 1975, p. 74.)

President Kimball's personal secretary, Arthur Haycock, said, "He never wanted the job, but was content to go along quietly and do the work. He had a common touch. He never worried about whether his shoes were shined or his suit was pressed. Some of his hard work seemed trying to compensate for his shortness and feelings of inadequacy in his callings. He ignited the Church with his simplicity, warmth and prodigious capacity for work. He wanted to die with his boots on and he did, having attended the general conference sessions just a few weeks before his death." (*CN*, Dec. 11, 1993, p. 10.)

Spencer W. Kimball's Testimony

"I know without question that God lives, and I have a feeling of sorrow for those people living in the world of doubt who do not have such assurance.

"I know that the Lord Jesus Christ is the Only Begotten Son of our Heavenly Father and that He assisted in the creation of man and in all that serves man, including this earth and all that is in the world, and that He was the Redeemer of mankind and the Savior of this world, the author of the plan of salvation for all men, and the exalter of all who live all the laws He has given. He it is who organized the true vehicle, this church, and called it after his own name, The Church of Jesus Christ of Latter-day Saints, and in it are all the saving graces.

"I know that there is contact between the Lord with his prophets and that he reveals the truth today to his servants as he did in the days of Adam, Abraham, Moses, and Peter, and numerous others throughout time. God's messages of light and truth are as surely given to man today as in any other

dispensation. Since Adam and Eve were placed in the garden, the Lord has been eager to reveal truth and light to his people, but there have been many times when man would not listen, and of course, 'where there is no ear there is no voice.' I know that the gospel truths will save and exalt mankind if men will accept the truths and fully live up to their commitments and covenants.

"I know this is true, and I bear this testimony to all the world. I urge all men to seriously accept and conform their lives totally to the precepts of the gospel. I bear this witness in all soberness and in the name of Jesus Christ. Amen." (Letter written by Spencer W. Kimball to Emerson R. West, March 11, 1974; quoted in *Profiles of the Presidents*.)

Teachings of Spencer W. Kimball

Abortion. Abortion must be considered one of the most revolting and sinful practices in this day, when we are witnessing a frightening evidence of permissiveness leading to sexual immorality. . . . We have repeatedly affirmed the position of the Church in unalterably opposing all abortions, except in rare instances. (*TSWK*, p. 189.)

Anger. We may get angry with our parents, or a teacher, or the bishop, and dwarf ourselves into nameless anonymity as we shrivel and shrink under the venom and poison of bitterness and hatred. . . . If you permit your anger to rise every time you are crossed . . . you are sure to be unhappy much of the time. We came to earth to learn to control ourselves, to test ourselves, and to see if we could do all the things whatsoever the Lord commanded us. (Abr. 3:25.) We did not come on earth to love ourselves, to appease our tempers, to satisfy our desires, lusts, and longings. We came to subjugate the flesh—to make our minds and bodies do the things which the Spirit knows are best in the long run. (*TSWK*, pp. 242-43.)

Child Abuse. Let no Latter-day Saint parent ever be guilty of the heinous crime of abusing one of Christ's little ones! (*TSWK*, p. 340.)

Consecration. Consecration is the giving of one's time, talents, and means. . . in the building of the Lord's kingdom. . . . We consecrate when we give of ourselves. (*Ensign*, Aug. 1984, p. 4)

Decisions. Indecision and discouragement are climates in which the adversary loves to function, for he can inflict so many casualties among mankind in those settings. . . . Right decisions are easiest to make when we make them well in advance, having ultimate objectives in mind; this saves a lot of anguish at the fork, when we're tired and sorely tempted. . . .

The time to decide on a mission is long before it becomes a matter of choosing between a mission and an athletic scholarship. The time to decide on temple marriage is before one has become attached to a boy friend or girl friend who does not share that objective. The time to decide on a policy of strict honesty is before the store clerk gives you too much change. The time to decide against drugs is before a friend you like teases you for being afraid or pious. The time to decide that you will settle for nothing less than an opportunity to live eternally with our Father is now, so that every choice we make will be affected by our determination to let nothing interfere with attaining that ultimate goal. (*TSWK*, pp. 164-65.)

Faith. In faith we plant the seed, and soon we see the miracle of the blossoming. Men have often misunderstood and reversed the process. They would have the harvest before the planting, the reward before the service, the miracle before the faith. Even the most demanding labor unions would hardly ask for wages before the labor. But many of us would have the vigor without the observance of the health laws, prosperity through the opened windows of heaven without the payment of our tithes. We would have the close communion with our Father without fasting and praying; we would have rain in due season and peace in the land without observing the Sabbath and keeping the other commandments of the Lord. We would pluck the rose before planting the roots; we would harvest the grain before sowing and cultivating. . . .

Faith can heal the sick, bring comfort to those who mourn, strengthen resolve against temptation, bring relief from the bondage of harmful habits, lend the strength to repent and change our lives, and lead to a sure knowledge of the divinity of Jesus Christ. (*FPM*, pp. 4, 12.)

Forgiveness. The pleading sinner, desiring to make restitution for his acts, must also forgive others of all offenses committed against him. The Lord will not forgive us unless our hearts are fully purged of all hate, bitterness, and accusation against our fellowmen. (*TSWK*, p. 102.)

God the Father. God, our Heavenly Father—Elohim—lives. That is an absolute truth. All four billion of the children of men on the earth might be ignorant of him and his attributes and his powers, but he still lives. All the people on the earth might deny him and disbelieve, but he lives in spite of them. They may have their own opinions, but he still lives, and his form, powers, and attributes do not change according to men's opinions. In short, opinion alone has no power in the matter of an absolute truth. He still lives. . . . It is not only a privilege to know God, it is a necessity if man wishes to gain highest blessings. . . .

The Lord has promised to make himself and these mysteries known to all flesh on condition that they reach and search in humility and teachableness. (*TSWK*, pp. 1, 3.)

Idolatry. Many people spend most of their time working in the service of a self-image that includes sufficient money, stocks, bonds, investments, portfolios, property, credit cards, furnishings, automobiles, and the like to guarantee carnal security. . . . We are, on the whole, an idolatrous people—a condition most repugnant to the Lord. (*Ensign*, June 1976, p. 5.)

Journals. We renew our appeal for the keeping of individual histories and accounts of sacred experiences in our lives—answered prayers, inspiration from the Lord, administrations in our behalf, a record of the special times and events of our lives. Stories of inspiration from our lives and those of our ancestors as well as stories from the scriptures and our history are powerful teaching tools.

I promise you that if you will keep your journals and records they will indeed be a source of great inspiration to you, each other, your children, your grandchildren, and others throughout the generations. (*TSWK*, pp. 349-50.)

Love Others. We must remember that those mortals we meet in parking lots, offices, elevators, and elsewhere are that portion of mankind God has given us to love and to serve. It will do us little good to speak of the general brotherhood of mankind if we cannot regard those who are all around us as our brothers and sisters. (*TSWK*, p. 483.)

Marriage. Marriage is perhaps the most vital of all decisions and has the most far reaching effects, for it has to do not only with immediate happiness but eternal joy as well. It affects not only two people but also their families and particularly their children and their children's children down through many generations. (*Marriage*, p. 31.)

Marriage. Your love, like a flower, must be nourished. There will come a great love and interdependence between you, for your love is a divine one. It is deep, inclusive, comprehensive. It is not like that association of the world which is misnamed love, but which is mostly physical attraction. When marriage is based on this only, the parties soon tire of one another. There is a break and a divorce, and a new, fresher physical attraction comes with another marriage which in turn may last only until it, too, becomes stale. The love of which the Lord speaks is not only physical attraction, but spiritual attraction as well. It is faith and confidence in, and understanding of, one another. It is a total partnership. It is companionship with common ideals and standards. It is unselfishness toward and sacrifice for one another. It is cleanliness of thought and action and faith in God and his program. It is parenthood in mortality ever looking toward godhood and creationship, and parenthood of spirits. It is vast, all-inclusive, and limitless. This kind of love never tires or wanes. It lives on through sickness and sorrow, through prosperity and privation, through accomplishment and disappointment, through time and eternity. (*FPM,* pp. 130-31.)

Missionary Work. If a person is old enough to be a member, he is old enough to be a missionary; and he doesn't need to be set apart especially for that calling. Every member has the obligation and the calling to take the gospel to those around him. We want every man, woman, and child to assume his rightful responsibility. . . . I know of no home that is not revitalized when the spirit of missionary work becomes part of that family's way of life. (*Ensign*, Feb. 1983, pp. 3-4.)

Morality. The earth cannot justify nor continue its life without marriage and the family. Sex without marriage for all people, young or older, is an abomination to the Lord, and it is most unfortunate that many people have blinded their eyes to these great truths. Husbands and wives should love and cherish their spouses. They must not break up their homes with divorce, and especially through infidelity and immorality. (*Ensign*, Nov. 1974, p. 8.)

Mortality. The Lord is omnipotent, with all power to control our lives, save us pain, prevent all accidents, drive all planes and cars, feed us, protect us, save us from labor, effort, sickness, even from death, if he will. But he will not.

The basic gospel law is free agency and eternal development. To force us to be careful or righteous would be to nullify that fundamental law and make growth impossible.

Is there not wisdom in his giving us trials that we might rise above them, responsibilities that we might achieve, work to harden our muscles, sorrows to try our souls? Are we not exposed to temptations to test our strength, sickness that we might learn patience, death that we might be immortalized and glorified?

If all the sick for whom we pray were healed, if all the righteous were protected and the wicked destroyed, the whole program of the Father would be annulled and the basic principle of the gospel, free agency, would be ended. No man would have to live by faith.

If joy and peace and rewards were instantaneously given the doer of good, there would be no evil—all would do good but not because of the rightness of doing good. There would be no test of strength, no development of character, no growth of powers, no free agency, only satanic controls.

Should all prayers be immediately answered according to our selfish desires and our limited understanding, then there would be little or no suffering, sorrow, disappointment, or even death, and if these were not, there would be no joy, success, resurrection, nor eternal life and godhood. *(FPM, pp. 96-97.)*

Prayer. Prayer is not an optional activity; it is basic to our religion . . . which includes establishing a prayer relationship with our Father. . . . For whom and what should we pray? We should express gratitude for past blessings. . . . We pray for the poor and needy, and at the same time remember our obligation to do something for them. . . . We pray for the missionaries. . . . We pray for our enemies. This will soften our hearts, and perhaps theirs, and we may better seek good in them. And this prayer should not be confined to national enemies but should extend to neighbors, members of the family, and all with whom we have differences. . . .

We pray for righteousness but do not expect the Lord to make us good. He will help us to perfect ourselves, and as we pray for controls and exercise those controls, we grow toward perfection. We pray for ourselves and our children and all that pertains to us. . . . We pray for the Church leaders. . . . We pray for our fellow believers. . . . We pray for our own family members. . . . We pray for enlightenment, then go to with all our might and our books and our thoughts and righteousness to get the inspiration. We ask for judgment, then use all our powers to act wisely and develop wisdom. We pray for success in our work and then study hard and strive with all our might to help answer our prayers. When we pray for health we must live the laws of health and do all in our power to keep our bodies well and vigorous. We pray for protection and then take reasonable precautions to avoid danger. There must be works with faith. How foolish it would be to ask the Lord to give us knowledge, but how wise to ask the Lord's help to acquire knowledge, to study constructively, to think clearly, and to retain things that we have learned. . . . We pray for forgiveness. . . . We pray for everything that is needed and dignified and proper. *(FPM, pp. 200, 202-207.)*

Repentance. When most of us think of repentance, we tend to narrow our vision and view it is as good only for our husbands, our wives, our parents, our children, our neighbors, our friends, the world—anyone and everyone except ourselves. Similarly there is a prevalent, perhaps subconscious, feeling that the Lord designed repentance only for those who commit murder or adultery or theft or heinous crimes. This is of course not so. If we are humble and desirous of living the gospel, we will come to think of repentance as applying to everything we do in life, whether it be spiritual or temporal in nature. Repentance is for every soul who has not yet reached perfection. *(MF, pp. 32-33.)*

Repentance. Repentance seems to fall into five steps: (1) Sorrow for sin, (2) Abandonment of sin, (3) Confession of sin, (4) Restitution for sin, (5) Doing the will of the Father. *(TSWK, pp. 84-86.)*

Temple Worthiness. Holy temples may be defiled and desecrated by members of the Church. . . .

When promises are made and covenants are entered into without serious or pure intent to magnify them, pollutions may occur in the holy temple. It is not only a matter of receiving a recommend to enter the temples of the Lord, but it is also a matter of one having a pure, sweet, and repentant spirit as well. . . .

All those who possess temple recommends should use them as often as possible to engage in baptisms, endowments, and sealings for the dead. *(TSWK, pp. 538, 540.)*

Testimony. You may know. You need not be in doubt. Follow the prescribed procedures, and you may have an absolute knowledge that these things are absolute truths. The necessary procedure is: study, think, pray, and do. Revelation is the key. God will make it known to you once you have capitulated and have become humble and receptive. *(TSWK, p. 63.)*

Women. No greater recognition can come to you in this world than to be known as a woman of God. No greater status can be conferred upon you than being a daughter of God who experiences true sisterhood, wifehood, and motherhood or other tasks that influence lives for good. *(My Beloved Sisters, p 38.)*

Worship. We do not go to Sabbath meetings to be entertained or even solely to be instructed. We go to worship the Lord. If the service is a failure to you, you have failed. No one can worship for you; you must do your own waiting upon the Lord. *(Ensign, Jan. 1978, p. 5.)*

EZRA TAFT BENSON
1899-1994
Thirteenth President

- **Born**: August 4, 1899, in Whitney, Idaho

- **Family**: Ezra Taft Benson was the son of George T. and Sarah Dunkley Benson, the first of eleven children. At age 27, he married Flora Amussen in the Salt Lake Temple on September 10, 1926 (she died on August 14, 1992); they had six children.

- **Missions**: Great Britain (1921-23); European Mission President (1945, 1964-65)

- **Education**: B.A. from Brigham Young University in animal husbandry; M.A. from Iowa State College in agricultural economics; graduate work at the University of California

- **Occupation**: Farmer, agricultural administrator, government service, Secretary of Agriculture in the Eisenhower administration (1953-1961)

- **Church Callings:** Missionary, stake YMMIA board, Scout executive, first counselor in stake presidency, stake president (twice), and apostle

- **Apostle**: Ordained by Heber J. Grant on October 7, 1943 (42 years; age 44-86)

- **President of the Quorum of the Twelve**: December 30, 1973, to November 10, 1985 (served 12 years)

- **Senior Apostle:** November 5 to November 10, 1985 (5 days)

- **President of the Church**: November 10, 1985, to May 30, 1994 (served 8½ years; age 86-94)

- **General Authority**: Served 50½ years

- **Temples: Rededicated**: Three: Alberta (1991); Swiss, London (1992); **Dedicated**: Nine: Seoul Korea (1985); Lima Peru, Buenos Aires Argentina, Denver Colorado (1986); Frankfurt Germany (1987); Portland Oregon, Las Vegas Nevada (1989); Toronto Ontario (1990); San Diego California

(1993); President Hinckley rededicated or dedicated nine of these temples.

- **Favorite Hymns**: "How Great Thou Art" and "Love at Home"

- **Selected Teachings**: *Come unto Christ, Teachings of Ezra Taft Benson,* and *A Witness and a Warning*

- **Special Interests and Hobbies**: Singing, playing horseshoes, riding horses, attending the theater, scouting, reading poetry, attending family reunions, and speaking on God, family, and country.

- **Appearance, Personality, and Qualities**: He stood six-feet, one-inch tall, weighed 200-220 pounds in his prime, and wore glasses. He had a sense of humor and showed integrity, moral courage, patriotism, and humility.

- **Died**: May 30, 1994, of heart failure in Salt Lake City (age 94)

- **1994**: Members: 8,688,511 Stakes: 1,980
    Missions: 295 Temples: 45
    Missionaries: 47,311
    General Authorities: 104

Biographical Highlights

"My life has been spared on more than one occasion in a miraculous manner, even at birth," said President Benson. Moments after he was born, the attending physician announced to the family, 'There is no hope for the child, but I think we can save the mother.' The faith of my father, the administrations of the priesthood and the quick action of my two grandmothers placing me first in a pan of cold water, and then warm water alternating, brought forth a husky yell, to the joy of all." (*CN*, Jan. 5, 1974, p. 7.) He was named Ezra Taft after his great-grandfather, who was one of the first pioneers to enter the Salt Lake Valley and who also served as an apostle from 1846 to 1869.

For young Ezra, agriculture was a way of life. At age four he could drive a team and was soon herding cattle and thinning beets on his parents' farm in Whitney, Idaho.

After completing his high school education, he attended Utah State Agricultural College (now Utah State University) in Logan where he met Flora Amussen. She was a popular young lady at school, and Ezra courted her with great perseverance until his mission call to Great Britain in 1921. After his return, Flora also decided to serve a mission. While she was gone, Ezra finished his education at Brigham Young University, and upon her return, they were married in 1926. He then accepted a scholarship to Iowa State College to continue his studies in agriculture.

President Benson served as president of the European Mission immediately following World War II. He reorganized branches and delivered much-needed supplies to the Saints there. He served for eight years as President Dwight D. Eisenhower's Secretary of Agriculture (1953-61) and as such was featured on the cover of *U. S. News & World Report*, *Time* (twice), *Newsweek*, and *Business Week*. He suggested that cabinet meetings be opened with prayer, and at the first one, President Eisenhower asked him to be voice. This tradition carried on during the eight years of the Eisenhower administration.

President Benson, known throughout the Church for his patriotism, was a bold spokesman for traditional American values and the U.S. Constitution. His book entitled *The Constitution: A Heavenly Banner* was published in 1986.

Throughout his life his health was generally good, except for a broken hip from a horse's kick in 1978 and a heart pacemaker operation in 1986.

President Benson gave special emphasis to personal and family preparedness and to the reading of the Book of Mormon. More copies of the Book of Mormon were distributed during the first six years of his administration than during all the years since 1830 combined.

During his administration, missionaries began serving in Russia, Poland, and Kenya; temple blessings were made available to all worthy members even if their spouses were not similarly interested (1986); stake seventies quorums were discontinued (1986); BYU Jerusalem Center for Near Eastern Studies was dedicated (1989); and Helvecio Martins of Brazil, the first black General Authority, was called to serve.

President Benson's Theme: "Seek the Spirit"

"*Seek the Spirit!*" was the single most recurring theme in the sermons and writings of President Ezra Taft Benson. It was also the most dominant theme in his life as well. In times of personal decision, trial, responsibility, or opportunity to serve the Lord, President Benson sought the Lord in deep humility, a manifestation of his earnest desire to do the will of God. He stated: "The most important thing in our work in the Church of Jesus Christ is the Spirit. I have always felt that. We must remain open and sensitive to the promptings of the Holy Ghost in this work as in all aspects of our lives." (*Come unto Christ*, p. 17.) He often quoted the counsel of his father: "Remember that whatever you do or wherever you are, you are never alone. Our Heavenly Father is always near. You can reach out and receive His aid through prayer." (Sheri L. Dew, *Ezra Taft Benson*, pp. 25-26.)

President Benson believed the home to be sacred. Seeking the Spirit, according to President Benson, begins in infancy at home and is nurtured within the circle of one's family. Good families invite and foster spirituality in the home.

Sister Benson was a wonderful wife and a great support to President Benson. "He wanted her to travel with him whenever possible, and he was delighted when she could participate. Her very presence provided him with strength and comfort. She was very proud of him.

When President Kimball died, President Benson wrote in his journal of his deep commitment to cultivate the Spirit. "I have never felt weaker and never before have I felt the influence of the Spirit in such great strength. . . . May the good Lord sustain me as I go forward humbly. I think it can be truthfully said, I will never acknowledge the Lord's hand as I have the last few hours." (Dew, *Ezra Taft Benson*, p. 481.)

Call to the Quorum of the Twelve Apostles

In 1943, while working in Washington, D.C., as executive secretary of the National Council of Farmer Cooperatives and serving as stake president, President Benson was offered a new job that would have provided a significant increase in salary but would have required him to move from the area. He traveled to Salt Lake City, hoping to obtain the advice of President David O. McKay, then a counselor in the First Presidency. He was surprised to be told that President Heber J. Grant, then recuperating in a summer cabin from an illness, wished to see him.

"President Grant took my right hand in both of his, and looked into the depths of my very soul, and said: 'Brother Benson, with all my heart I congratulate you and pray God's blessings to attend you. You have been chosen as the youngest apostle of the Church.'

"The whole world seemed to sink. I could hardly believe it was true, that such a thing could happen; and it has been difficult since for me to realize that it is a reality." (*CR*, Oct. 1943, p. 19.)

Ezra Taft Benson's Testimony

"As a special witness of Jesus Christ, and as His humble servant, it is now my obligation and privilege, as the Spirit dictates, to bear pure testimony and witness to that which I know to be true. This I will do.

"I testify that we are the spirit offspring of a loving God, our Heavenly Father. He has a great plan of salvation whereby His children might be perfected as He is, and might have a fulness of joy as He enjoys. I testify that in our premortal state our Elder Brother in the spirit, even Jesus Christ, became our foreordained Savior in the Father's plan of salvation. He is the captain of our salvation and the only means through whom we can return to our Father in Heaven to gain the fulness of joy. . . .

"I testify that during His mortal ministry Christ established His church on the earth. He called and ordained men to be apostles and prophets with authority so that what they bound on earth would be bound in heaven. . . .

"I testify that God the Father and His Son, Jesus Christ, appeared to Joseph Smith in the spring of 1820, thus bringing to an end the long night of apostasy. To Joseph Smith appeared other beings, including John the Baptist and Peter, James, and John, who ordained him with authority to act in the name of God. The church and kingdom of God was restored in these latter days, even The Church of Jesus Christ of Latter-day Saints, with all the gifts, rights, powers, doctrines, officers, and blessings of the former-day Church.

"I testify that through the Book of Mormon God has provided for our day tangible evidence that Jesus is the Christ and that Joseph Smith is His prophet. This other testament of Jesus Christ is a scriptural account of the early inhabitants of America. . . .

"I testify that America is a choice land. God raised up the founding fathers of the United States of America and established the inspired Constitution. . . .

"I testify that there has been, and there is now, and there will be legal successors to the Prophet Joseph Smith who hold the keys of the kingdom of God on earth, even the President of The Church of Jesus Christ of Latter-day Saints. He receives revelation from God to direct His kingdom. . . .

"I testify that it is time for every man to set in order his own house both temporarily and spiritually. It is time for the unbeliever to learn for himself that this work is true. . . . It is time for us, as members of the Church, to walk in all the ways of the Lord. . . .

"I testify to you that a fulness of joy can only come through the atonement of Jesus Christ and by obedience to all of the laws and ordinances of the gospel, which are found only in The Church of Jesus Christ of Latter-day Saints.

"To all these things I humbly testify and bear my solemn witness that they are true, and I do so in the name of Him who is the head of this church, even Jesus Christ, Amen." (*Ensign*, Nov. 1988, pp. 86-87)

Teachings of Ezra Taft Benson

Abuse/Wife and Child. A priesthood holder who would curse his wife, abuse her with words or actions, or do the same to one of his own children is guilty of grievous sin. (*TETB*, p. 446.)

Book of Mormon. There are three ways in which the Book of Mormon is the keystone of our religion. It is the keystone in our witness of Christ. It is the keystone of our doctrine. It is the keystone of testimony. . . . [The Book of Mormon] helps us draw nearer to God. Is there not something deep in our hearts that longs to draw nearer to God, to be more like Him in our daily walk, to feel His presence with us constantly? If so, then the Book of Mormon will help us to do so more than any other book. The Book of Mormon teaches truth . . . [and] bears testimony of Christ. There is power in the book which will begin to flow into your lives the moment you begin a serious study of the book. (*Ensign*, Nov. 1986, pp. 5, 7.)

Book of Mormon. From the Book of Mormon we learn how disciples of Christ live in times of war. From the Book of Mormon we see the evils of secret combinations portrayed in graphic and chilling reality. In the Book of Mormon we find lessons for dealing with persecution and apostasy. We learn much about how to do missionary work. And more than anywhere else, we see in the Book of Mormon the dangers of materialism and setting our hearts on the things of the world. Can anyone doubt that this book was meant for us and that in it we find great power, great comfort, and great protection? (*Ensign*, Nov. 1986, pp. 6-7.)

Cheerfulness. Be cheerful in all that you do. Live joyfully. Live happily. Live enthusiastically know-ing that God does not dwell in gloom and melancholy, but in light and love. (*NE*, Sept. 1979, p. 42.)

Citizenship. History teaches that when individuals have given up looking after their own economic needs and transferred a large share of their responsibility to the government, both they and the government have failed. At least twenty great civilizations have disappeared. The pattern of the downfall is shockingly similar. All, before collapse, showed a decline in spiritual values, in moral stamina, and in the freedom and responsibility of their citizens. They showed such symptoms as excessive taxation, bloated bureaucracy, government paternalism, and generally a rather elaborate set of supports, controls, and regulations affecting prices, wages, production, and consumption.

Only an alert and informed citizenry can insure that the "sentinels on the country's watchtower" do their duty. If we continue to sleep—as we have been doing—we may one day awake to find that the sentinels have been overpowered and replaced by the godless soldiers of the enemy. We must never cease to exercise our God-given rights as citizens to criticize, to suggest alternatives, and to vote new men into office. (*TETB*, pp. 674-75.)

Faith in Jesus Christ. Faith in Him is more than professing belief. Faith in Jesus Christ consists of complete reliance on Him. As God, He has infinite power, intelligence, and love. There is no human problem beyond His capacity to solve. Because He descended below all things (see D&C 122:8), He knows how to help us rise above our daily difficulties. (*Ensign*, Nov. 1983, p. 8.)

Family. A Formula for Successful Families.
1. Successful families have love and respect for each family member. Family members know they are loved and appreciated. . . .
2. Strong families cultivate an attribute of effective communication. They talk out their problems, make plans together, and cooperate toward common objectives.
3. Fathers and mothers in strong families stay close to their children. They talk. . . .
4. Successful families try to work together toward solutions instead of resorting to criticism and contention. They pray for each other, discuss, and give encouragement. . . .

5. Strong families support each other.
6. Successful families do things together: family projects, work, vacations, recreation, and reunions.
7. Successful parents have found that it is not easy to rear children in an environment polluted with evil. Therefore, they take deliberate steps to provide the best and most wholesome influences. Moral principles are taught. Good books are made available and read. Television watching is controlled. Good and uplifting music is provided. But most importantly, the scriptures are read and discussed. . . .
8. In successful Latter-day Saint homes, parents teach their children to understand faith in God, repentance, baptism, and the gift of the Holy Ghost.
9. Family prayer is a consistent practice in [successful] families. (*Ensign*, May 1984, pp. 6-7.)

Freedom. What can we do to keep the light of freedom alive? Keep the commandments of God. Walk circumspectly before Him. Pay our tithes and fast offerings. Attend our temples. Stay morally clean. Participate in local elections, for the Lord has said, "Honest men and wise men should be sought for diligently, and good men and wise men ye should observe to uphold" (D&C 98:10). Be honest in all our dealings. Faithfully hold our family home evenings. Pray—pray to the God of heaven that He will intervene to preserve our precious freedoms, that His gospel may go to every nation and people. Yes, in the words of the Lord Himself: "Stand ye in holy places, and be not moved until the day of the Lord come" (D&C 87:8). Those "holy places" are our temples, stakes, wards, and homes. (*This Nation Shall Endure*, pp. 9-10.)

Government. Since God created man with certain inalienable rights, and man, in turn, created government to help secure and safeguard those rights, it follows that man is superior to government and should remain master over it. . . .

There is only one way to reverse greatly increasing expenditure of money by the federal government and that is to have an awakening to the dangers of excessive spending, and start eliminating programs which require these huge funds. Our government cannot continue to overspend its annual income indefinitely any more than your family or mine can do it. (*TETB*, pp. 680-82.)

Health. The condition of the physical body can affect the spirit. That's why the Lord gave us the Word of Wisdom. He also said that we should retire to our beds early and arise early (see D&C 88:124), that we should not run faster than we have strength (see D&C 10:4), and that we should use moderation in all good things. In general, the more food we eat in its natural state and the less it is refined without additives, the healthier it will be for us. Food can affect the mind, and deficiencies in certain elements in the body can promote mental depression. A good physical examination periodically is a safeguard and may spot problems that can be remedied. Rest and physical exercise are essential, and a walk in the fresh air can refresh the spirit. Wholesome recreation is part of our religion, and a change of pace is necessary, and even its anticipation can lift the spirit. (*Ensign*, Nov. 1974, p. 66.)

Holy Ghost. We hear the words of the Lord most often by a feeling. If we are humble and sensitive, the Lord will prompt us through our feelings. That is why spiritual promptings move us on occasion to great joy, sometimes to tears. Many times my emotions have been made tender and feelings very sensitive when touched by the Spirit. The Holy Ghost causes our feelings to be more tender. We feel more charitable and compassionate with each other. We are more calm in our relationships. We have a greater capacity to love each other. People want to be around us because our very countenances radiate the influence of the Spirit. We are more godly in our character. As a result, we become increasingly more sensitive to the promptings of the Holy Ghost and are thus able to comprehend spiritual things more clearly. (*Ensign*, Apr. 1988, p. 4.)

Home Teaching. Brethren, home teaching is not just another program. It is the priesthood way of watching over the Saints and accomplishing the mission of the Church. Home teaching is not just an assignment. It is a sacred calling. Home teaching is not to be undertaken casually. A home teaching call is to be accepted as if extended to you personally by the Lord Jesus Christ. (*CR*, Apr. 1987, p. 60.)

Honor. An honorable man or woman is the one who is truthful; free from deceit; above cheating, lying, stealing, or any form of deception. An honorable man or woman is one who learns early that one cannot do wrong and feel right. A man's character is judged on how he keeps his word and his agreements.

I speak of honor—your honor to God—your honor to country—your honor to self. I sincerely believe it to be the cure to most of our ills, both on a national or individual basis. (*TETB*, pp. 368-69.)

Hope. We must not lose hope. Hope is an anchor to the souls of men. Satan would have us cast away that anchor. In this way he can bring discouragement and surrender. But we must not lose hope. The Lord is pleased with every effort, even the tiny, daily ones in which we strive to be more like Him. Though we may see that we have far to go on the road to perfection, we must not give up hope. (*TETB*, p. 398.)

Love God. To love God with all your heart, soul, mind, and strength is all-consuming and all encompassing. It is no lukewarm endeavor. It is a total commitment of our very being—physically, mentally, emotionally, and spiritually. . . .

We should give God, the Father of our spirits, an exclusive preeminence in our lives. He has a prior parental claim on our eternal welfare ahead of all other things that may bind us here or hereafter. Should we not love Him for it and honor Him first? (*TETB*, pp. 349-50.)

Love Others. We must develop a love for people. Our hearts must go out to them in the pure love of the gospel, in a desire to lift them, to build them up, to point them to a higher, finer life and eventually to exaltation in the celestial kingdom of God. We emphasize the fine qualities of the people with whom we associate, and love them as children of God whom the Lord loves. (*TETB*, p. 276.)

Love of Wife. What does it mean to love someone with all your heart? It means with all our emotional feelings and with all our devotion. Surely when you love your wife with all your heart, you cannot demean her, criticize her, find fault with her, nor abuse her by words, sullen behavior, or actions. What does it mean to "cleave unto her"? It means to stay close to her, to be loyal and faithful to her, to

communicate with her, and to express your love for her. (*TETB*, p. 508.)

Music. Inspiring music may fill the soul with heavenly thoughts, move one to righteous action, or speak peace to the soul. . . . 'Memorize some of the inspiring songs of Zion and then, when the mind is afflicted with temptations, sing aloud, keep before your mind the inspiring words and thus crowd out the evil thoughts.' This could also be done to crowd out debilitating, depressive thoughts. (*TETB*, p. 324.)

Patience. Patience is another form of self-control. It is the ability to postpone gratification and to bridle one's passions. . . . Patience is composure under stress. A patient man is understanding of others' faults. A patient man also waits on the Lord. We sometimes read or hear of people who seek a blessing from the Lord, then grow impatient when it does not come swiftly. Part of the divine nature is to trust in the Lord enough to "be still and know that [he] is God." (D&C 101:16.) (*TETB*, p. 446.)

Patriarchal Blessings. I would encourage you . . . to receive a patriarchal blessing. Study it carefully and regard it as personal scripture to you—for that indeed is what it is. A patriarchal blessing is the inspired and prophetic statement of your life's mission together with blessings, cautions, and admonitions as the patriarch may be prompted to give. (*TETB*, p. 214.)

Patriotism. Let us do our part to stay free; let us stand eternal watch against the accumulation of too much power in government. . . . Let us all reaffirm our patriotism, our love of country. It is how we respond to public issues. . . . Let us all rededicate our lives and our nation to do the will of God. (*TETB*, p. 655.)

Pride. Pride is essentially competitive in nature. We pit our will against God's. When we direct our pride toward God, it is the spirit of "my will and not thine be done". . . . Our will in competition to God's will allows desires, appetites, and passions to go unbridled.

The proud cannot accept the authority of God giving direction to their lives. . . . They pit their perceptions of truth against God's great knowledge, their abilities versus God's priesthood power, their accomplishments against His mighty works. Our enmity toward God takes on many labels, such as rebellion, hard-heartedness, stiff-neckedness, unrepentant, puffed up, easily offended, and sign seekers. The proud wish God would agree with them. They aren't interested in changing their opinions to agree with God's. Another major portion of this very prevalent sin of pride is enmity toward our fellowmen. We are tempted daily to elevate ourselves above others and diminish them. . . .

The proud make every man their adversary by pitting their intellects, opinions, works, wealth, talents, or any other worldly measuring device against others. (*Ensign*, May, 1989, p. 4.)

Prophet. You sustain the President of the Church as a prophet, seer, and revelator. Have you ever thought about the significance of those terms? Prophet: An inspired teacher of known truths. Seer: One who sees with spiritual eyes—one who foresees the future. Revelator: A revealer of new truth. (*TETB*, p. 141.)

Purity. Stay morally clean. This means that you keep a clean mind. Your thoughts will determine your actions, and so they must be controlled. It's difficult to control thoughts if you submit to temptation. So you will have to carefully select your reading material, the movies you see, and the other forms of entertainment in order to have good thoughts rather than unwholesome desires. (*Ensign*, May 1985, p. 36.)

Scouting. I would to God that every boy of Boy Scout age in America could have the benefits and the blessings of the great Boy Scout program. It is truly a noble program; it is a builder of character, not only in the boys, but also in the men who provide the leadership. I have often said that Scouting is essentially a spiritual program, a builder of men. It is established, as is our government and its Constitution, upon a deeply spiritual foundation. (*TETB*, p. 235.)

Self-Esteem. If we love God, do His will, and fear His judgment more than men's, we will have self-esteem. (*Ensign*, May 1989, p. 6.)

Temple. When you attend the temple and perform the ordinances that pertain to the house of the Lord, certain blessings will come to you: You will receive the spirit of Elijah. . . .You will receive the key of the knowledge of God. You will learn how you can be like Him. Even the power of godliness will be manifest to you. You will be doing a great service to those who have passed to the other side of the veil. . . .We should seek for the blessings and ordinances of the temple. This means that we are keeping the commandments of the Lord–honesty, integrity, personal chastity—and sustaining the Lord's priesthood. (*TETB*, pp. 254-55.)

Testimony. A testimony is one of the few possession we may take with us when we leave this life. (*Ensign*, May 1982, p. 62.)

Trials. There are times when you simply have to righteously hang on and outlast the devil until his depressive spirit leaves you. To press on in noble endeavors, even while surrounded by a cloud of depression, will eventually bring you out on top into the sunshine. . . . While you are going through your trials, you can recall your past victories and count the blessings that you do have with a sure hope of greater ones to follow if you are faithful. (*TETB*, p. 396.)

Women. Since the beginning, a woman's first and most important role has been ushering into mortality spirit sons and daughters of our Father in Heaven. Since the beginning, her role has been to teach her children eternal gospel principles. She is to provide for her children a haven of security and love. . . .

Some sisters are widowed or divorced. My heart is drawn to you who are in these circumstances. The Brethren pray for you, and we feel a great obligation to see that your needs are met. Trust in the Lord. Be assured He loves you and we love you. Resist bitterness and cynicism. . . .

Not all women in the Church will have an opportunity for marriage and motherhood in mortality. But if you in this situation are worthy and endure faithfully, you can be assured of all blessings from a kind and loving Heavenly Father. (*TETB*, pp. 546, 549-50.)

HOWARD W. HUNTER
1907-1995
Fourteenth President

- **Born**: November 14, 1907, in Boise, Idaho

- **Family**: Howard William Hunter was the son of John William and Nellie Rasmussen Hunter, the oldest of two children. At age 23, he married Clara Jeffs on June 10, 1931, in the Salt Lake Temple (she died on October 9, 1983; they had three sons). At age 82, he married Inis Bernice Egan in the Salt Lake Temple on April 10, 1990.

- **Mission**: None

- **Education**: Southwestern University Law School, 1939 (graduated cum laude; admitted to practice law in 1940)

- **Occupation**: Banker; attorney (specialized in corporate, business, and probate law)

- **Church Callings**: Stake scout leader, genealogy teacher, scoutmaster and bishop (concurrently during wartime shortage of male leadership), high priest group quorum leader, high councilor, stake president, chairman of regional council of stake presidents and apostle.

- **Apostle**: Ordained by David O. McKay on October 15, 1959 (served 35 years; age 51-86)

- **President of the Quorum of Twelve**: June 2, 1988, to June 5, 1994 (served 6 years)

- **Senior Apostle**: May 30 to June 2, 1994 (4 days)

- **President of the Church**: June 5, 1994, to March 3, 1995 (served nine months; age 86-87; shortest period of any president up to that time.)

- **General Authority**: Served 35½ years

- **Temples Dedicated**: Two: Orlando Florida and Bountiful Utah (1994)

- **Favorite Hymns**: "How Great Thou Art" and "Abide with Me!"

- **Selected Teachings**: *Teachings of Howard W. Hunter* and *That We Might Have Joy*

- **Special Interests and Hobbies**: Scouting; wild bird egg, stamp, and coin collecting; playing the piano, clarinet (his favorite), drums, trumpet, violin, marimba, and saxophone. Had his own band. Did home repairs, kept an extensive journal, was an historian, was interested in world history, geology, business, economic systems, genealogy, and the Dead Sea scrolls.

- **Appearance, Personality, and Qualities**: He was six feet tall, weighed 185 pounds (in his prime), and had a medium build. He was humorous, kind, fair, compassionate, courageous, and had an indomitable spirit and determination to serve despite his many health problems. He had great concern and compassion for others.

- **Died**: March 3, 1995, of prostate cancer in Salt Lake City, Utah (age 87)

1995: Members: 9,025,914 Stakes: 2,029
Missions: 303 Temples: 47
Missionaries: 48,631
General Authorities: 97

Biographical Highlights

As a youth, Howard W. Hunter loved animals and regularly brought home strays as pets. He sought employment early in life, selling newspapers on street corners, delivering telegrams, and working in a newspaper office. Although his father was a nonmember, his mother reared Howard in the Church. When Howard was twelve, his father reluctantly gave permission for his baptism. His father later joined the Church, and his parents were sealed in the temple.

Howard learned to play the piano when he was six years old and soon took up the violin, marimba, drums, clarinet, and saxophone. During his college years in Seattle, he and some friends formed a band called "Hunter's Croonaders." The group secured a gig on the *SS President Jackson*, enjoying a five-month cruise of Asia. The band also played in hotels and dinner clubs in Tokyo, Shanghai, Hong Kong, and Manila.

Elder Hunter later moved to Los Angeles, where he clerked at a bank during the day and played music for a radio program at night. He gave up professional music in 1931 when he and Clara May (Claire) Jeffs were married in the Salt Lake Temple. He eventually was promoted to bank examiner in the California State Banking Department. He attended law school at night, passed the bar examination in 1939, and worked as a corporate attorney from 1941 to 1959. During this time he also served as a bishop and as a stake president. He and Claire had three sons, the first of whom died in infancy.

President Hunter was thoughtful of his family, especially during trials or while facing some crisis. He was often prompted to phone someone at the right moment the call was needed. Even after his call to the apostleship, he often juggled his schedule to share in family events. When his son Richard was called as a bishop in San Jose, California, President Hunter met him in the United Airlines terminal in San Francisco between flight connections to set him apart.

He was named president of the Genealogical Society of Utah (1964) and served as Church Historian and Recorder (1970). He is the only Church President who has ever served as a bishop. He was the keynote speaker at the first-ever satellite address to all full-time missionaries which originated from the Missionary Training Center (1994).

President Hunter displayed great courage during his speech on February 7, 1993, at Brigham Young University, when a young man leaped to the stage and threatened to detonate a bomb. President Hunter refused when the assailant demanded that he read aloud a letter. The crowd spontaneously burst into the hymn, "We Thank Thee O God for a Prophet," and after a few tense minutes, the assailant was apprehended. Calmly, President Hunter then continued his speech.

President Hunter spent his life preaching the gospel. He was admired for his intellectual integrity as well as his holiness. He was a student of the teachings of the Savior and encouraged everyone to study the restored gospel. He exemplified humility in the face of adversity, particularly the health problems that he and Claire had experienced. Although he endured much pain in his later years, he avoided some medications because he wanted to be able to function well in his calling; he took only mild nonprescription drugs. He counseled, "Prophets and apostles of the Church have faced . . . personal difficulties. I acknowledge that I have faced a few. . . . When these experiences humble us and refine us and teach us and bless us, they can be powerful instruments in the hands of God to make us better people, to make us more grateful and more loving, more considerate of other people in their own times of difficulty." (*CN*, Feb. 13, 1993, p. 2.)

President Hunter's health problems were many. On June 4, 1980, he underwent surgery to remove a benign tumor. He suffered a heart attack on July 23, 1980, then had quadruple bypass heart surgery in October 1986. In April 1987, he had surgery for a bleeding ulcer; in June 1988, he had back surgery. The nerves in his legs deteriorated as a complication of diabetes, and he lost the use of his legs. He fell backward while speaking at the April 1988 general conference and broke three ribs, but he finished his talk. In 1990, he was hospitalized for pneumonia, and in 1992, he was treated for gastrointestinal bleeding. In 1993, complications from gall bladder surgery resulted in a three-week coma. In January 1995, he was hospitalized with prostate cancer.

He was known for his quick wit. On one occasion in 1994, as he was going to speak at the conclusion of his ward sacrament meeting, two brethren helped President Hunter to the stand. President Hunter said, "Brethren, I hope the next time you two have to speak that I don't have to help you to the podium." He then spoke of the Savior and the blessings of the gospel.

During his presidency, President Hunter set a tone of reconciliation. He invited all estranged members who were offended or hurt to come back to the Church. He invited all who met him to become his friend. He traveled almost continuously, even when his health made such travel inconvenient, until December 1994, when he became too ill. He met with the Saints and blessed them with his wisdom and counsel. He organized the 2,000th stake (in Mexico).

His sermons were given in a spirit of love; his words were powerful and rich in meaning, and were always worth rereading. He was never demanding or overbearing. His message to the Saints was to live a Christlike life. A 1995 *BYU Studies* article pointed out that President Hunter had spoken more on the Savior and New Testament gospel themes than any other General Authority up to that time. (*THWH*, p. xii.)

He emphasized temple worthiness and temple attendance, and asked members to be kinder, gentler, more tolerant, forgiving, and more Christlike. A close friend of many years, who suffered from health problems and who had been blessed by President Hunter, called him "a wonderful example of Christlike living, a testament of compassion and love."

He was the first Church President born in the twentieth century and served the shortest term as president—nine months.

Showing Compassion for His Wife

Claire Hunter suffered from a lingering illness for many years before she died. Her daughter-in-law, Louine Hunter, said: "Dad was her loving caretaker, and I doubt that ever a man was more patient, caring, sensitive and thoughtful than he was during those difficult years.

"When he could no longer take her with him when he traveled, he hired live-in care for her during the day, but he always took over her care when he returned home at night, which meant getting up several times during the night and sleeping very little. He kept this up until he had a heart attack and his doctor said if he didn't get night help for Claire, he wouldn't survive to take care of her.

"Unfortunately, Claire spent her last 18 months in a nursing facility, in a coma. Although it was a long drive from his office, Dad visited twice a day. When he was away on Church trips, he would call and discuss the positives of her condition. To the very end he did what few—if any—men have been called upon to do, to combine the endless duties and travels of an apostle with the constant care of his wife. It was a remarkable love story." (*CN*, Mar. 11, 1995, p. 16.)

Howard W. Hunter's Testimony

"My greatest strength through these past months has been my abiding testimony that this is the work of God and not of men. Jesus Christ is the head of this church. He leads it in word and deed. I am honored beyond expression to be called for a season to be an instrument in his hands to preside over his church. But without the knowledge that Christ is the head of the Church, neither I nor any other man could bear the weight of the calling that has come.

"In assuming this responsibility, I acknowledge God's miraculous hand in my life. . . . Like my Brethren before me, I receive with this calling the assurance that God will direct his prophet. I humbly accept the call to serve. . . . My brothers and sisters, I testify that the impressions of the Spirit have weighed heavily upon me in considering these matters. Our Eternal Heavenly Father lives. Jesus Christ, our Savior and Redeemer, guides his church today through his prophets. I invoke his blessings upon you in your homes, in your work, in your service in his church. I pledge my life, my strength, and the full measure of my soul to serving him. May we have ears to hear and hearts to feel, and the courage to follow, I humbly pray in the name of Jesus Christ, Amen." (*Ensign*, Nov. 1994, pp. 7-9.)

Teachings of Howard W. Hunter

Adversity. Adversity touches many, many lives. What makes the difference is how we accept it. It's important to know it's all within the purposes of the

Lord, whatever they are for us. If we can submit ourselves to that, we can go forward in faith and understanding. (*CN*, Mar. 11, 1995, p. 13.)

Church of Jesus Christ. I submit that the Church of Jesus Christ is as necessary in the lives of men and women today as it was when established by him, not by passive interest or a profession of faith, but by an assumption of active responsibility. In this way the Church brings us out of the darkness of an isolated life into the light of the gospel, where belief is turned into doing according to the admonitions of scripture. This is the hope of the individual, the family, the Church, the nations of the earth. (*CR*, Oct. 1967, pp. 13-14.)

Courage. Courage is acting in spite of fear. (*CR*, April 1967, p. 117.)

Endure to the End. It appears to me that the kind of greatness that our Father in Heaven would have us pursue is within the grasp of all who are within the gospel net. We have an unlimited number of opportunities to do the many simple and minor things that will ultimately make us great. . . .To those who are doing the commonplace work of the world but are wondering about the value of their accomplishments; to those who are the workhorses of this Church, who are furthering the work of the Lord in so many quiet but significant ways; to those who are the salt of the earth and the strength of the world and the backbone of each nation—to you we would simply express our admiration. If you endure to the end, and if you are valiant in the testimony of Jesus, you will achieve true greatness and will live in the presence of our Father in Heaven. (*Ensign*, May 1982, p. 20.)

Equality. As members of the Lord's church, we need to lift our vision beyond personal prejudices. We need to discover the supreme truth that indeed our Father is no respecter of persons. Sometimes we unduly offend brothers and sisters of other nations by assigning exclusiveness to one nationality of people over another. . . . Imagine a father having many sons, each having different temperaments, aptitudes, and spiritual traits. Does he love one son less than another? Perhaps the son who is least spiritually inclined has the father's attention, prayers, and pleadings more than the others. Does that mean he loves the others less? Do you imagine

our Heavenly Father loving one nationality of his offspring more exclusively than others? As members of the Church, we need to be reminded of Nephi's challenging question: "Know ye not that there are more nations than one?" (*Ensign*, June 1979, p. 74.)

Example. I would encourage all present today to live in such a way as to be an example of the teachings of the Savior. Ways to be an example: Pay an honest tithing. Live the Word of Wisdom. Read and study the scriptures. Pray night and day every day. Prepare and receive and accept the ordinances and covenants. (*CN*, Sept. 24, 1994, p. 4.)

Faith. There is no tangible, concrete evidence of the existence of God or the divinity of the Master in the legal sense, but not all inquiry for truth results in proof by real or demonstrative evidence. It is fallacious to argue that because there is no demonstrative evidence of the existence of God he does not in fact exist. In the absence of evidence often thought necessary by the scientific world for positive proof, our search may take us unto the realm of circumstantial evidence. We could spend hours describing the wonders of the universe, of the earth, of nature, of the human body, the exactness of the laws of physics, and a thousand things, all of which dictate to the conscience of a truth seeker that there is a creator and one who rules over the universe.

Suppose that all things could be proven by demonstrative evidence. What then would become of the element of faith? There would be no need for faith and it would be eliminated, giving rise then to this query: If faith is the first step or principle of the gospel and is eliminated, what happens to the gospel plan? The very foundation will crumble. I submit that there is a divine reason why all things cannot be proven by concrete evidence. (*CR*, April 1975, pp. 57-58.)

Family. In the ordinances of the temple, the foundations of the eternal family are sealed in place. The Church has the responsibility—and the authority—to preserve and protect the family as the foundation of society. The pattern for family life, instituted from before the foundation of the world, provides for children to be born to and nurtured by a father and mother who are husband and wife, lawfully married. Parenthood is a sacred obligation and privilege with children welcomed as a "heritage of the Lord." (Ps. 127:3.) (*Ensign*, Nov. 1994, p. 9.)

Family History/Temple Work. In our hands lie the sacred powers of being saviors on Mount Zion in the latter days. As we attend the temple and perform work for the dead, we acquire a deep sense of alliance with God and a better understanding of His plan for the salvation of the human race. Truly there is no work equal to that done in the temple. (*CN*, Mar. 11, 1995, p. 7.)

General Conference. Conference time is a season of spiritual revival when knowledge and testimony are increased and solidified that God lives and blesses those who are faithful. It is a time when an understanding that Jesus is the Christ, the Son of the living God, is burned into the hearts of those who have the determination to serve him and keep his commandments. Conference is the time when our leaders give us inspired direction in the conduct of our lives—a time when souls are stirred and resolutions are made to be better husbands and wives, fathers and mothers, more obedient sons and daughters, better friends and neighbors. (*Ensign*, Nov. 1981, p. 12.)

God the Father. He loves God with all his soul, or rather with all his life, who is ready to give up his life for his sake and to be deprived of the comforts of the world to glorify Him. He loves God with all his strength who exerts all the powers of his body and soul in the service of God. He loves with all his mind who applies himself only to know God and his will, who sees God in all things and acknowledges him in all ways. (*CR*, April 1965, p. 58.)

God the Father. With the advance of knowledge has come a reliance upon scientific principles of proof, and [in] consequence, there are some who do not believe in God because his existence cannot be substantiated by such proof. In reality, scientific research is an endeavor to ascertain truth, and the same principles which are applied to that pursuit are used in the quest to establish the truth of religion as well. . . . As important as scientific research may be, the greatest quest is a search for God—to determine his reality, his personal attributes, and to secure a knowledge of the gospel of Jesus Christ. It is not easy to find a perfect understanding of God. The search requires persistent effort, and there are

some who never move themselves to pursue this knowledge. . . . We have the formula for the search for God and the tools to accomplish the quest—faith, love and prayer. (*Ensign*, Nov. 1974, p. 96-97.)

Gospel Imperatives. The best goals, the best friends, and the best of opportunities are all meaningless unless they are translated into reality through our daily actions. Real Christians must understand that the gospel of Jesus Christ is not just a gospel of belief—it is a plan of action. His gospel is a gospel of imperatives. . . . He did not say "observe" my gospel; he said "live" it! He did not say, "Note its beautiful structure and imagery," he said, "Go, do, see, feel, give, believe!" The gospel of Jesus Christ is full of imperatives, words that call for personal commitment and action—obligatory, binding, compulsory. . . . Merely saying, accepting, believing are not enough. They are incomplete until that which they imply is translated into the dynamic action of daily living. (*CR*, April 1967, pp. 115-16.)

Husband and Father. Any man who abuses or demeans his wife physically or spiritually is guilty of grievous sin and in need of sincere and serious repentance. Differences should be worked out in love and kindness and with a spirit of mutual reconciliation. A man should always speak to his wife lovingly and kindly, treating her with the utmost respect. Marriage is like a tender flower, brethren, and must be nourished constantly with expressions of love and affection. You who hold the priesthood must not be abusive in your relationship with children. Seek always to employ the principles of priesthood government set forth in the revelations (see D&C 93:40; 121:34-36, 41-45). . . . No man who has been ordained to the priesthood of God can with impunity abuse his wife or child. (*Ensign*, Nov. 1994, p. 51.)

Jesus Christ, Our Exemplar. I would invite all members of the Church to live with more attention to the life and example of the Lord Jesus Christ. . . . I pray that we might treat each other with more kindness, more courtesy, more humility, patience and forgiveness. (*CN*, June 11, 1994, p. 14.)

Love Others. We cannot love God unless we love his children also. These are our neighbors, and true love of them knows no class or culture, race, color, or creed. (*That We Might Have Joy*, p. 25.)

Marriage. Tenderness and respect—never selfishness—must be the guiding principles in the intimate relationship between husband and wife. Each partner must be considerate and sensitive to the other's needs and desires. Any domineering, indecent, or uncontrolled behavior in the intimate relationship between husband and wife is condemned by the Lord. (*Ensign*, Nov. 1994, p. 51.)

Missionary Work. A great indicator of your personal conversion to the gospel of Jesus Christ is the desire to share it with others. . . . The Lord gave a charge to every member of the Church to be a missionary. Each of us present today has a duty to bear faithful testimony of our Lord and Savior and His restored gospel. (*CN,* Mar. 11, 1995, p. 7.)

Parents. There are many in the Church and in the world who are living with feelings of guilt and unworthiness because some of their sons and daughters have wandered or strayed from the fold. Parents' hearts are ofttimes broken, yet they must realize that the ultimate responsibility lies with the child after parents have taught correct principles. A successful parent is one who has loved, one who has sacrificed, and one who has cared for, taught, and ministered to the needs of a child. If you have done all these and your child is still wayward or troublesome or worldly, it could well be that you are, nevertheless, a successful parent. Perhaps there are children who have come into the world that would challenge any set of parents under any set of circumstances. Likewise, perhaps there are others who would bless the lives of, and be a joy to, almost any father or mother.

My concern today is that there are parents who may be pronouncing harsh judgments upon themselves and may be allowing these feelings to destroy their lives, when in fact they have done their best and should continue in faith. (*Ensign*, Nov. 1983, pp. 63-65.)

Problems. Every generation since time began has had things to overcome and problems to work out. Furthermore, every individual person has a set of challenges which sometimes seem to be earmarked for him individually. We understood that in our premortal existence. When these experiences hum-

ble, refine, and teach us, they make us better people, more grateful, loving and considerate of other people in their own times of difficulty. Even in the most severe of times, problems and prophecies were never intended to do anything but bless the righteous and help those who are less righteous move toward repentance. (*NE*, Jan. 1994, p. 6.)

Spirituality. Developing spirituality and attuning ourselves to the highest influences of godliness is not an easy matter. It takes time and frequently involves a struggle. It will not happen by chance, but is accomplished only through deliberate effort and by calling upon God and keeping his commandments. (*Ensign*, May 1979, p. 25.)

Temple. I also invite the members of Church to establish the temple of the Lord as the great symbol of their membership and the supernal setting for their most sacred covenants. It would be the deepest desire of my heart to have every member of the Church be temple worthy. (*Ensign*, July 1994, p. 5.)

Testimony. The objectives of the Church are to teach the laws of the Lord and the principles of the gospel, to assist individuals in religious education, to implant the firm testimony that God lives and that Jesus is the Christ and Savior of the world, and to help and encourage each member along the path to celestial and eternal exaltation through the opportunity of "doing." (*CR*, Oct. 1967, p. 13.)

Truth. The knowledge explosion of which the world is so proud is not of man's creation. It is his discovery of portions of the unlimited knowledge and information which are part of God's knowledge. How we use it is determined by whether we are of the eternal kingdom of God or a part of the temporary understanding of the world. (*Ensign*, Jan. 1974, p. 56.)

Women. As our Lord and Savior looked to the women of his time for a comforting hand, a listening ear, a believing ear, a believing heart, a kind look, an encouraging word, loyalty—even in his hour of humiliation, agony, and death—it seems to me that there is a great need to rally the women of the Church today to stand with and for the Brethren in stemming the tide of evil that surrounds us. (*Ensign*, Nov. 1994, p. 97.)

GORDON B. HINCKLEY
1910 - Present
Fifteenth President

- **Born**: June 23, 1910, in Salt Lake City

- **Family**: Gordon Bitner Hinckley is the son of Bryant S. and Ada Bitner Hinckley, the first of five children. At age 26, he married Marjorie Pay on April 29, 1937, in the Salt Lake Temple; they have five children, twenty-five grandchildren, and eighteen great-grandchildren

- **Mission**: Great Britain (1933-35)

- **Education**: A University of Utah graduate in English (1933)

- **Occupation**: Church business executive

- **Church Callings:** Stake Sunday School superintendent (1936-37), Sunday School General Board (1937-46), stake president's counselor (1946-56), stake president (1956-58), Assistant to the Quorum of the Twelve (1958-61), apostle (1961-95), additional counselor in the First Presidency (1981-82), Second Counselor (1982-85), First Counselor (1985-95). Served 14 years in the First Presidency

- **Apostle**: Ordained by David O. McKay on October 5, 1961 (has served 34 years; age 51-84)

- **President of the Quorum of the Twelve**: June 5, 1994, to March 3, 1995 (served 9 months)

- **Senior Apostle**: March 3-11, 1995 (9 days)

- **President of the Church**: Ordained March 12, 1995, age 84

- **General Authority**: Has served 39 years

- **Temples:** As a member of the First Presidency, he has dedicated or rededicated 29 of the 50 operating temples (1983 to 1997).

Rededicated: Four: Manti (1985), Alberta (1991), Swiss, London (1992). **Dedicated**: Twenty-five: Atlanta Georgia, Apia Samoa, Nuku'alofa Tonga, Papeete Tahiti, Santiago Chile, Mexico City (1983); Boise Idaho, Sydney Australia, Manila Philippines, Dallas Texas, Taipei Taiwan, Guatemala City (1984); Freiberg Germany, Stockholm Sweden, Chicago Illinois, Johannesburg South Africa, Seoul Korea, (1985); Lima Peru, (1986), Portland Oregon, Las Vegas Nevada (1989), Toronto Ontario (1990), San Diego California (1993), Hong Kong, Mount Timpanogas Utah (1996), and St. Louis Missouri (1997).

- **A Favorite Hymn:** He wrote, "My Redeemer Lives" (*Hymns,* no. 135).

- **A Favorite Scripture**: "Be not afraid, only believe." (Mark 5:36.)

- **Selected Teachings**: *Be Thou an Example* and *Faith: The Essence of True Religion*

- **Special Interests and Hobbies**: Reading English and American literature, Church history, and current events; carpentry; home repairs; gardening; pruning trees; planting flowers and bushes.

- **Appearance, Personality, and Qualities**: He stands five-feet, ten inches tall, weighs 175 pounds, has a medium build, wears glasses, and is in excellent health. He is known for his sense of humor and for being optimistic, valiant, eloquent, persuasive, honorable, and hard working. He is also known for his breadth of knowledge, his problem-solving capability, his straightforwardness in counsel, and his interest in interfaith cooperation.

- **Personal Motto**: "Carry on. Things will work out. If you keep trying and praying and working, things will work out. They always do. If you want to die at an early age, dwell on the negative. Accentuate the positive, and you'll be around for a while." (Dew, *GBH*, p. 423.)

- **Favorite Saying**: "Keep trying. Be believing. Be happy. Don't get discouraged." (Jeffrey R. Holland, "President Gordon B. Hinckley," *Ensign*, June 1995, p. 4.)

- **1997**: Members: Est. 9,900,000 (August)
 Stakes: 2,325 Temples: 50
 Missions: 318; Missionaries: 56,000
 General Authorities: 103

Biographical Highlights

During his youth, Gordon B. Hinckley learned from his parents the importance of work. He developed a great love for good literature, especially the scriptures. He also developed a great love for Joseph Smith and for the Savior. During the Great Depression, few young men were financially able to serve missions. In fact, the bank failed where Gordon had his savings, and he lost all his missionary funds. However, his mother, who had died three years before he accepted a call to Great Britain, had left him some funds for his mission. His father and brother also helped. As a missionary, he experienced opposition and discouragement and wrote to his father that he felt he was wasting time and money. His father wrote back: "Forget yourself and go to work." It was then that he knelt down and made a life-changing pledge to the Lord: "I covenanted that I would try to forget myself and lose myself in His service. That July day in 1933 was my day of decision. A new light came into my life and a new joy into my heart. The fog of England seemed to lift and I saw the sunlight. I had a rich and wonderful experience." ("Taking the Gospel to Britain: A Declaration of Vision, Faith, Courage and Truth," *Ensign*, July 1987, p. 7.)

He recalled this experience from his labors: "I had been called to labor in the European Mission Office in London under President Joseph F. Merrill of the Quorum of the Twelve, then President of the European Mission. One day, three or four of the London papers carried reviews of a reprint of an old book, snide and ugly in tone, indicating that the book was a history of the Mormons. President Merrill said to me, 'I want you to go down to the publisher and protest this.'"

Elder Hinckley accepted the assignment, said a prayer, and met with the publisher. "I held in my hand the reviews, I do not recall what I said after that. Another power seemed to be speaking through me. At first [the publisher] was defensive and even belligerent. Then he began to soften. He concluded by promising to do something. Within an hour word went out to every book dealer in England to return the books to the publisher. At great expense he printed and taped in the front of each volume a statement to the effect that the book was not to be considered as history, but only as fiction, and that no offense was intended against the respected Mormon people. Years later he granted another favor of substantial worth to the Church, and each year until the time of his death, I received a Christmas card from him.

"I came to know that when we try in faith to walk in obedience to the requests of the priesthood, the Lord opens the way, even when there appears to be no way." ("If Ye Be Willing and Obedient," *Ensign*, July 1995, pp. 4-5.)

When Gordon returned from his mission, where he had served as assistant to President Merrill, he was asked to report to the First Presidency about his missionary efforts in Great Britain. He entered the office of President Heber J. Grant and his counselors, J. Reuben Clark and David O. McKay. President Grant said, "We'll give you fifteen minutes." However, the interview lasted more than an hour, and the Brethren were so impressed with his talents and abilities that a few days later President McKay offered him the position of executive secretary of the Church's Radio, Publicity, and Mission Literature Committee, forerunner to the Public Communications Department. Young Gordon wrote numerous missionary tracts but said, "The most persuasive gospel tract is the exemplary life of a faithful Latter-day Saint." ("Five Million Members—A

Milestone and Not a Summit," *Ensign*, May 1982, p. 45.)

Trained at the University of Utah in journalism and public relations, President Hinckley spent many years developing materials and programs using the rapidly evolving communications technology. He wrote radio scripts, including thirty-nine half-hour Church history segments broadcast as "The Fulness of Times," some of which aired on 400 radio stations nationwide. He supervised translations of the Book of Mormon and wrote "A Short History of the Church of Jesus Christ of Latter-day Saints" (1947) as part of a larger work, *What of the Mormons?* Later it was reprinted as *Truth Restored* (1979). He was also instrumental in creating Church displays for the San Francisco World's Fair and other major exhibits.

Gordon B. Hinckley's other callings have included serving as stake Sunday School superintendent and a member of the Sunday School General Board, as a counselor in a stake presidency, as stake president, and an Assistant to the Twelve. He has traveled thousands of miles to many places in the world to preach the gospel and encourage the Saints. He is known everywhere as a warm and loyal friend. He has made many visits to servicemen in Korea and Vietnam and is a special friend to those in the military.

It is interesting to note that President Hinckley is the Church's senior employee and senior apostle. He has been a Church employee since 1935, except one year during World War II when he was assistant manager of mail and baggage for the Denver and Rio Grande Western Railroad Co. The railroad made him an attractive financial offer to retain his services, but he declined it to return to Church service.

He is the first President since the mid-1970s to have good health. He has spent only one night in the hospital as a patient, and that was when he was seventy-five years of age.

He is well read and well informed and has a great love for the stories of faithful pioneers. He frequently tells about their sacrifices and loyalty in his talks. He served on the committee that produced the LDS temple ceremony in thirteen languages and helped initiate temple work in several non-English-speaking countries. Through his extensive travel, he has become familiar with the large and culturally diverse membership of the Church.

In 1951, he was called to serve as Executive Secretary of the General Missionary Committee. For many years he was the general authority adviser to the Mormon Tabernacle Choir. He has always been a great champion of music in the Church.

President Hinckley took a personal interest in the Church film *Legacy*, and according to writer and director Kieth Merrill, he removed obstacles that could have caused a three-year delay in completing the film. President Hinckley envisioned the transformation of the Hotel Utah into the Joseph Smith Memorial Building, a reflection of his love for the Prophet Joseph Smith.

In November 1995, he met with President Bill Clinton, gave him a six-generation Clinton family history, and spoke with him about the importance of the family as the fundamental unit of society. He presented to President Clinton a copy of "A Proclamation to the World."

He has carried the message of the Church to influential people. During his 1995 trip to Washington, D.C., he spoke in New York City to a group of corporate executives, representatives of the national media, and heads of charitable organizations. After setting a friendly tone with his wonderful humor, he told the executives about the Church. In speaking of missionary work, he said "There is a tremendous vigor and vitality about this work." He explained that there are more than 49,000 missionaries serving in 307 missions all around the world and that these men and women are trying to lift people up, helping them understand the purpose of life. He said, "It is a great, sobering thing that builds a consciousness of the world and its problems and its people." He concluded by telling the executives that the Church works to bring peace. "Our objective is to make bad men good and good men better."

President Hinckley commented about this experience: "It was a satisfying experience, and those who were there were respectful, gracious and interested. I enjoyed meeting these people who have so much influence in the world." (*CN*, Nov. 18, 1995, p. 12.)

President Hinckley loves people everywhere, which is why he keeps such a busy schedule and extends himself as much as he can for the good of the members of the Church. He understands people and their problems wherever he travels. He is a tireless traveler and makes it a point to know something about the history of the area and its people wherever he travels. He has a remarkable way of making an audience feel as though he is one of them.

He refers to the missionaries as ambassadors of the Lord Jesus Christ with authority given by the Lord to represent Him in this work of teaching the gospel to others. He encourages the missionaries to work hard, love the people, stick to mission rules, and look for the good in their companions. He says, "You can never foretell the consequences of your service as a missionary. Do not get discouraged." (*CN*, Nov. 18, 1995, p. 3.)

President Hinckley is recognized as a very good listener with the ability to remain calm in stressful situations.

President Hinckley has received many academic honors, including the Distinguished Alumni Award from the University of Utah and five honorary doctorates. Other honors include the Silver Buffalo Award from the Boy Scouts of America and a distinguished citizen award from the National Conference of Christians and Jews for his contributions to tolerance and understanding in the world.

Elder Russell M. Nelson gave insight into President Hinckley's quest for knowledge. "He is a multifaceted genius. He understands anatomy and physiology better than any non-physician I have worked with . . . whether it is medicine or law, education or plumbing, it doesn't matter. He grasps things quickly, has an amazing breadth of knowledge, and can apply what he knows." (Dew, *GBH*, p. 449.)

Although President Hinckley's life has been filled with many positive experiences, his life has "not been without challenges. In the summer of 1981, President Spencer W. Kimball called Elder Hinckley to serve as an additional counselor in the First Presidency. At that time, the entire First Presidency was experiencing declining health. Since then, President Hinckley has remained a member of the First Presidency. He said, 'That was a very heavy

and overwhelming responsibility. It was an almost terrifying load at times. Of course, I consulted with our brethren of the Twelve.'

"I recall on one particular occasion getting on my knees before the Lord and asking for help in the midst of that very difficult situation. And there came into my mind those reassuring words, 'Be still and know that I am God' (D&C 101:16). I knew again that this was His work, that He would not let it fail, that all I had to do was work at it and do my very best, and that the work would move forward without letup or hindrance of any kind." (Jeffrey R. Holland, "President Gordon B. Hinckley—Stalwart and Brave He Stands," *Ensign*, June 1995, p. 12.)

"His empathy for those who had suffered may have been developed partly in the crucible of his own experience. He himself was forced to suffer—almost always in silence—over vicious attacks from enemies determined to humiliate and disgrace him. As the only visible member of the First Presidency, he was an easy target, a lightning rod of sorts. There were those who apparently believed that if they could discredit President Hinckley, they would also undermine and threaten the stability of the Church hierarchy. Consequently, over time he was accused of everything." (Dew, *GBH*, pp. 422-23.) Most of these attacks came from people within the Church.

President Hinckley called Area Authority Seventies in 1997, a move toward a decentralization of the leadership and operation of the Church and greater efficiency in working in more than 160 nations. Members of the Third, Fourth, and Fifth Quorums of the Seventy were called to serve for a period of years in a voluntary capacity in the area in which they reside. "We have established a pattern under which the Church may grow to any size with an organization of Area Presidencies and Area Authority Seventies, chosen and working across the world according to need." (*Ensign*, May 1997, p. 6.)

"I have a desire to get out and meet the people of the Church, and not just in huge conferences. I just want to look into the eyes of the good Saints, wherever they are. We find good Saints wherever the Church is. I am so optimistic about this work and the way it is moving forward." (*CN*, Sept. 9, 1995, p. 5.)

"Fortunately, we live in a season of good will. There has come down to us an inheritance of respect and honor to our people. We must grasp the torch and run the race." (*CN*, April 12, 1997, p. 18.)

Personal Spiritual Experience

At age twelve, sitting on the back row at a stake priesthood meeting, during the singing of "Praise to Man," there came into my heart a great surge of love for and belief in the mighty Prophet of this dispensation. In my childhood I had been taught much about him in meetings and classes in our ward as well as in our home, but my experience in that stake priesthood meeting was different. I knew then, by the power of the Holy Ghost, that Joseph Smith was indeed a prophet of God." (Hinckley, *Faith: The Essence of True Religion*, pp. 92-93.)

Marriage and Family Life

While growing up, Marjorie and Gordon lived across the street from each other. They were attracted to each other's sense of humor, love for the gospel, innate optimism, and love of life. President Hinckley says that his marriage to Marjorie was a key decision in his life. He has said, "She is a woman of great faith. She is a wonderful mother. How I love her." (*Ensign*, May 1995, p. 74.) Sister Hinckley says that she is grateful for his "integrity and loyalty. He has never hesitated to do whatever was needed to make me and my family more comfortable." He always expressed complete confidence in his wife and children, giving them the encouragement that caused them "to reach beyond themselves."

President Hinckley reflected back to the time of his marriage when he said, "My mind goes back almost sixty years. It was the bottom of the Depression. If ever the world looked dark in terms of economics, it looked dark then. The unemployment rate in the state of Utah was 34 percent. We grumble now about 5 or 6 percent. I finished the university in the very bottom of the Depression when we were married. I had a little job with a salary of $165 per month, and we had no savings. I do not know how we had the nerve to get married. I guess we just got married because we loved each other, and we closed our eyes and jumped. But I think we did so with faith.

"We were seated in our home the other evening. The lights were low and I looked over at my wife. I looked at her hands. . . .We are getting old. We don't stand as tall as we once did. Our hands are wrinkled and the veins show and there is a little arthritis. You get that way when you get in your 80s. Tears came into my eyes as I thought of our life together, of the sorrows we have known, of the defeats we have known, of the struggles we have had, of the triumphs we have enjoyed, the glad times, the sad times, the good times, and the bad times. We are still here. It reminds me of a sign on a barbed wire fence on a farm down in Texas during the Depression, which read: 'Sold out by sheriff, 'et out by jackrabbits, drowned out by flood waters, still here.' That is the way life is. And that is the way our lives have been."

He said he and Sister Hinckley struggled in their early years, when there was never enough money. "Those were tough times, but rich and beautiful and wonderful because we loved one another. How thankful I am for this companion." (*CN*, Feb.17, 1996, p. 3.)

"Through all of these years we have been blessed in marvelous and remarkable ways. I feel only a great sense of gratitude. I thank the Lord for my beloved companion, for her loyalty, her love, her encouragement, her companionship. I thank the Lord every day for her, for our children and our posterity.

"I think of how empty my life would have been without her. I think we have experienced the problems that most people experience. But somehow, with the blessings of the Lord, we have made it to this station along the road of immortality and eternal life. All in all, it has been a wonderful journey." (*CN*, May 6, 1995, p. 11.)

In one interview, President and Sister Hinckley listed some of their essentials for a happy marriage: "live the gospel; love, appreciate each other; develop self-discipline; curb temper and tongue; look on the bright side of things; develop, maintain respect for one another; give soft answer[s]; speak quietly; don't be selfish; look after one another; develop talents, opportunities of companion; recognize differences; pay tithing, stay out of debt; develop ability to communicate with each other." (*CN*, April 19, 1997, p. 3.)

Sister Hinckley stated that the family received inspiration from President Hinckley's "beautiful and articulate daily prayers." In addition, "he was always optimistic, always encouraging and told us that things will come out well in the end. His love of music and literature and of life itself has made being with him a great adventure." (Neal A. Maxwell, "President Gordon B. Hinckley, The Sculpturing of a Righteous Soul." (*Ensign,* Jan. 1982, p. 10.)

He taught these "four simple principles parents might consider in rearing their children: to love them, to teach them, to respect them, and to pray with and for them." (Dew, *GBH,* p. 175.)

With all his responsibilities, President Hinckley has maintained a marvelous sense of humor. His son, Clark, recalls that with all of his dad's pressures at work, the family did not feel a lot of pressure from him. "He had a great sense of humor. He had a great ability to laugh. That was another aspect of our dinners together as a family. There was a lot of laughter that took place. I remember his coming home from the office and repeating a joke he had heard and laughing so hard he couldn't tell it and he got so red in the face that he couldn't breathe, and he still does that." Sister Hinckley added, "His sense of humor has gotten us through the crises in our lives. He never took himself or anything else too seriously except things that should be taken seriously, of course. But he was not a worrier." President Hinckley said, "Humor is a very important element in life. It is wonderful to be able to laugh—to laugh at ourselves, particularly, not to have fun at the expense of others, but to see the bright side of things. There is a little streak of humor in almost every situation and it is the thing that gives sparkle and makes life tolerable. What a great thing is a little humor." (*Gordon B. Hinckley: Man of Integrity, 15th President of the Church,* 1995 videotape.)

Temple Visit As Senior Apostle

After President Hunter's death and funeral, early on March 9, 1995, President Hinckley went to the Salt Lake Temple to be alone. He entered the meeting room of the First Presidency and Quorum of the Twelve and locked the doors.

"It was a wonderful experience. I read from the scriptures, from the Old Testament, the New Testament, the Book of Mormon, and the Pearl of Great Price. On the west wall are three paintings of the Savior—one depicts the calling of the Twelve, two depicts the Crucifixion, three depicts the Resurrection. . . . There by myself, as I reflected, I thought much of the price my Savior paid for my redemption. I thought of the overwhelming responsibility of standing as His prophet in the earth. I was subdued and wept over my feelings of inadequacy.

"On the north wall is a portrait of the Prophet Joseph Smith, on the south wall is a portrait of his brother, Hyrum. Between these and reaching around along the east wall are portraits of all of the Presidents of the Church from Brigham Young to Howard W. Hunter. I walked around in front of these portraits and looked into the eyes of the men there represented. I felt almost as if I could speak with them. I felt almost as if they were speaking to me and giving me reassurance. . . . I sat down in the chair which I have occupied as first counselor to the President. I spent a good deal of time looking at those portraits. Every one seemed almost to come alive. Their eyes seemed to be upon me. I felt that they were encouraging me and pledging their support. They seemed to say to me that they had spoken in my behalf in a council held in the heavens, that I had no need to fear, that I would be blessed and sustained in my ministry.

"I got on my knees and pleaded with the Lord. I spoke with Him at length in prayer. . . . I am confident that by the power of the Spirit, I heard the word of the Lord, not vocally, but as a warmth that was felt within my heart concerning the questions I had raised in prayer." (*Personal Journal of Gordon B. Hinckley,* March 9, 1996, as quoted in Dew, *GBH,* pp. 507-508.)

Regarding this temple experience, President Hinckley wrote, "With the confirmation of the Spirit in my heart, I am now ready to go forward to do the very best work I know how to do. It is difficult for me to believe that the Lord is placing me in this most high and sacred responsibility. . . . I hope that the Lord has trained me to do what He expects of me. I will give Him total loyalty, and I will certainly seek His direction." (Dew, *GBH,* p. 508.)

The Church and the Media

President Hinckley has largely pioneered the use of media in the Church and is an excellent communicator with reporters wherever he travels. He said, "I feel very strongly that we ought to be friendly with the media. We have nothing to fear from the media. We have a story to tell. We can speak honestly and frankly and candidly, and they respond in the same way." (*CN*, March 15, 1997, p. 7.) This was especially true when President Hinckley was interviewed on a segment of television's *60 Minutes*. The prime-time program included a profile of the Church, and President Hinckley honestly and articulately answered questions, shared his humor and wit, and bore his testimony to the viewers. His noble bearing and demeanor represented the Saints well.

In a personal, one-on-one interview with Mike Wallace on April 6, 1996, President Hinckley gave some twenty million viewers a firsthand look at not only his testimony and articulateness, but also his quick wit and humor. In the first-ever interview with an LDS Church President, Mike Wallace was obviously charmed by President Hinckley's gracious but forthright manner. One could not help coming away from the program with admiration and respect for Church members and with a sense of awe for its prophet, President Gordon B. Hinckley.

President Hinckley loves missionary work and envisions an increase in the use of the media for missionary work. "There are so many people in the world, and there really is not any other way to reach them, at least to do things that will disabuse their minds of a lot of false notions concerning us and to have them feel something of the kind of people we hope we are and of the message which we have to give. I think we can use the media more and more to open the way for our missionaries." (*CN*, Sept. 9, 1995, p. 5.)

Sheri Dew, who wrote the authorized biography of President Hinckley, says: "[In] general [President Hinckley] followed a simple maxim that he has preached all his life—that the only way to get anything done is to get on your knees and ask for the Lord's help, and then get to your feet and go to work. . . . I have personally seen him bolster the missionaries and inspire the members. . . . His preparation and gifts of expression have been evident as he has been interviewed by journalists from a host of countries and has described the work of the Church to nonmembers, and at times non-Christian, reporters without being preachy, patronizing, or overbearing. . . . I have witnessed the tremendous affection he has for the peoples of the world, as well as the love they have for him." (Dew, *GBH*, pp. x-xiii.)

President Hinckley said: "One of the purposes of a prophet is to seek the wisdom and the will of the Lord and to teach his people accordingly. It was the case with Moses when he led the children of Israel out of Egypt. It was the case for the Old Testament prophets when people were faced with oppression and trouble and difficulty. That is the purpose of a prophet, to give answers to people for the dilemmas in which they find themselves." ("This Thing Was Not Done in a Corner," *Ensign*, Nov. 1996, p. 51.)

"Carry On" is the theme of his administration. "I think we must go forward with our regular programs that have been established and have functioned through the years of the Church," says President Hinckley. (*CN* Mar. 18, 1995, p. 10.)

Gordon B. Hinckley's Testimony

"This is God's holy work. I haven't the slightest doubt of that. This is the little stone which was cut out of the mountain without hands which should roll forth to fill the whole world. It's on its way. It's happening. It's wonderful and it's tremendous.

God, our Eternal Father, lives. He is the Creator and Ruler of the universe and yet He is our Father. He is the Almighty and is above all. He can be reached in prayer. . . . Does He hear a child's prayer? Of course He does. Does He answer it? Of course He does. Not always as we might wish, but He answers. He hears and answers.

"I know that He lives. I know that Jesus is the Redeemer of the world, the Savior of mankind. Without His divine sacrifice all of this through which we go would be in vain, but it is not in vain because of that atonement which ensures for all of us the resurrection and for all who walk in obedience to His commandments, growth and progress and eternal glory beyond bounds.

"I know that the conversation which took place in the grove was as real and as personal and as intimate as is my conversation with you this morning. The priesthood is upon the earth. The Book of Mormon stands as a witness to the world of the reality and divinity of the Son of God. We are partakers of these marvelous blessings." (*CN*, July 22, 1995, p. 4.)

Teachings of Gordon B. Hinckley

Abuse (child). I do not hesitate to say that no one who is a professed follower of Christ, and no one who is a professed member of Christ's Church, can engage in the abuse of children without offending God, who is their Father, and repudiating the teachings of the Savior and his prophets. (*Faith: The Essence of True Religion*, p. 70.)

Atonement. If there is any question in anyone's mind about the divinity of this work, let him ponder the importance of the universality of the richest fruits of the Atonement. Resurrection, yes, through the grace of God to all men, but beyond that the magnificent concept of exaltation and eternal life through acceptance and living the principles of the gospel. How thankful I feel about this matter. (*CN*, March 2, 1996, p. 2.)

Attitude. Attitude has more to do with personality, with attractiveness, with getting along with others than does any other attribute. (*Ensign*, March 1997, p. 60.)

Blessings. Great are the promises of the Lord. The marvelous thing to me is that the Lord never asks us to do anything that He does not attach to it a blessing. It is not a sacrifice to live the gospel of Jesus Christ. It is never a sacrifice when you get back more than you give. It is an investment. And the living of the gospel of Jesus Christ becomes a greater investment because its dividends are eternal and everlasting. (*CN*, Aug. 26, 1995, p. 4.)

Book of Mormon. I know the Book of Mormon is true. You only have to read it, prayerfully, and you'll know it is true. It speaks for itself. It is its own greatest testimony of its truth. And the marvelous thing is, every time you read it you see things you never saw before. (*CN*, Jan. 6, 1996, p. 1.)

Challenge. The time has come for us to stand a little taller, to lift our eyes and stretch our minds to a greater comprehension and understanding of the grand millennial mission of The Church of Jesus Christ of Latter-day Saints. This is a time to be strong. It is a time to move forward without hesitation, knowing well the meaning, the breadth and the importance of our mission. It is a time to do what is right regardless of the consequences that might follow. It is time to be found keeping the commandments. It is a season to reach out with kindness and love to those in distress and to those who are wandering in darkness and pain. It is time to be considerate and good, decent and courteous toward one another in all our relationships. In other words, to become more Christlike. (*CN*, April 9, 1995, p. 17.)

Church. We have basic cornerstones on which the Latter-day church has been established by the Lord and built "fitly framed together". . . . The first, or chief, cornerstone we recognize and honor as the Lord Jesus Christ. The second is the vision given the Prophet Joseph Smith when the Father and the Son appeared to him. The third is the Book of Mormon, which speaks as a voice from the dust with the words of ancient prophets declaring the divinity and reality of the Savior of mankind. Fourth is the priesthood with all of its powers and authority, whereby men act in the name of God in administering the affairs of his kingdom. (*Faith: The Essence of True Religion*, p. 8.)

Compassion. Nursing homes are filled with the aged and the infirm who cry out for a listening ear and a comforting word. There are the sick and dying who live in pain and fear for whom the holding of a hand and a few quiet words could make all the difference in the world. (*Ensign*, Nov. 1985, p. 87.)

Death. What a wonderful thing is death, really, when all is said and done. It is the great reliever. It is a majestic, quiet passing on from this life to another life, a better life, I'm satisfied of that. We go to a place where we will not suffer as we have suffered here, but where we will continue to grow, accumulating knowledge and developing and being useful under the plan of the Almighty made possible through the atonement of the Son of God. (*CN*, Feb. 3, 1996, p. 2.)

Discipleship. As [Christ's] followers, we cannot do a mean or shoddy or ungracious thing without tarnishing his image. Nor can we do a good and gracious and generous act without burnishing more brightly the symbol of him whose name we have taken upon ourselves. And so our lives must become a meaningful expression, the symbol of our declaration of our testimony of the living Christ, the Eternal Son of the living God. It is that simple and that profound and we'd better never forget it. (*Be Thou an Example*, p. 90.)

Divine Birthright. I believe that I am a child of God, endowed with a divine birthright. I believe that there is something of divinity within each of you. I believe that we have a godly inheritance and that it is our responsibility, our obligation and our opportunity to cultivate and nurture the very best of these qualities within us. (*Ensign*, Aug. 1992, pp. 6-7.)

Education (for youth). Education is the key that unlocks opportunity. I hope . . . that you will not cut short your education for some frivolous reason. It is so very, very important to you, and it is important to the Church because you will make a contribution to society in terms of your capacity and ability to do so. The Church will be honored and respected more because of the way in which you deport yourselves, having educated your minds and your hands and qualified yourselves for the work of the world. (*CN*, Feb. 1, 1997, p. 2.)

Equality in Membership. We should not be classified as married or single but as members of the Church, each worthy of the same attention, the same care, the same opportunities to be of service. We are all individuals, men and women, sons and daughters of God, not a mass of "look-alikes" or "do-likes." All of us are very much alike in our capacity to think, to reason . . . to be happy, to love and be loved. (*Ensign*, March 1997, p. 59.)

Evil Speaking of Others. Do not do it. It does injury. It hurts. Think of the Golden Rule: Whatsoever one should do unto you, do ye even so unto them. . . . Never, never, never run down another. (*CN*, March 30, 1996. p. 3.)

Example. [Our] test lies in our capacity to live the gospel rather than adopt the ways of the world. I do not advocate a retreat from society. On the contrary, we have a responsibility and a challenge to take our places in the world of business, science, government, medicine, education, and every other worthwhile and constructive vocation. We have an obligation to train our hands and minds to excel in the work of the world for the blessing of all mankind. In so doing we must work with others, but this does not require a surrender of standards. We can maintain the integrity of our families if we will follow the counsel of our leaders. As we do so, those about us will observe with respect and be led to inquire how it is done. We can oppose the tide of pornography and lasciviousness, which is destroying the very fiber of nations. We can avoid partaking of alcoholic beverages and drugs and stand solidly for measures designed to lessen their use. As we do so, we shall find others who feel as we do and who will join hands in the battle. We can more fully care for our own who may be in need rather than pass the burden to government and thereby preserve the independence and dignity of those who must have and are entitled to help.

We can refrain from buying on the Sabbath day. . . . As we observe these and other standards taught by the Church, many in the world will respect us and find strength to follow that which they too know is right. . . . We must not compromise. . . . Beginning with you and me, there can be an entire people who, by the virtue of our lives in our homes, in our vocations, even in our amusements, can become as a city upon a hill to which men may look and learn, and an ensign to the nations from which the people of the earth may gather strength. (*Ensign*, July 1990, p. 5.)

Family. It is a God-given calling. And it's worth every effort that one can put into it to make it successful. There is no greater work. There is too much worldliness in our homes. There is too much selfishness. We need to get back to the basics of respect one for another, concern one for another, love and appreciation one for another, and working and worshiping together and living together as families who love the Lord and look to Him for light and strength and comfort. I just want to see our people walk in the light of the Lord. That is where they will find their happiness; that is where they will find their progress; that is where they will find their prosperity, in walking the paths that the Lord has laid out for us. Happiness and peace lie in living the gospel. (*CN*, June 24, 1995, p. 7.)

Fellowshipping [new convert members]. This places upon each of us an urgent and pressing need to fellowship those who join our ranks. Each convert needs three things: a friend, a responsibility and a nurturing "with the good word of God." I plead with you . . . I ask of you, each of you, to become part of this great effort. Every convert is precious. Every convert is a son or daughter of God. Every convert is a great and serious responsibility. (*CN*, April 12, 1997, p. 15.)

Forgiveness. If there are any who nurture in their hearts the poisonous brew of enmity toward another, I plead with you to ask for strength to forgive. This expression of desire will be of the very substance of your repentance. It may not be easy, and it may not come quickly. But if you will seek it with sincerity and cultivate it, it will come. And even though he whom you have forgiven continues to pursue and threaten you, you will know you have done what you could to affect reconciliation. (*Ensign*, June 1991, p. 5.)

God the Father. I believe, without equivocation or reservation, in God, the Eternal Father. He is my Father, the Father of my spirit and the Father of the spirits of all men. He is the great creator, the Ruler of the Universe. He directed the creation of this earth on which we live. In His image man was created. He is personal. He is real. He is individual. He has "a body of flesh and bones as tangible as man's (D&C 130:22). . . . I worship Him "in spirit and in truth." I look to Him as my strength. I pray to Him for wisdom beyond my own. I seek to love Him with all my heart, might, mind, and strength. His wisdom is greater than the wisdom of all men. His power is greater than the power of nature. His love is greater than the love of any other for His love encompasses all of His children, and it is His work and His glory to bring to pass the immortality and eternal life of His sons and daughters of all generations. (*Ensign*, Nov. 1986, pp. 49-50.)

Honesty. The Lord requires his people to be honest. May we desire with all our hearts to be honest in all our relationships and in all the things that we do. God will help us if we seek the strength that comes from him. Sweet then will be our peace of mind and our lives. (*Ensign*, Oct. 1990, p. 5.)

Hope. I know that each of us gets discouraged on occasion. Most of us feel at one time or another that we have failed. . . . I have seen President David O. McKay discouraged. I have seen President Joseph Fielding Smith and President Harold B. Lee and President Spencer W. Kimball discouraged. All of us can become discouraged. . . .

It is important to know, when you feel down, that many others do also and that their circumstances are generally much worse than yours. And it is important to know that when one of us is down, it becomes the obligation of his friends to give a lift. I hope that each of us will cultivate a sensitivity toward the feelings of others, and when encouragement is needed, make an effort to extend it . . . .

There is also in our society a sad tendency among many of us to belittle ourselves. Other persons may appear to us to be sure of themselves, but the fact is that most of us have some feelings of inferiority. The important thing is not to talk to yourself about it. All of us cannot be tall, dark, and handsome. All of us cannot be trim of figure or have a beautiful face. The important thing is to make the most of all that we have. Don't waste your time feeling sorry for yourself. Don't belittle yourself. Never forget that you are a child of God. You have a divine birthright. (Hinckley, in *Hope*, pp. 32-33.)

Humor. We need to have a little humor in our lives. We better take seriously that which should be taken seriously, but at the same time we can bring in a touch of humor now and again. If the time ever comes when we can't smile at ourselves, it will be a sad time. (*CN*, Feb. 3, 1996, p. 3.)

Jesus Christ. [On why the cross is not used.] And so because our Savior lives, we do not use the symbol of his death [the cross] as the symbol of our faith. But what shall we use? No sign, no work of art, no representation of form is adequate to express the glory and the wonder of the living Christ. He told us what that symbol should be when he said, "If ye love me, keep my commandments." (John 14:15.) (*Be Thou an Example*, p. 90.)

Learning. We must continually learn. It is a divinely given mandate that we go on adding to our knowledge. We have access to institute of religion classes, extension courses, education weeks, and many other opportunities where, as we study and match our minds with others, we will discover a tremendous reservoir of capacity within ourselves. (*Ensign*, March 1997, p. 62.)

Loneliness. The best medicine for loneliness is work and service in behalf of others. . . . There are many others whose problems are more serious than yours. Reach out to serve them. . . . If you are fed up with your life, if you feel an oppressive loneliness, if you feel you are of no worth, go out and look up somebody who is in worse condition than you are—and you will find very many of them. Read to the blind, read to the aged, help those in distress, comfort those who are in sorrow. (*Ensign*, March 1997, p. 61.)

Marriage. Every marriage is subject to occasional stormy weather. But with patience, mutual respect, and a spirit of forbearance, we can weather these storms. Where mistakes have been made, there can be apology, repentance, and forgiveness. But there must be willingness to do so on the part of both parties. . . . I have learned that the real essence of happiness in marriage lies not so much in romance as in anxious concern for the comfort and well-being of one's companion. Thinking of self alone and of the gratification of personal desires will build neither trust, love nor happiness. Only when there is unselfishness will love, with its concomitant qualities, flourish and blossom. (*Ensign*, Aug. 1992, pp. 5-6.)

Mercy. Mercy is the very essence of the gospel of Jesus Christ. The degree to which each of us is able to extend it becomes an expression of the reality of our discipleship under Him who is our Lord and Master. (*Ensign*, May 1990, p. 69.)

Missionary Work. Be a part of this great process which constantly adds to the vitality of the Church. Every time a new member comes into the Church something happens. There is an infusion of strength and faith and testimony that is wonderful. Think of what this Church would be without the missionary program. Think of it! I think this is the greatest age in the history of the world. I think this is the greatest time in the history of the Church. I believe that. I think there will be greater times in the future. We are growing ever and ever stronger. (*CN*, March 2, 1996, p. 2.)

Motherhood. The greatest job that any mother will ever do will be in nurturing, teaching, lifting, encouraging, and rearing her children in righteousness and truth. None other can adequately take her place. (*Ensign*, Nov. 1996, p. 69.)

Obedience. I give you my testimony that the happiness of the Latter-day Saints, the prosperity of the Latter-day Saints, and the eternal salvation and exaltation of this people lie in walking in obedience to the counsels of the priesthood of God. We sing, "We thank thee, O God for a prophet to guide us in these latter-days." (*Hymns*, no. 19.) Let us always follow that guidance. (*Ensign*, July 1995, p. 5.)

Optimism. I am asking that we stop seeking out the storms and enjoy more fully the sunlight. I am suggesting that as we go through life we "accentuate the positive." I am asking that we look a little deeper for the good, that we still the voices of insult and sarcasm, that we more generously compliment virtue and effort. . . . Growth comes of correction. Strength comes of repentance. . . . I have little doubt that many of us are troubled with fears concerning ourselves. . . . There are occasionally hard days for each of us. Do not despair. Do not give up. Look for the sunlight through the clouds. Opportunities will eventually open to you. (*Faith: The Essence of True Religion*, pp.74 -76.)

Peace. The gospel of Jesus Christ is the only element that will destroy the hatred that exists among people. If they will bring this gospel into their lives and recognize the fatherhood of God and the brotherhood of man and the effects of the atonement of Christ, there will be a far greater measure of peace in the world. That is why we are here, brothers and sisters, you and I. That is the objective of our work—to teach the gospel of the Lord Jesus Christ and touch the hearts of people so that they can look upon one another as brothers and sisters, as children of our Father in Heaven. (*CN*, March 2, 1996, p. 2.)

Pioneers. What a grand thing to know that there are those who have gone before us and laid out the way we should walk, teaching those great eternal principles which must be the guiding stars of our lives and of those who come after us. We today can follow their example. The pioneers were people of great faith, of tremendous loyalty, of unthinkable industry and of absolutely solid and unbending integrity. (*CN*, Feb. 8, 1997, p. 3.)

Prayer. Be prayerful. I hope that every one of you gets on your knees every morning and every night and expresses gratitude to the Lord, that you share with Him the righteous desires of your hearts, that you pray for those in need and distress wherever they may be. *(Ensign*, March 1997, p. 63.)

Priesthood. All of you, of course, are familiar with binoculars. When you put the lenses to your eyes and focus them, you magnify and in effect bring closer all within your field of vision. But if you turn them around and look through the other end, you diminish and make more distant that which you see. So it is with our actions of the priesthood. When we live up to our high and holy calling, when we show love for God through service to fellowmen, when we use our strength and talents to build faith and spread truth, we magnify our priesthood. When, on the other hand, we live lives of selfishness, when we indulge in sin, when we set our sights on the things of the world rather than on the things of God, we diminish our priesthood. (*Ensign*, May 1989, p. 47.)

Priesthood. Paul wrote concerning the priesthood: "No man taketh this honour unto himself, but he that is called of God, as was Aaron." (Hebrews 5:4.) We have not acquired it through purchase or bargain. The Lord has given it to men who are considered worthy to receive it, regardless of station in life, the color of their skin, or the nation in which they live. It is the power and the authority to govern in the affairs of the kingdom of God. It is given only by ordination by the laying on of hands by those in authority to do so. The qualification for eligibility is obedience to the commandments of God. There is no power on the earth like it. Its authority extends beyond life, through the veil of death, to the eternities ahead. It is everlasting in its consequences. (*Faith: The Essence of True Religion*, p. 11.)

Reading. The best books are the scriptures. Read the Church magazines. There are many other worthwhile things to read. Reading will sharpen your mind. It will clean up your intellect. But be careful of what you read. Avoid pornography as you would a plague because it is as deadly as a deadly disease. Avoid the foul language, the titillating rubbish of many TV programs, of videotapes, or sensual magazines, of 900-numbers, and the filth that I am told is now found on the Internet. These will bring you no benefit, and they could destroy you. (*Ensign*, March 1997, p. 62.)

Reading. We live in a world where knowledge is developing at an ever-accelerating rate. Drink deeply from this ever-springing well of wisdom and human experience. If you should stop now, you will only stunt your intellectual and spiritual growth. Keep everlastingly at it. Read. Read. Read. Read the word of God in sacred books of scripture. Read from the great literature of the ages. Read what is being said in our day and time and what will be said in the future. (*CN*, May 6, 1995, p. 11.)

Repentance. If there be those throughout the Church who by word or act have denied the faith, I pray that you may draw comfort and resolution from the example of Peter, who, though he had walked daily with Jesus, in an hour of extremity momentarily denied the Lord and also the testimony which he carried in his own heart. But he rose above this and became a mighty defender and a powerful advocate. So, too, there is a way for any person to turn about and add his or her strength and faith to the strength and faith of others in building the kingdom of God. *(Ensign*, Mar. 1995, p. 6.)

Respect. [Husbands and wives,] respect one another. [Have] that respect which comes of the knowledge that she is a daughter of God and that I am a son of God, that we are children of God, that God loves us, His children, and that if I offend her, I offend our Father in Heaven. Never forget that—mutual respect, the kind of respect that manifests itself in courtesy and kindness and patience and forgiveness and deference. . . . What a difference it would make if there were a greater measure of respect in the homes of our people. It is my sad responsibility to sit in judgment in the office which I hold concerning those who once loved one another, joined hands over the altar in the temple, and then for one reason or another became disillusioned, found themselves in troubled circumstances and now request a cancellation of their temple sealings. It comes from selfishness in so very, very many cases. It comes of disloyalty one to another. It comes of lack of respect. I sometimes sit in the evening . . . as we read together and just look over at this little lady with whom I have been so closely associated for nearly six decades and marvel at what I see. We are just very ordinary people, but I think of her unflagging loyalty toward me and that stirs within me a desire to be unflagging in my loyalty toward her.

My brethren, you will never have in all of your lives a greater asset than the women into whose eyes you looked as you joined hands over the altar in the House of the Lord. . . . Respect her and live with honor together and there will be happiness in your lives. (*CN*, Feb. 17, 1996, p. 3.)

Revelation. [Revelation comes] in a very quiet way. . . . When we have a problem, we pray about it, we ponder it, gradually the answer comes. There isn't a voice that comes, generally, but there is a very strong impression that gives one confidence to speak up and move ahead. (*CN*, March 15, 1997, p. 7.)

Spirit. The Spirit of the Lord . . . is the great conversion principle. From my point of view, it is strictly the Spirit of the Lord which enters into the heart of an individual which makes all the difference in the world, which causes him to say, "It is true. I know it is true and I can't deny it." And he builds his life accordingly. (*CN*, March 15, 1997, p. 7.)

Scriptures. Read the word of the Lord. I know that with the demands of daily living there is little time to read anything. But I promise that if you will read that which we call scripture, there will come into your heart an understanding and a warmth that will be pleasing to experience. (*Ensign*, Apr. 1983, p. 7.)

Service. I speak of that service which is given without expectation of monetary reward. Most of the troubles of the world come because of human greed. What a therapeutic and wonderful thing it is for a man or woman to set aside all consideration of personal gain and reach out with strength and energy and purpose to help the unfortunate, to improve the community, to clean up the environment and beautify our surroundings. (*Ensign*, Aug. 1992, p. 5)

Smith, Joseph. We do not worship the Prophet [Joseph Smith]. We worship God our Eternal Father, and the risen Lord Jesus Christ. But we acknowledge him, we proclaim him, we respect him, we reverence him as an instrument in the hands of the Almighty in restoring to the earth the ancient truth of the divine gospel. (*Ensign*, May, 1977, p. 65.)

Standards (drinking, drugs, profanity). It happens around us every day as men and boys drink alcoholic beverages and use illegal drugs. What a scourge these are. . . . Be clean in language. There is so much of filthy, sleazy talk these days. . . . A filthy mind expresses itself in filthy and profane language. . . .

I urge you to be clean in manner, to be courteous, to be respectful, to be honest. . . . To practice the kind of self-discipline which can control one's temper in the little things that happen almost every day is an expression of emotional cleanliness. (*Ensign*, May 1996, pp. 48-49.)

Temple. Qualify for a temple recommend and live worthy of it at all times and in all circumstances. The vicarious service you do in behalf of others will bring a measure of satisfaction that will come from no other source. (*Ensign*, March 1997, p. 63.)

Temple. The temple is a place of personal inspiration and revelation. Legion are those who in times of stress, when difficult decisions must be made and perplexing problems must be handled, have come to the temple in a spirit of fasting and prayer to seek divine direction. Many have testified that while voices of revelation were not heard, impressions concerning a course to follow were experienced at that time or later which became answers to their prayers. . . . And here I have entered to do that for which this house was designed, always leaving a better man than I was when I entered. (*Ensign*, March 1993, p. 6.)

Testimony. We have become as a great family spread across the world. We speak different tongues. We live under a variety of circumstances. But in the heart of each of us beats a common testimony. You and I know that God lives and is at the helm of His holy work. We know that Jesus is our Redeemer, who stands at the head of this Church which carries His name. We know that Joseph Smith was a prophet and is a prophet who stands at the head of this the dispensation of the fulness of times. We know that the priesthood was restored upon his head and that it has come down to us in this day in an unbroken line. We know that the Book of Mormon is a true testament of the reality and divinity of the Lord Jesus Christ. Our testimony of these and other matters will be strengthened, our faith will be deepened as we participate together in this great and sacred convocation. (*Ensign*, Nov. 1996, p. 5.)

Tolerance. I plead with our people everywhere to live with respect and appreciation for those not of our faith. There is so great a need for civility and mutual respect among those of differing beliefs and philosophies. We must not be partisans of any doctrine of ethnic superiority. We live in a world of diversity. We can and must be respectful toward those with whose teachings we may not agree. We must be willing to defend the rights of others who may become the victims of bigotry. (*Ensign*, May 1995, p. 71.)

Trials. The only consolation [for tragedy] comes in the gospel. Life is eternal. Death is a part of our eternal journey. . . . [Life] is a time of testing, a time of trials, a time of education. It is a time of gaining experience a time of trying to qualify for things that lie ahead. (See D&C Section 76 and John 14.) You rise above them to see the big, wonderful picture of that millennial vision. You get that picture and things look different. Live the gospel. Carry on, keep the work growing. Be happy as you serve. (*CN*, June 24, 1995, p. 7.)

Virtue. There is no substitute for virtue. Keep your thoughts virtuous. Rise above the filth that's all around you in this world and stand tall in strength and virtue. You can do this and you will be happier for it as long as you live. (*CN*, March 2, 1996, p. 2.)

Women. I am grateful that women today are afforded the same opportunity to study for science, for the professions, and for every other facet of human knowledge. You are as entitled as are men to the Spirit of Christ, which enlightens every man and woman who comes into the world. (See D&C 84:46.) Set your priorities in terms of marriage and family, but also pursue educational programs which will lead to satisfying work and productive employment in case you do not marry, or to a sense of security and fulfillment in the event you do marry. It is also important to enhance one's appreciation of the arts and culture which are of the very substance of our civilization. . . .

Please know that you are deeply appreciated. Please know that your place in the divine plan is no less important, no less great, and no less necessary than that of men. . . . Count your wonderful blessings. Do not worry away your lives with concerns over "rights," so-called, but move forward, concerned with responsibilities and opportunities. Your potential is limitless. You are daughters of God, endowed by inheritance with marvelous gifts and immeasurable potential.

Accept the challenge. Go forward with confidence in the knowledge that the differences you face are not those which come of discrimination so much as those which come of designation. [I pray] that you may be happy, and that your lives may be rich with that satisfaction which comes from the development of your spiritual gifts. (*Ensign*, Nov. 1985, p. 89.)

Work. There is no substitute under the heavens for productive labor. It is the process by which dreams become realities. It is the process by which idle visions become dynamic achievements. . . . It is work that spells the difference in the life of a man or woman. It is stretching our minds and utilizing the skills of our hands that lift us from mediocrity. It is work that provides the food we eat, the clothing we wear, the homes in which we live. (*Ensign*, Aug. 1992, p. 7.)

Youth. You are great young people. I have said again and again, we have the finest generation of young people ever in the history of this Church. I believe it. You know the gospel better. You come to seminary and you learn about the things of the Lord here. You know more about the gospel than those of my generation at your age did without any question. Furthermore, you are intrinsically better. You are wonderful people! (*CN*, Sept. 2, 1995, p. 2.)

PROFILES OF THE WIVES OF THE PRESIDENTS

The wives of Church presidents comprise a diverse and impressive group. The women of the early Church coped with persecution, physical hardship, plural marriage, and poverty in their efforts to help their husbands establish a home for the new church. In recent years, the wives of the Church presidents, like their husbands, have been advanced in years when they received the challenge of reaching out to the diverse members of a worldwide church. The task has required travel, correspondence, public speaking, media interviews, and television appearances.

Space precludes providing even abbreviated profiles of all of the presidents' wives. None of the plural wives of Joseph Smith has been included, and only a few of the plural wives of Brigham Young are represented here. Heber J. Grant, who practiced polygamy in years prior to becoming President of the Church, had three wives, all included in this section. Subjects of these profiles were selected on the basis of their accomplishments, their children's prominence, and the material available—which is, regrettably, unequal in quantity. In the twentieth century, George Albert Smith, David O. McKay, Spencer W. Kimball, and Ezra Taft Benson married once; Joseph Fielding Smith, Harold B. Lee, and Howard W. Hunter remarried after the deaths of earlier spouses. These women are included, along with the wife of Gordon B. Hinckley.

Men can learn a great deal from the prophets about how they should treat their wives: with gentleness, kindness, respect, and devotion. Women can learn a great deal from the wives of the prophets about faith, adversity, work, devotion, accomplishment, suffering, patience, education, hope, and service.

❖❖❖❖❖❖❖❖❖❖❖❖❖❖❖❖❖❖❖❖❖

JOSEPH SMITH

Emma Hale Smith (1804-1879) was born in Harmony, Pennsylvania, on July 10, 1804, the daughter of Lewis and Elizabeth Hale. She married Joseph Smith, Jr., on January 18, 1827, at age twenty-two. They were married for seventeen years, had eleven children, including two adopted ones. Five of the children died in early childhood. Emma died on April 30, 1879, at age seventy-four.

Emma had a happy childhood, learned to ride horses, and enjoyed canoeing on the Susquehanna River with her brothers. Her education included one year beyond the common grammar school education.

Emma met Joseph when he and his father arrived in Harmony to work for an acquaintance of the Hales, Josiah Stowel. During the two years Joseph worked in the area, he twice asked Emma's father for permission to marry her, but was twice refused because he was a "stranger." In 1827, Emma married Joseph without her father's permission when she and Joseph eloped to South Bainbridge, New York.

Emma is described as being tall, attractive, quickwitted, compassionate, courageous, and charismatic. By profession, Emma was a schoolteacher. She was known for a lovely singing voice. She was the scribe for the Book of Mormon for a time.

A woman of intelligence and spirit, she defended Joseph tenaciously, nursed him in illness, and was his strongest supporter except on the sensitive issue of plural marriage. Because of this, she suffered greatly and was torn between her love for her husband and obedience to God's commands concerning plural marriage. Emma said: "First of all that I would crave as the richest of heaven's blessings would be wisdom from my Heavenly Father." (Cannon, *Notable Quotables from Women to Women,* p. 35.)

Oliver Cowdery baptized Emma in June of 1830. In July 1830, the Prophet received a revelation addressed to her in which she was called an "Elect Lady." She was instructed to "expound scriptures, and to exhort the church"(D&C 25:7) and to compile a hymnal for the church. (See D&C 25:11-12.) Published as *A Collection of Sacred Hymns, for the Church of the*

Latter Day Saints in 1835, this hymnal contained the text only for ninety hymns. Thirty-four of the hymns were written by Latter-day Saints; the remainder were Protestant hymns.

"She was a partner in his [Joseph's] business affairs, a spokeswoman for the Church when he was away in hiding, and a confidante in his most private concerns. In Joseph's diary are countless references to his life with Emma. Mercy Thompson recalled his tenderness with Emma: 'I saw him by the bedside of Emma, his wife, in sickness, exhibiting all the solicitude and sympathy possible for the tenderest of hearts and the most affectionate of natures to feel.' His letters to Emma and Emma's letters to him suggest a warm and affectionate relationship." (Arrington, "Joseph Smith," *TPC*, p. 35.)

Emma had a strong testimony of the divine authenticity of the Book of Mormon. She said, "I have not the slightest doubt that book is of divine origin. I sat across the table from my husband. I wrote with my own pen the words as they fell from his inspired lips. . . . I knew it would be impossible for a learned man to produce or fabricate that work, much less the unlearned man I knew my husband to be." (R. Scott Lloyd, "Events in the Life of A Prophet, 'Elect Lady,'" *CN*, Sept. 10, 1994, p. 7.)

In 1842, Joseph chose Emma to be the first president of the Nauvoo Female Relief Society, a name which she suggested. According to Joseph, this fulfilled an earlier revelation identifying her as an "elect lady" (D&C 25:3). Her complaint after cleaning the tobacco mess left by men attending the School of the Prophets contributed to Joseph's receiving the revelation called the Word of Wisdom. (D&C 89.)

Emma sheltered the homeless, nursed the sick, and fed the hungry, often suffering fatigue from overwork and illness. In 1842, she led a delegation of Relief Society women to the governor of Illinois, petitioning him to protect Joseph and the Saints. She also penned a letter to the governor. After Joseph's death, she, with the help of others, hid his body as well as Hyrum's to prevent their mutilation by the mob.

Emma exhibited great courage and faith to endure when Joseph was imprisoned in Liberty Jail. "While her husband languished there through the winter of 1838-1839, Emma, with two babies in her arms and two at her skirts, walked across Missouri, finally crossing the frozen Mississippi to seek refuge in Quincy, Illinois, carrying the manuscript of her husband's translation of the Bible hidden in pockets in her clothing. From there she wrote to her husband in March 1839 of the trials she had endured, but vowed that she was 'yet willing to suffer more if it is the will of kind heaven.'" (Carol Cornwall Madsen, *EnM* 3:1324.)

Emma was sealed to Joseph for time and eternity on May 28, 1843, having been the first woman in this dispensation to receive the full temple endowment. She then performed anointings and endowments for other women.

Emma had a beautiful relationship with Joseph's mother, Lucy Mack Smith, and cared for her until Lucy's death in 1856. Lucy had great respect for Emma. "I have never seen a woman in my life, who would endure every species of fatigue and hardship, from month to month, and from year to year with that unflinching courage, zeal, and patience, which she has ever done." (Lucy Mack Smith, *History of Joseph Smith*, pp. 190-91.)

"Enduring her husband's frequent absences on Church business, Emma was obliged to support herself and the children by taking boarders into her already crowded quarters, an expedient that she would frequently employ throughout her life." (Madsen, *EnM* 3:1324.)

After Joseph's death, Emma, unwilling to accept plural marriage, remained in Nauvoo with her children and, in 1847, married one of the defenders of Nauvoo, Lewis C. Bidamon, a nonmember. She remained in Illinois, never moving to the Utah Great Basin. On April 30, 1879, Emma Hale Smith Bidamon died and was buried by the Mississippi River, as she had requested, near Joseph Smith.

Eleven children: **Alva** was born and died on June 15, 1828; **Thaddeus** and **Louisa** (twins) were born and died on April 30, 1831; **Joseph** and **Julia** were born on April 30, 1831 to John and Julie Murdock and were adopted by Joseph and Emma upon their mother's death. Little Joseph died shortly after a mobbing on March 24, 1832, after exposure to cold weather. Julia died in Nauvoo at the age of forty-nine. **Joseph III** was born on November 6, 1832, and became the first president of the Reorganized Church of Jesus Christ of Latter-day Saints in 1860 and served as president until his death in 1914. **Frederick Madison Smith** was born on June 30, 1836, and died in 1860. **Alexander Hale Smith** was born on June 2, 1838. He supported Joseph III in the "reorganization" and became a general authority and presiding patriarch in the reorganized church. He died in 1909. **Don Carlos** was born on June 13, 1840, and died in 1841. An **infant son** (unnamed) was born and died on December 26, 1842. **David Hyrum** was born on November 17, 1844, and became a painter and poet. He was also active in the "reorganization." He died at the state mental hospital in Elgin, Illinois, in 1904.

BRIGHAM YOUNG

Brigham Young had twenty-seven wives, sixteen of whom bore a total of fifty-seven children. He married his first plural wife in 1842. His wives include: Miriam Works, Mary Ann Angell, Lucy Ann Decker (first plural wife), Harriet E. Cook, Augusta Adams, Clarissa Decker, Susannah Snively, Eliza R. Snow, Clarissa Ross, Emily Dow Partridge, Olive Grey Frost, Maria Lawrence, Louisa Beaman, Martha Bowker, Ellen A. Rockwood, Margaret Maria Alley, Namah K. J. Carter, Emmeline Free, Margaret Pierce, Zina D. Huntington, Mary Jane Bigelow, Lucy Bigelow (divorced in 1851), Eliza Burgess, Harriet Barney, Harriet Amelia Folsom, Mary Van Cott, and Ann Eliza Webb (divorced in 1876). (Arrington, *Brigham Young: American Moses*, pp. 420-21.)

The first plural marriages in the Church were performed secretly. The revelation commanding its practice was not written until July 1843 but was not publicly announced until 1852, the practice itself being confined to a limited group until the Saints moved to the Great Basin. "The practice of plural marriage has never been general in the Church and at no time have more than three per cent of the families in the Church been polygamous." (Stephen L Richards, *About Mormonism*, p. 1.) In 1890, conditions were such that the Lord by revelation withdrew the command to continue the practice of plural marriage.

Miriam Angeline Works Young (1806-1832) was born on June 7, 1806, in Aurelius, New York, the daughter of Asa and Jericho Works. She married Brigham on October 5, 1824, at age eighteen. They were married for eight years and had two daughters. She died on September 8, 1832, age twenty-six, after a long illness from chronic tuberculosis contracted after the birth of her first child.

Miriam was self-educated and is described as an excellent housekeeper with blond wavy hair, blue eyes, a fine face, and a gentle and uncomplaining spirit. She and Brigham became members of the Methodist Church in 1824. They read the Book of Mormon together from 1830 to 1831 and both gained testimonies. It was a snowy day when Brigham was baptized in April 1832, and because of the severe weather, Miriam waited until May to be baptized.

She became a semi-invalid and was bedfast for most of the two years before her death. Brigham worked only part-time so he could tend to the domestic work. He prepared breakfast for himself, Miriam and the girls, dressed the children, cleaned the house, and carried Miriam to the rocking chair. When he came home from work at night, he cooked the evening meal, read to Miriam from the Bible, and put her to bed. During the final stages of Miriam's illness, Vilate Kimball, wife of Heber C. Kimball, cared for her. On her deathbed, strong in the faith, Miriam clapped her hands to emphasize her joy and asked all those around her to do likewise. In later years, Brigham referred to her great faith at the time of her death.

Mary Ann Angell Young (1803-1882) was born on June 8, 1803, in Seneca, New York, the daughter of James William and Phoebe Morton Angell. She married Brigham on February 18, 1834, at age thirty. They were married for forty-eight years, had six children, and reared

Miriam's two daughters. Mary Ann died on June 27, 1882, at age seventy-nine.

In her early years before hearing the gospel message, Mary Ann was a student of the scriptures and a Baptist Sunday School teacher. She resolved not to marry until she found "a man of God." In 1830, while working in Providence, Rhode Island, she heard the gospel message from missionaries.

In 1832, she moved to Ontario County, met Joseph, Phinehas, and Lorenzo Young, who encouraged her to join the Church. She was finally baptized along with her parents.

In the spring of 1833, she went to Kirtland and it was there where she met Brigham. When Brigham heard her "bear testimony," he was impressed, as she had been when she heard him preach. Brigham and Mary Ann were married in 1834 in Kirtland, Ohio. (*Arrington*, Brigham Young: American Moses, p. 37.)

On December 22, 1837, Brigham left Ohio to escape the threats of apostates. Joseph Smith and the remainder of the Saints left Kirtland in January. "Meanwhile, until friends took Mary Ann west, she and the children were terrorized by apostates who frequented their property, pretending to believe that Brigham was 'hid up there.' They used 'threats and vile language' that undid her emotions until her health became frail. This was, she told her biographer, 'undoubtedly the severest trial of my life.'" (*Brigham Young: American Moses*, p. 61.)

Before arriving at the Mississippi River gathering place in the spring of 1839, Mary Ann had "kept house in eleven different places." She was subjected to the persecutions of the mob in Missouri and traveled with the other exiled Saints across the state and into Illinois. She was able to endure, displaying a resourceful and self-reliant character.

In 1839, "her husband took his departure on a mission to England, in connection with other brethren, to preach the gospel to that nation, leaving his wife and almost helpless family in the depths of poverty. This brave woman urged him on saying, 'God will provide for us; go, and fulfill your mission.'" ("In Memoria, Death of Mary Ann Angel Young," *DN*, July 5, 1882, p. 1.)

It is unclear the extent to which Brigham knew of his family's desperate plight. One day "she left the older

girls with the rest of her children while she crossed the Mississippi in an open boat, her baby bundled tight against the cold. She hoped to obtain food from the Nauvoo bishops. Years later, one Nauvoo veteran described her arrival that stormy, November day with her baby Alice in her arms, almost fainting with cold and hunger, and dripping wet with spray from crossing the river. . . . I tried to persuade her to stay, but she refused, saying, 'the children at home are hungry, too.' I shall never forget how she looked, shivering with cold and thinly clad. I kept the baby while she went to the tithing office. She came back with a few potatoes and a little flour, for which she seemed very grateful, and taking her baby with her parcels . . . weak as she was from ague and fever, wended her way to the river bank." (*Brigham Young: American Moses*, p. 86.)

While Brigham served a mission in England, Mary Ann preserved her children's lives, despite having few resources. She sewed for others and raised a small garden. During the greater part of 1834-49, Brigham was absent on missions, and the responsibility of rearing the family was upon her alone.

A peacemaker, she helped resolve conflicts among her husband's many plural wives and children. She was known to many for her kindness and hospitality and was honored with the title "Mother Young." She truly proved to be an angel in Brigham Young's household. Many trying and bitter experiences came to Brigham and his family, but Mother Young endured them all with the knowledge that they were laboring in a much greater cause.

The *Deseret News* said of her: "In all trying circumstances never was [she] disheartened nor lost her faith in God. For twenty-five years she has scarcely known a day of good health. In March last, her feet began to swell. This affliction had been on her more or less for years, and in the course of a few weeks reached her body [her vital organs] and ultimately caused her death." (*DN*, July 5, 1882, p. 1.)

Six children: Joseph A. (apostle, but not a member of the Quorum of the Twelve), **Brigham, Jr.** (member of the Quorum of the Twelve and counselor in the First Presidency), **Mary Ann**, **Alice**, **Luna**, and **John W.** (First Counselor in the First Presidency).

Zina Huntington Jacobs Smith Young (1821- 1901) was born on January 31, 1821, in Watertown, New York, the daughter of William and Zina Baker Huntington. She married Brigham on February 2, 1846, at age twenty-five. They were married for thirty-one years and had one daughter. She also reared four of Brigham's children by Clarissa Chase after Clarissa's death. Zina died on August 28, 1901, at age eighty.

Zina acquired a basic education as a young girl. She developed musical talent by playing the cello. In 1835, at age fourteen, she and her family, except her oldest brother, were converted to the Church by the missionary efforts of Hyrum Smith and David Whitmer, after which the family moved to Kirtland.

Zina possessed great faith, courage, compassion, spiritual sensitivity, and remarkable composure in the face of adversity. A gifted speaker, she exercised the gift of tongues and their interpretation throughout her life.

In addition to teaching school, she "studied obstetrics and became a midwife and helped deliver the babies of many women, including those of the plural wives of Brigham Young. At their request, she anointed and blessed many of these sisters before their deliveries. Other women in need of physical and emotional comfort also received blessings under her hands." (Carol Firmage Woodward, "Zina D. H. Young," *EnM* 4:1612.)

Although she abhorred silkworms, she tended cocoons and supervised a large cocoonery and mulberry orchard. She was founding president of the Silk Association, organized in 1876, traveling extensively to promote this short-lived home industry.

Zina helped to establish the Deseret Hospital, served as its vice-president, organized its nursing school, and taught in its school for obstetrics. She served as its president for twelve years.

In the East during the winter of 1881-1882, she advocated women's suffrage and dispelled misinfor-

mation about the Church. She attended the National Women's Suffrage Association convention in New York. In 1891, she was elected vice president of the National Council of Women. She also addressed many temperance societies.

Zina worked in the Endowment House and the Salt Lake Temple. She served as first counselor in the Relief Society to Eliza R. Snow and became the Relief Society's third general president (1888- 1901).

She advised: "Seek for a testimony, as you would for a diamond concealed. If someone told you by digging long enough in a certain spot you would find a diamond of unmeasured wealth, do you think you would begrudge time or strength or means to obtain that treasure? Then I will tell you that if you will dig in the depths of your own hearts you will find with the aid of the Spirit of the Lord, the pearl of great price, the testimony of the truth of this work." *(Young Woman's Journal,* April 1892, p. 319.) Her epitaph is the Relief Society motto, "Charity never faileth."

One child: Zina Prescinda

JOHN TAYLOR

John Taylor had seven wives and thirty-five children. He married Leonora Cannon, Elizabeth Kaighin, Jane Ballantyne, Mary Ann Oakley, Sophia Whitaker, Harriet Whitaker, and Margaret Young.

Leonora Cannon Taylor (1796-1868) was born on October 5, 1796, in Peal, Isle of Man (off the coast of Great Britain), the daughter of George and Leonora Callister Cannon. She married John on January 28, 1833, at the age of thirty-six. They were married for thirty-five years and had four children; one died in infancy. She died on December 9, 1868, at age seventy-two.

She is described as "refined both by nature and education, gentle and ladylike in manner, witty, intelligent, gifted with rare conversational powers, possessed of a religious sentiment, and withal, remarkable for the beauty of her person." (Roberts, *Life of John Taylor*, p. 475.)

"She did not know why [after leaving her native land] she should go to Canada, yet she felt that it was the will of God. . . .

"Subsequent events have proved the correctness of her impressions, and she was led by Him; in carrying out this decision she herself was brought to the knowledge of the truth of the everlasting gospel, and was the means through the instrumentality of her husband, to impart that knowledge to many of her kinfolk, who yet live to bless her memory for her faithfulness in following the counsel of God in this matter." *(DNW 17:354.)*

Very spiritual and a devout Methodist, Leonora met John Taylor, then a Methodist preacher, while living in Canada. When he proposed marriage, she first rejected his proposal but changed her mind after a persuasive dream.

In 1836, Parley P. Pratt introduced the gospel to them. Leonora persuaded John, who was initially not as interested, to listen again; both were baptized in May 1836.

Leonora suffered greatly. She wrote in her diary [original spelling and punctuation retained.]: "Mr. Taylor returned 3rd of July I had gone through all but death during his absence lived in an old barrack room twenty feet square with one small window the back door of the hinges and walls so open that a skunk came in every night one Winter twice I found a large Snake in the room, naturally nervous and timid my sleep nearly left me—twice when my children were Sick and had a light in the middle of the night drunken Indians came to the door and there quarreled some to get in others keeping them back, and I alone with three small children.

. . . . " I was a stranger in a strange land without a friend or relative near me, my Heavenly Father who has watched over me did not forsake me in the day of my adversity but inclined the heart of my neighbors to be kind to me which I give him thanks." (Roberts, *Life of John Taylor*, p. 474.)

Four children: **George John, Mary Ann, Joseph James,** and **Leonora Agnes** (died as an infant).

Sophia Whitaker Taylor (1825-1887) was born April 21, 1825, in Blakedown, England, the daughter of Sophia Turner and Thomas Whitaker. She married John on April 23, 1847, at age twenty-two. They were married forty years and had eight children. She died of a stroke on February 27, 1887, at age sixty-two, John being absent for fear of arrest on charges of cohabitation by federal agents who were guarding the house.

In 1840, at age fifteen, she was living in Liverpool, England, probably with a married sister, Mary Ann, when she heard the gospel preached. She was baptized on April 28. Her mother died in 1841, and her father asked her to keep house for him. She introduced her family to the Church, and several of them joined. She immigrated to America in a company under the direction of John Taylor.

She is described as a strict disciplinarian, a good homemaker, capable in every respect, dignified, and possessing strong convictions.

Eight children: **Harriet Ann, James Whitaker, Hyrum Whitaker, John Whitaker** (member of the Quorum of the Twelve), **Helena Whitaker, Moses Whitaker, Fredrick Whitaker** (prominent physician in Provo, Utah), and **Nettie Jones** (adopted).

WILFORD WOODRUFF

Wilford Woodruff had five wives and thirty-three children. He married Phoebe Whittemore Carter, Mary Ann Jackson (divorced), Emma Smith, Sarah Brown, and Sarah Delight Stocking.

Phoebe Whittemore Carter Woodruff (1807-1885) was born on March 8, 1807, in Scarboro, Maine, the daughter of Ezra and Sarah Fabyau Carter. She married Wilford on April 13, 1837, at age thirty; they were married for forty-eight years and had nine children. She died of

pneumonia on November 10, 1885, at age seventy-eight.

Phoebe worked as a tailor and school teacher. She joined the Church in 1834, the only member of her family to do so at that time. (Both parents were eventually baptized.) Her mother was grief-stricken when Phoebe decided to join the Saints in Kirtland. "She was relieved only by Phoebe's promise to return if she lost faith in Mormonism. Phoebe traveled with a small band of converts to Kirtland, where she met and married Wilford Woodruff in 1836." (Madsen, Carol Cornwall, *In Their Own Words*, Deseret Book Co., 1994, p. 134.)

She served as the first president of the 14th Ward Relief Society in Salt Lake City, as an officer in the Deseret Agricultural and Manufacturing Society, and as a member of the board of the Deseret Hospital. She accompanied her husband on missions to the Fox Islands and to Europe. She was a faithful companion in tribulation and assisted in the pioneers' efforts to settle Utah Territory. She was known for her spiritual and physical strength, wise counsel, and good works.

Nine children: **Sara Emma**, **Wilford Jr.**, **Phoebe Amelia**, **Susan Cornelia**, **Joseph Woodruff**, **Ezra**, **Sarah Carter**, **Beulah Augusta**, and **Aphek**.

Emma Smith Woodruff (1838-1912) was born on
March 1, 1838, in Spring Hill, Missouri, the daughter of Samuel and Martishia Smoot Smith. She married Wilford on March 13, 1853, at age fifteen, and they were married for forty-five years and had eight children. She died on March 4, 1912, at age seventy-four.

When Emma was very young, she and her family joined the Church and shortly thereafter moved to Nauvoo. As a child, she was impressed by the Prophet Joseph Smith and all her life remembered his kindly attitude toward her. In 1850, she started west with her parents and four siblings. Her father died suddenly, and three days later her mother gave birth to another child. Emma, only twelve years old, was left to assume the responsibility of looking after the

bereaved family. She drove the wagon until they reached the Salt Lake Valley. She had a large responsibility, but accepted her duties willingly.

She was a member of the General Relief Society Board from 1892 to 1910. She was a charter member of the Retrenchment Society and later presided over the Farmers Ward Relief Society. She was a member of the first Salt Lake Relief Society Board and president of the Granite Stake Relief Society. When the Salt Lake Temple was opened in 1893, she was chosen as one of the first ordinance workers.

"[Being] the wife of President Woodruff was an honor to her all her life, and that their children were willing always to take his counsel was her greatest blessing." (Jenson, *LDS Biographical Encyclopedia* 4:201, 2:805-807.)

Loved by all who knew her, she was known for her spirituality and kindness to everyone. She was a hard worker, full of zeal, generous, but prudent and thrifty. She was gifted with a rare executive ability and was an excellent housekeeper.

Eight children: **Hyrum Smith**, **Emma Manella**, **Asahel Hart**, **Ann Thompson**, **Clara Martishia**, **Abraham Owen** (member of the Quorum of the Twelve), **Winnifred Blanch**, and **Mary Alice**.

LORENZO SNOW

Lorenzo Snow had nine wives and forty children. He married Charlotte Squires, Mary Adeline Goddard, Sarah Ann Prichard, Eleanor Houtz, Harriet Amelia Squires, Caroline Horton, Mary Elizabeth Houtz, Phoebe Amelia Woodruff, and Sarah Minnie Jensen.

Sarah Minnie Jensen Snow (1854-1908) was born
on October 10, 1854, in Brigham City, Utah, the daughter of J.P. and Sarah Clawson Jensen. She married Lorenzo on June 12, 1871, at age sixteen. They were married for thirty years and had five children. She died on January 2, 1908, at age fifty-three.

Sarah was well educated. She taught a Book of Mormon class in Sunday School at age twelve and became the organist for the stake choir at age fourteen. Her goal was to marry a man who loved God. Referring to Lorenzo, she said: "No harsh words have ever passed between us." She represented Church organizations at the National Council of Women in 1895, 1899, and 1906. She served as a private secretary to her husband, took dictation from him for his journal, and helped him in many ways. She was a temple worker for many years.

A friend wrote of her, "She never allows herself to indulge in slander. She plans with wise and careful forethought, and executes with promptitude and decision, preventing delay or waste of time." (*CN* Sept. 15, 1979, p. 12.)

President Snow wrote a tribute to Minnie: "Thy husband dear, now oft calls, Thy burden's borne mid cares and toils, With cloudless brow and smiling face, With spirit bright and charming grace." (*Ibid.*, p. 12.) She died of heart failure.

Five children: **Clarence LeRoi** (journalist), **Minnie Mabel**, **Cora Jeane**, **Lorenzo**, and **Lucile**.

JOSEPH F. SMITH

Joseph F. Smith had six wives and forty-eight children (three adopted). He married Levira Annett Clark Smith (divorced), Julina Lambson, Sarah Ellen Richards, Edna Lambson, Alice Ann Kimball, and Mary Taylor Schwartz.

Julina Lambson Smith (1849-1936) was born in Salt Lake City on June 18, 1849, the daughter of Alfred B. and Melissa June Bigler Lambson. She married  Joseph F. on May 5, 1866, at age seventeen. They were married fifty-two years and had thirteen children, two of whom were adopted. She died on January 10, 1936, at age eighty-six.

Julina spent part of her childhood in the home of her aunt and uncle, Bathsheba and George Smith, where the Historian's Office was located. Here she met Joseph F. Smith, then a clerk. At eighteen, Julina was appointed president of the Sixteenth Ward Retrenchment Society, the forerunner of today's Young Women's organization.

She received a medical certificate from the examining board of the Utah Territory as a licensed practitioner in obstetrics and was commissioned by the Church to serve as a midwife. Known as a great organizer, she helped her husband arrange his personal and business effects. She was skilled in sewing and cooking.

During "the Raid" on plural families, she left five small children, took her baby, and accompanied Joseph F. to Hawaii for a short mission of two months; she stayed for two years.

When Julina's son, Joseph Fielding, was ten years old, he became her assistant in her midwifery At all hours of the day or night, when the call came for her services, Julia was driven by Joseph to the home of the patient. Altogether, she brought nearly 1,000 babies into the world, never losing a mother or baby. Sometimes she received as much as five or six dollars for her services, sometimes spending five or six days caring for the mother and child. On other occasions, she would receive nothing. (See *Life of Joseph Fielding Smith*, p. 52.)

When her husband became President of the Church, Julina moved into the Beehive House and was a gracious hostess to visitors, dignitaries, and friends. She was a member of the General Relief Society Board for twenty-nine years (1892-1921) and a counselor to the president, Emmeline B. Wells. In 1912, she helped establish a department for temple and burial clothing. She was a charter member of the Daughters of Utah Pioneers, an active worker in the Endowment House, and one of the first workers called after the Salt Lake Temple was dedicated in 1893. After Joseph F.'s death in 1918, Julina spent many hours as a temple worker.

Her diary records her daily activities in Laie, Hawaii, on February 27 and 28, 1886 [original spelling retained]: "worked very hard scrubbing and cleaning all day. . . . A little before twelve o'clock in the night bro Gates came for me. Susie [Susa Young Gates] was sick. . . . Her watter had broke but her pains were very light. I staid till half past three then came home and went to bed, got up and went over again at six to see if I could go on with getting breakfast. . . . I sent word to Sister Farr who got breakfast. Susies ten pound boy was born ten minutes to seven Feb 28th. . . . [I] got back in time to help wash the breakfast dishes and get dinner." (Godfrey, Godfrey & Derr, *Women's Voices*, p. 356.)

Thirteen children: **Mercy Josephine, Mary Sophronia, Donette, Joseph Fielding** (Church President), **David Asael** (counselor in the Presiding Bishopric), **George Carlos, Julina Clarissa, Elias Wesley, Emily, Rachel, Edith Eleanor, Marjorie Virginia** (adopted), and **Edward Arthur** (adopted).

Edna Lambson Smith (1851-1926) was born on March 3, 1851, in Salt Lake City, Utah, daughter of Alfred B. and Melissa Jane Bigler Lambson. She married Joseph F. on January 1, 1871, at age nineteen. They were married forty-seven years and had ten children. She died on February 28, 1926, at age seventy-four.

Edna, like her sister Julina, was a skilled and licensed obstetrical practitioner who delivered many babies. "She graduated from Maggie Shipp's school of obstetrics. Most of her work was charity work for most people who sent for her were unable to pay for this service. She never refused to go when called whether it was night or day, and in the hundreds of cases she waited upon, she never lost a mother or baby. The fee charged, when someone could pay was $5.00." ("Edna Lambson Smith," *The Descendants of Joseph F. Smith (1838-1918), compiled by the Joseph F. Smith Family Genealogical Committee.*)

She and Julina waited upon each other and upon other wives, and when the babies came they all rejoiced equally with the mother. All of the children recognized each other as full-fledged brothers and sisters.

In 1893, Edna was chosen to work in the Salt Lake Temple. In 1910, she became the President of the Women Workers, a position she held until her release in 1922. In 1916, because of her long experience in temple work, she was again selected by Joseph F. Smith and Charles W. Nibley to supervise extensive improvements in the Logan Temple.

She was a student of the scriptures and very knowledgeable about the doctrines of the Church. In 1906, she accompanied her husband to Europe where they visited the European Missions. She accepted a position in the Endowment House in 1874 and labored there until it was closed in 1884. "Duty first, pleasure afterwards," was Edna's creed, symbolic of her firm and devoted character.

Edna worked in Relief Society and served on the Salt Lake Stake Primary Board for many years. She spoke in many wards on the importance of temple work. She participated in the Daughters of the Utah Pioneers. Edna suffered an accident on February 26, 1926.

Edna passed away in her home in Salt Lake City on February 28, 1926.

Ten children: **Hyrum Mack** (member of the Quorum of the Twelve), **Alvin, Alfred Jason, Edna Melissa, Albert Jesse, Robert, Emma, Zina, Ruth**, and **Martha.** Four died in childhood: **Alfred Jason, Albert Jesse, Robert**, and **Ruth**.

HEBER J. GRANT

Lucy Stringham Grant (1858-1893) was born on April 29, 1858, in Salt Lake City, the daughter of Briant and Lucy Ashby Stringham. She married Heber on November 1, 1877, at the age of nineteen, in the St. George Temple—a great sacrifice to the young couple because of the time and money required for the journey. Lucy and Heber were married for sixteen years and had five daughters and one son, who died at age seven. Lucy died on January 3, 1893, at age thirty-five.

Lucy's father died when she was thirteen, leaving her mother, who was in frail health, with seven children, four of whom were younger than Lucy. Lucy was courageous and showed responsibility in helping to care for her brothers and sisters.

She was well educated and taught school at age fourteen to help the family. After her marriage to

Heber, she was a good homemaker and mother, with a particularly good business sense, helping her husband with his early financial success. She loved to attend the theater but was equally dedicated to her other responsibilities, which included caring for Heber's mother, who lived with them and was nearly completely deaf.

Lucy later developed health problems exacerbated by both the fear that Heber would be imprisoned for polygamy and by the strain of his long absences. She was bedfast for months and patiently endured many years of pain before her death. Heber scarcely left her side the last few weeks of her life.

Daughter Lucy gives this interesting and intimate account of her mother: "Mother was medium in height. She stood erect. Her hair was almost black and very abundant. She wore it in the style of the day, with bangs in front and a high bob. Her features were marked and distinct, but her eyes were the loveliest I have ever seen. Many people who knew Mother have remarked what a fine-looking woman she was, so gracious and pleasing were her manners.

"Mother was artistic and loved beautiful things. She did some pen and ink sketches which Father had framed, and they were in our house for years. I am sure if she had [had] the opportunity for even a little instruction she would have excelled in some of the fine arts. She was exceptionally kind and was greatly loved by all who worked in the home.

"Mother was an executive. She wasted no time. She planned everything. Theater tickets were always available. Mother, however, did not turn us over to the hired help. It seemed to me she always knew where we were and what we were doing. She took a special interest in all of our activities and in all of our friends.

"She made our home so pleasant and happy that we always loved to be there. I love to think back over those happy times when Mother sat under the gas light and we gathered around while she read from the *Youth's Companion, Hans Brinker* or the *Silver Skates, Little Lord Fauntleroy*, or some of Louisa Alcott's works." (Bryant S. Hinckley, *Life of a Great Leader*, pp. 79-80.)

Six children: Rachel, Lucy, Florence, Edith, Anna, Heber (died at age seven).

Hulda Augusta Winters Grant (1856-1952) was born on July 7, 1856, in Pleasant Grove, Utah, the daughter of Oscar and Mary Ann Stearns Winters. She married Heber on May 26, 1884, at age twenty-seven. They were married for sixty-one years and had one child. Augusta died of a stroke on June 1, 1951, at age ninety-four.

At age thirteen, Augusta was an assistant teacher to her mother in a one-room school where they taught as many as seventy students. Augusta later became the principal. She also taught school for ten years before her marriage. She was known to thousands as "Aunt Gusta."

Augusta was a graduate of the University of Deseret in Utah. She traveled widely when Heber was Church President and helped him in his numerous acts of charity and friendship toward the widow, the fatherless, and the needy. She organized night school in Pleasant Grove, Utah, in 1885-86 for young workers. Her *Deseret News* obituary included this tribute: "She possessed a rare gift of understanding and the ability to inspire children with a desire for knowledge and development." ("Mrs. Grant Dies at Home," *DN*, June 2, 1952, p. A-1.) With a wide range of interests, she studied French and learned to speak Japanese quite fluently. The knowledge of the Japanese language enabled her to do much good while she was in Japan with her husband, who served as mission president. For several years she was secretary of the Free Kindergarten in Salt Lake City, established to provide training for the children of underprivileged families. Sister Grant decided early in life that she would "always like to do what she had to do" and never want anything that she could not have. (Susa Young Gates, "Augusta Winters Grant," *RSM*, May 1931, p. 250.)

She possessed great leadership abilities but accepted only minor offices and duties so she could take care of family responsibilities and help her husband.

She enjoyed both art and music, and attended the theater regularly. Her favorite form of entertainment was grand opera, and Wagner's operas were her favorites. However, she preferred to read Shakespeare rather than to see the performances on stage. (*Ibid*, p. 252.)

She was a member of the Young Women's General Board where she assisted in establishing traveling libraries, served on the editorial committee of the *Young Woman's Journal*, and suggested the idea and selected the site for the Girls' Summer Home in Brighton, Utah.

She was interested in books, magazines, and current events. She attended the temple weekly and gave liberally to fund genealogical research. She was known to have a good sense of humor, and she enjoyed laughing at herself. The question with her was not what she could get, but rather what she could give.

One child: **Mary Judd**

Emily Harris Wells Grant (1857-1908) was born on April 22, 1857, in Salt Lake City, the daughter of Daniel H. and Martha Harris Wells. She married Heber on May 27, 1884, at age twenty-seven. They were married for twenty-four years, had four daughters and one son, who died at the age of three. Emily died of stomach cancer on May 25, 1908, at age fifty-one.

Emily grew up in a wholesome and happy home environment; the Wells children were well educated for their day and were taught to work, to shun idleness and to improve their talents. She was a University of Deseret (Utah) graduate. Friends came to her for advice and sympathy because she was known as a peacemaker.

During the first six years of her married life she lived on "the underground," which forced her to live away from home under an assumed name and to never disclose her identity. During this twenty-two month period, she lived with her father in England where he was serving as president of the European Mission.

Later, Heber took her and the children to Europe where he served as president of the European Mission from

1904-1906. Upon their return, Heber built Emily her "dream house," but she was able to live in it only briefly as she passed away shortly thereafter.

Their daughter Dessie relates this concerning her parents: "We are proud to be their children. They taught us to love life, without fearing death; to be happy in the face of trials; to make our Heavenly Father our best friend." (*Life of a Great Leader*, p. 92.)

Five children: **Daniel** (died at age three); **Dessie G. Boyle**, **Grace G. Evans**, **Emily G. Madsen**, and **Frances Marian Bennett**.

GEORGE ALBERT SMITH

Lucy Emily Woodruff Smith (1869-1937) was born in St. Thomas, Arizona (now Nevada), on January 10, 1869, the daughter of Wilford and Emily Jane Smith Woodruff, Jr., and the granddaughter of President Wilford Woodruff. She married George Albert on May 29, 1892, at age twenty-three. They were married for forty-five years and had three children. She died on November 5, 1937, after a long illness, at age sixty-eight.

She attended the University of Deseret and studied math and surveying. She enjoyed gardening and raised four thousand tulips and other flowers each spring, giving many flowers to hospitals and friends. She worked with the city and county of Salt Lake as a surveyor, most unusual in that day. She later worked in the City Recorder's Office and completed several engineering projects before her marriage.

She was a charter member of both the Daughters of Utah Pioneers and Utah State Society of Daughters of the American Revolution. She was an active Sigma Chi mother and a collector of art objects.

She supported her husband in service to the Church and to the Boy Scouts of America. "She mothered and furnished a home to a number of other children, all of whom loved and admired her. Her home was always open to relatives and friends and many notables have been entertained there." (*DN*, Nov. 6, 1937, p. 8.)

She was a member and former president of the Salt Lake Stake Young Women's Mutual Improvement Association; served many years on the general board of the YWMIA; served for many years as a guide at Temple Square; and served missions with her husband in the southern states and also in England.

She was admired for her wisdom, strong faith, gentleness, kindness, consideration for others and a sense of justice. "She inspired many thousands to better living. She will continue to live in the hearts of countless numbers." *(Ibid.*, pp. 1, 8.)

Three children: **George Albert, Jr**. (Harvard business professor), **Emily Stewart**, and **Edith Elliot.**

DAVID O. McKAY

Emma Ray Riggs McKay (1877-1970) was born on June 23, 1877, in Salt Lake City, the daughter of O.H. Robbins and Emma Robbins Riggs. She married David on January 2, 1901, at the age of twenty-three. They were married for sixty-nine years and had seven children. Emma died of congestive heart failure on November 14, 1970, at age ninety-three.

Upon seeing his baby daughter, Emma's father said, "She is like a ray of sunshine. Her name shall be Ray—Emma Ray Riggs." She was an 1898 graduate of the University of Utah, where she met her future husband, David O. McKay. David and his brother were renting a house from Emma's mother.

After graduation and before her marriage, Emma taught at Madison School in Ogden. David and Emma were the first couple to be married in the Salt Lake Temple in the twentieth century. The newlyweds made their home in Ogden, where they welcomed seven children into their family. Emma served in Primary and Relief Society presidencies and as a teacher.

Emma later studied at the Cincinnati College of Music and was an accomplished pianist. She taught piano lessons to all of her children. In 1954 she received an honorary doctorate from Utah State Agricultural College (now Utah State University). Emma and

David's six surviving children all graduated from the University of Utah.

Emma Ray was a superb cook, especially noted for her pies. She was very patient with her children and her friends. She loved to attend plays, symphony concerts, and motion pictures, and she enjoyed reading English literature and about current world affairs.

Two of her most quoted sayings are: "I never ask anyone to do something for me that I can do for myself," and "Life's finest blessing is the ability to find joy in doing something for somebody else."

When her husband was away, Emma did not stay home and mope; she took her children to the movies, read to them from good literature, told them stories, sang songs, and played games with them. David and Emma made it a point never to disagree in front of their children. Neither believed in spanking, but both were good disciplinarians and gave wise counsel.

Emma and her husband were a model for the ideal marriage and always kept romance alive. President McKay credited his "sweetheart-wife" for keeping their sixty-nine years of marriage on an even keel: "She has never spoken a harsh word to me during the many years we've spent together."

"In 1952, when Mother and Father had been married for fifty-one years, Mother gave an address to the women students at Brigham Young University. [Reprinted in 1967 as a pamphlet that sold more than 25,000 copies.] Although the topic was the art of rearing children peacefully, she also included a solid section of advice to young wives about how to build a happy marriage. 'A [husband] wants to see a wife who has made herself as beautiful as she can, a woman who has poise and charm, who greets him lovingly and cheerfully, who studies his every mood, and can tell when he wants to talk and when he would like a complete rest. . . .

'There are many qualifications that a woman should have to be a good wife and mother, but the most important is patience—patience with children's and husband's tempers, patience with their desires, with their actions.'" (David Lawrence McKay, *My Father, David O. McKay*, pp. 12-13.)

David O. McKay expressed his feelings about his wife in an October 25, 1939, letter to his children. "I want to acknowledge to you and to her, how greatly her loving devotion, inspiration and loyal support have contributed to whatever success may be ours. Willingly and ably she has carried the responsibility of the household.

"Sometimes I have come home tired and irritable and have made remarks provocative of retaliating replies; but never to this day have you heard your mother say a cross or disrespectful word. This can be said truthfully I think of but few women in the world.

"Under all conditions and circumstances, she has been the perfect lady. Her education has enabled her to be a true helpmate; her congeniality and interest in my work, a pleasing companion, her charm and unselfishness, a lifelong sweetheart; her unbounded patience and intelligent insight into childhood, a most devoted mother; these and many other virtues, combined with her loyalty and self-sacrificing devotion to her husband, impel me to crown her the sweetest, most helpful, most inspiring sweetheart and wife that ever inspired a man to noble endeavor." (McKay, *My Father, David O. McKay*, pp. 194-95.)

Seven children: **David Lawrence**, attorney; **Llewelyn Riggs**, language professor at the University of Utah; **Louise Jeannette Blood**; **Royle Riggs**, died at age three; **Emma Rae Ashton**; **Edward Riggs**, physician; **Robert Riggs**, jeweler.

JOSEPH FIELDING SMITH

Louie Emily Shurtliff Smith (1876-1908) was born on June 16, 1876, in Plain City, Utah, the daughter of Lewis Warren and Emily Wainwright Shurtliff. She married Joseph Fielding on April 26, 1898. They were married for nine years and had two daughters. She died of complications during pregnancy on March 30, 1908, at age thirty-one.

Louie was slightly taller than her five-feet nine-inch husband. Graduating from the University of Utah, she became a teacher. She enjoyed books, the outdoors, and playing the piano. She moved into her parents' home when Joseph Fielding was called on a mission in 1899 and worked to help support him on his mission. She later became a temple worker.

To Louie, Joseph paid this heartfelt tribute: "She died firm in the faith and true to every principle of the gospel which she lived in righteousness. A purer, nobler, truer companion and mother there is not to be found in the whole earth. Her entire life was devoted to the gospel and the love of her fellows. She was constantly engaged in doing good. She loved her husband and babies dearer than her life and for them she laid it down. Every action on her part for them was one of love and unselfish devotion. She sacrificed self and her own comfort for those she loved and her example is one to be emulated by her children and all her loved ones. She received the blessings of the house of the Lord and lived the law of the Celestial Kingdom." (Smith and Stewart, *The Life of Joseph Fielding Smith*, p. 162.)

Two children: Josephine Reinhardt and **Julina Hart.**

Ethel Georgina Reynolds Smith (1889-1937) was born on October 23, 1889, in Salt Lake City, daughter of George and Amelia Schofield Reynolds. She married Joseph Fielding on November 2, 1908, at age eighteen, with President Joseph F. Smith performing the sealing ceremony. They were married for twenty-eight years and had  nine children. Ethel died on August 26, 1937, at age forty-seven.

Ethel managed her household with skill. She cared not only for her own children and for Joseph Fielding's two daughters from his previous marriage, but she also raised the son of a man who had been killed while washing her windows. When someone asked how it was possible for her to assume the responsibility for still another child when she had so many of her own, Ethel responded simply that when you love them, "one more does not make any difference." (Gibbons, *Joseph Fielding Smith: Gospel Scholar, Prophet of God*, pp. 155-56.)

She was educated through home study, and she loved to read Church history. She was never satisfied with mediocrity, and she became an outstanding writer and speaker. She taught piano lessons and was a ward organist at age eleven. She became a member of Relief Society General Board and served on various stake boards. She worked in the Church Office Building and was known for her kind and gentle manner. She was both industrious and interested in people; many confided in her. Sister Smith was released from the Relief Society General Board in 1936 due to failing health, and she died the following year.

Nine children: **Emily Myers**, **Naomi Brewster**, **Lois Fife**, **Joseph Fielding Jr.** (account executive), **Amelia Smith McConkie**, **Lewis Warren** (killed in World War II), **George Reynolds** (loan officer), **Douglas Alan** (business secretary), and **Milton Edmund** (BYU business professor)

Jessie Ella Evans Smith (1902-1971) was born on December 29, 1902, in Salt Lake City, the daughter of Jonathan W. and Jeanette Buchanan Evans. She married Joseph Fielding on April 12, 1938, at age thirty-five. They were married for thirty-three years. She died on August 3, 1971, at age sixty-eight.

Jessie Evans attended the Stevens-Henager College of Business. She became a widely-acclaimed soloist with the Tabernacle Choir and sang with the choir for more than fifty years. Known in the Church as the "First Lady of Song," she performed on radio and TV programs and sang at hundreds of branch, ward, and stake meetings, conferences, and funerals throughout the Church. She recorded three albums. She was offered the role of Mother Superior in the movie *The Sound of Music*, but she declined.

She served in Church auxiliaries as a teacher, chorister, and organist. She traveled with her husband to conferences where she would often speak and sing duets with him. Elder Smith referred to these performances as "do its," humorously implying that he allowed Jessie to cajole him into joining her. (Gibbons, *Joseph Fielding Smith*, p. 281.) She served as matron in the Salt Lake Temple (1945-49) while her husband was president of the temple. She was called "Aunt Jessie" by the children of his two previous marriages. She enjoyed doing needlepoint and crocheting, and she collected old ties to make quilts. She was described as a witty and magnetic woman, and people often commented that she helped her husband stay young in spirit.

She received many awards, such as the Young Women's Mutual Improvement Association Honorary Golden Gleaner Award in 1954 and the David O. McKay Humanities Award from Brigham Young University in 1966. She also received the Annual Distinguished Achievement Award from the Ricks College women students in 1967, the Eternal Quest of Womanhood Award from the Latter-day Saint Women students at Utah State University in 1968, and the MIA Combined Arts Award plaque in 1970.

HAROLD B. LEE

Fern Lucinda Tanner Lee (1896-1962) was born on November 14, 1896, in Salt Lake City, the daughter of Stewart T. and Janet Coats Tanner. She married Harold on November 14, 1923, in the Salt Lake Temple, at age twenty-seven. They were married for thirty-eight years and had two daughters. She died of a stroke on September 24, 1962, at age sixty-five.

A scriptorian of unusual ability, Fern met Harold while serving as a missionary in the Western States Mission. She was the Primary organist at age fourteen; later she wrote and successfully directed many prize-winning road shows and dramas. She served in various auxiliaries and presidencies and was a gracious presence in the bride's room of the Salt Lake Temple.

She attended the LDS Business College. She was employed at Druehl Drug, where she eventually had complete charge of the office. She also worked in the county clerk's office, later for the Utah State Legislature, and then as a stenographer in the office of the Utah Secretary of State.

Fern made the Lee home an enjoyable place for their daughters to have parties and get-togethers after school or in the evening. It was common for thirty young people to show up for a gathering. Young people enjoyed her so much that they adopted her as "mother."

She was known as "Aunt Fern" to all the neighborhood children, as she always had time to help when someone needed her. She was interested in plays, music, reading, and writing, but she said to her daughters, "You are the only books I shall ever write: the only pictures I shall ever paint."

Her daughter, Helen, describes her feelings about her mother and her relationship with the family: "Mother was small of stature, quiet and unassuming, but was always a source of great spiritual strength in our home. She sincerely felt that a man's home should be his castle, that it should be an oasis where he could return from the battles of the day and find there a tranquil, quiet atmosphere of peace to rebuild him for future struggles. . . .

"There is no doubt that Mother had a most profound influence on my father's life. When one recalls that he grew up in a very small community in Idaho, it is easy to understand that he needed the refining influence of a loving companion to introduce him to gracious living. She incorporated those values as well as spiritual dimensions, into their home.

"Her inner strength was unquestioned as a powerful influence upon all who knew her. Her mind was filled with wisdom and her heart with empathy as she met my father's needs, as well as the needs of others around her. She had a remarkable sense of fairness.

"My father's personality was one of being very quick, moving ahead into a situation, making a decision and taking action promptly, regardless of whether the given situation was in Church work, employment, or in a family setting. He needed the influence of a wife who would say to him, as Mother would, 'Now, dear, you need to think about this and you must not fail to look at the other side of the situation.' She balanced him in this way.

"Mother was his inspiration. My father has often said, 'The loftiest thoughts for which I have been given credit were first expressed to me by my dear wife.' That is true. I've heard him use phrases that were originally spoken by Mother, as he would deliver a sermon or counsel others. Although she was quiet in manner, her influence extended to many lives, and was most keenly felt by my father. . . .

"There had been a very fine man in our ward who had lost his wife and he had remarried quite soon after his first wife had died. I said to Mother: 'I think that's just terrible! I think that's being so disrespectful to his first wife. He must not have loved her very much!' My mother then turned quietly to me and said: 'Oh, my dear, you don't understand what it is to love someone. If I were to go before Daddy, and I think that we will have to face that possibility, I could never rest until I knew that your father was happily married again. I just couldn't bear to think of his being alone.' I replied, 'Mother, how can you say that? Don't you love him enough so that you just couldn't stand to see another woman taking care of him and living with him'. . . .

"She answered, 'It's because I do love him so much that I can think of it, and that's what I want for him. I cannot bear the thought of his being alone and lonesome and not having his needs cared for by someone who loves him as I do. I would want him to remarry, and I mean soon after I go, so that he will not be lonely—don't you see?'

"That was one of the most profound lessons of my life. Mother described to us that day what true love really is. My mother possessed it for my father, to a degree seldom achieved." (Goates, *Harold B. Lee*, pp. 137-39.)

"Fern knew also the blessings derived from sharing material goods, for she gave freely of that which she had on shelves, as well as the baked goodies she often brought forth from her oven.

"The doors of her home were always open to those who needed a place to stay, either temporarily or more permanently. She kept a 'spare bedroom' ready, and there were many who enjoyed being a part of her home for short or longer periods of time." (Goates, *Fern Lucinda Tanner Lee*, p. 5.)

Two children: Helen L. Goates and **Maurine L. Wilkens**.

Freda Joan Jensen Lee (1897-1981) was born on July 2, 1897, in Provo, Utah, the daughter of Hermina Thuesen and Christine Julius Jensen. She married Harold on June 17, 1963, at age sixty-five. She died on July 1, 1981, at age eighty-three.

Tall and slender, Freda was friendly and helpful, always remembered names, and possessed a good sense of humor. A graduate of BYU, she did graduate work at University of Utah, University of California, and Columbia University. She taught school and was a district school supervisor of elementary education for thirty years. She was an expert in children's literature.

She traveled worldwide on Church assignments, often working with and speaking to youth groups. She loved children and devoted much of her professional and private life to them.

Freda played the piano, loved music, and believed that "music is the universal language that opens the windows of the soul."

Freda served as a member of the Primary General Board, Young Women's General Board, and General Music Committee, in addition to various stake boards and several educational societies and boards. She was a life member of the Board of the American Cancer Society (Utah Division) and a member of Phi Kappa Phi Scholastic Society.

In 1969, at the YWMIA Centennial Conference, Freda was presented with a gold plaque for devotion to the youth of the Church. She was also honored as Woman of the Year in 1971 by the Associated Women Students of Ricks College, and in 1972 by the Utah Women's Review and Utah State Fair (Women's Division). In 1979 she received the Distinguished Service Award from BYU Alumni Association.

As a young woman, she was engaged to a widower who had three children. When he died of a ruptured appendix before they could be married, she raised one of his children to adulthood. After Freda married Elder Lee, she became "Aunt Joan" to his daughters.

Speaking at Freda's funeral, her nephew, Dr. Stanford Cazier, then president of Utah State University, said that from the time of accountability to the day of her death, her life had been one of "whole-souled devotion to the gospel. She walked humbly with our Father in Heaven in the spirit of faith, hope and charity. She did not turn away the needy and the naked. She did visit the sick and afflicted. She did impart of her substance. She was a sanctuary to the troubled and heavily burdened. She was a haven to those who had temporarily lost their way. Little wonder that the Lord wanted her for a model of sisterhood in leadership responsibility at the ward and stake levels and on the general boards of the Church." (Gerry Avant, "Freda Joan Lee Eulogized by Family and Friends July 6," *CN*, July 11, 1981, p. 6.)

SPENCER W. KIMBALL

Camilla Eyring Kimball (1894-1987) was born on December 7, 1894, in Colonia Juarez, Mexico, the daughter of Edward Christian and Caroline Romney Eyring. She married Spencer on November 16, 1917, at the age of twenty-two, and they were sealed in the Salt Lake Temple in 1918. She and Spencer were married for sixty-eight years and had four children. She died on September 20, 1987, at age ninety-two.

As a young girl, Camilla had been forced to flee with her family from Mexico during the Revolution in 1912. Camilla attended BYU Academy from 1912 to 1914. She earned a teaching certificate and taught school. A disciple of learning, she spent much of her life acquiring knowledge. "I have always had an inquiring mind. I am not satisfied just to accept things. I like to follow through and study things out." (*DN*, Sept. 21, 1987, p. B-1.)

She attended the University of California in 1915 and Utah State Agriculture College in 1917. She nourished her love of learning by frequently taking classes at the University of Utah. She loved to learn new things—Spanish, typing, literature, and especially things relating to religion. She read biographies to "see how God's plan works itself out in the lives of men and women." She believed education enlarged one's capacity to serve. All of her children earned college degrees—a total of ten degrees among them.

Shortly after Elder Kimball's mission, he read in the local paper about Camilla Eyring, a new teacher at Gila Academy in Arizona. He had met her just before his mission and now was greatly interested. "As soon as I got back down in the valley and was finished with the well work, I looked her up and a courtship was started. I was in the military service, waiting to be called, so my courtship was mostly in a khaki uniform, but she seemed not to be too much offended by my appearance. We were married in November, 1917." (*CN*, Jan 5, 1974, p. 4.)

He was not called up for active duty in the military, and after saving every penny they could for seven months, Spencer and Camilla were able to travel to Salt Lake City to be sealed in the temple.

President Kimball had a deep love for Camilla. On one occasion he wrote this after the two had been clothes shopping for her. "She is very pretty and looks very well in red. She is a lovely lady and she adds so much to my peace and well being." (*SWK*, p. 275.)

Camilla was an inspiring speaker, highly intelligent, loving, patient, generous, and very supportive of her husband. She was an excellent cook and an exquisite seamstress.

She enjoyed gardening, needlepoint, and reading. She studied oil painting after she was ninety. She reviewed books for clubs, sometimes over the radio, and became a popular lecturer on Indian tribes and their cultures.

Sister Kimball made her kitchen the heart of her home. There she cooked, baked, bottled fruit, and ironed. In her home a child could find a ready listener in this patient and loving mother. She uncomplainingly scrubbed clothes on a washboard during the early days of their marriage.

She served as a hospital and library volunteer and was the first president of the Safford, Arizona, PTA, the Safford Women's Club, and the Southeastern Arizona Federation of Women's Clubs. Sister Kimball served as Primary president and also on Relief Society boards. She was a woman of prayer and had great spiritual

reserves, which she drew on during the various illnesses of her family. She cared for her son, Edward, when he contracted polio as a child. She was beside her husband as he underwent open-heart surgery and additional surgeries for throat cancer and subdural hematomas, among other illnesses and problems.

She dealt privately with her agonizing fears, finding strength to show compassion and composure at the bedside of the sufferer. She also lovingly cared for her deaf sister, Mary, who lived with the Kimballs for twenty-five years.

She strongly advocated woman's overall development. Her example inspired her husband to encourage and challenge women to have a program of self-improvement. She believed that education for women was as important as for men. She said, "A woman needs to be concerned with church, school and community. If she buries herself inside four walls, she does not reach her potential. She needs to keep growing, to keep aware of the world in which her children are growing."

She also said, "The pursuit of knowledge is part of the gospel plan for men and women. . . . We should all be resourceful and ambitious, expanding our interests. Forget self-pity and look for mountains to climb. . . .

Any woman should be alive to opportunities—alive to public interests, to her family, to growth, for Church service. Life is so interesting, it worries me that I can't get it all done. And I have no patience with women whose lives 'bore' them." (*DN*, Sept. 21, 1987, p. 2-B)

Camilla counseled every girl and woman to "qualify in two vocations—that of homemaking, and that of preparing to make a living outside the home, if and when the occasion requires. A married woman may become a widow without warning. . . . Thus a woman may be under the necessity of earning her own living and helping to support her dependent children." (*Ensign*, March 1977, p. 59.)

She traveled more with her prophet-husband than any other President's wife up to that time. In her biography, entitled *Camilla*, published by Deseret Book in 1980, it states that her motto was "Never suppress a generous impulse." She believed that "our basic responsibilities are love and service. I learned long ago that with God's help there is no difficulty too great to overcome. That knowledge keeps me from being discouraged for long. . . .

"I love to read and to explore ideas and see new places. . . . Living in this world has proven to be a voyage of continual discovery." (Miner and Kimball, *Camilla*, p. 211.)

Because Camilla was a strong-willed individual, "there were occasional disagreements, of course. One summer when Camilla wanted to save their extra cash for a new house and Spencer wanted to travel, they simply did not come to an agreement. So Spencer loaded the car and took the trip alone and had a good time." (SWK, p. 115.)

President and Sister Kimball were married for sixty-eight years and had a wonderful marriage. Despite the challenges they faced, they had an interesting and enjoyable life together. They loved dancing, singing, and entertaining.

As the wife of an apostle and then the wife of the Church President, Sister Kimball was forthright, highly intelligent, and committed to the gospel. Ever supportive, she perfectly complemented President Kimball in his Church assignments.

She received many awards, including an honorary doctorate from the University of Utah. She earned Exemplary Womanhood Awards from Brigham Young University and Ricks College. She also was given an honorary Golden Gleaner award from the YWMIA and the Ka Hoa Pono Award from BYU-Hawaii. BYU established the Camilla Eyring Kimball Chair of Home and Family Life and a scholarship to honor her for her dedication to the nurturing and perfecting of families. Those who knew her best said her lifelong commitment to excellence in whatever she undertook kept her excited and exciting to know.

Four Children: **Spencer LeVan** (law professor), **Olive Beth K. Mack**, **Andrew Eyring** (business executive), and **Edward Lawrence** (law professor).

EZRA TAFT BENSON

Flora Smith Amussen Benson (1901-1992) was born on July 1, 1901, in Logan, Utah, the daughter of Carl and Barbara Amussen. She married Ezra on September 10, 1926, at age twenty-five. They were married for sixty-six years and had six children. She died on August 14, 1992, at age ninety-one.

Flora was popular in school, always showed a good sense of humor, and was a very happy person. She served as student body vice-president in high school. She developed her athletic ability and, while attending Utah State Agriculture College, became the Women's Singles Tennis Champion. She also had theatrical talent and was elected to the honorary dramatic fraternity for her Shakespearean acting, particularly for the lead role in *Twelfth Night*. She played the piano and had a natural ability in music.

Ezra Taft recalled their "glorious perfect courtship during which I discovered in Flora a great character and a rare combination of virtues." They made plans to marry, but plans were delayed for several years, first while Elder Benson completed a mission in England and then upon his return, Flora decided to go on a mission and served in Hawaii. For a few months, she was a missionary companion with her mother.

After their marriage, Flora's primary interests in life were to support her husband in his work and his Church activities, to make a happy home, and to rear a family. Husband, family, and church were Sister Benson's profession and life. For many years she had to manage the household on a meager allowance. She was a nonmaterialistic parent and a loving disciplinarian. She was also encouraging and protective of her family. She met every problem or emergency with calm assurance that if she did all she could, everything would work out for the best.

When her husband was U.S. Secretary of Agriculture, Flora often accompanied him to press and congressional committee meetings and prayed for him in his service to the nation. She was always very spiritual and prayerful.

Flora's sense of humor found its match in President Benson. As she was giving a speech in 1986, she turned to her husband and said, "When I was a little girl, I used to wonder if I would ever meet the Prophet." Ezra immediately and spontaneously replied, "Did you ever imagine you would have to live with him?" (Dew, *Ezra Taft Benson*, p. 503.)

Flora managed the rearing of the children alone in 1946, while Elder Benson was directing the distribution of food and clothing to the people of war-torn Europe. When her children were young, she declined many invitations, preferring to stay home with them. She did not believe in having hired help in her home "unless absolutely necessary." She felt that the children were part of the home organization and should learn to work and take care of themselves. She exemplified the dedicated mother when, on September 24, 1954, she appeared with her family on Edward R. Murrow's nationally televised Friday night show, "Person to Person." Flora introduced the family, the girls sang, and Beth tap-danced. Reed and Mark explained the Church's missionary program, and the family sang, "Love at Home."

She was a devoted wife, mother, and homemaker. She was always home when the children returned from school or a day's activities and she made home a fun place to be. She played tennis, basketball, and badminton, and rode a bicycle with her family. She always told her children she loved them; Her favorite phrase was "The Lord bless you and the devil miss you." She taught her children to have faith in the Lord by encouraging them to fast and pray for each other. Her favorite song and motto was taken from "Do What Is Right." Her son, Reed, said, "When mother prayed, you knew her prayers were getting through the roof." (*ETB*, p. 139.)

Family home evening at the Bensons was enjoyable and religious. After the opening song, prayer, and scripture reading, there was a discussion of family matters. Then the parents and children played games, gathered around the piano to sing, or put on some records for dancing. Sister Benson was often quoted as saying, "We often dance away our troubles."

Many who knew the family were impressed with how well she organized and managed her home affairs. She had the gift of discernment and often jotted down a note with ideas to help her husband or one of the children. Perhaps the finest tribute to Sister Benson is found in her husband's words: "She has taken her family and other responsibilities most seriously. She has played, sung, cried and studied with them and considered faithfully their every need. Her great faith knows no bounds. When problems arise, she always goes to the Lord in prayer, usually with the family, and often in a special prayer with those most directly concerned. She has instilled in all her children a strong testimony of the gospel." (*Ibid.*, p. 506.)

She served, among other callings, in a stake Relief Society presidency, and as a stake board member in the Young Women, a teacher in the Primary and Sunday School, and other ward callings.

Flora was honored as Homemaker of the Year by the Washington, D.C., Chapter of the National Home Fashion Magazine, received the Distinguished Achievement Award from Ricks College, was the Lambda Delta Sigma Woman of the Year, and the recipient of the BYU Exemplary Womanhood Award.

Six children: **Reed** (professor of religion at BYU), **Mark** (sales manager), **Barbara B. Walker, Beverly B. Parker, Bonnie B. Madsen,** and **Beth B. Burton.**

HOWARD W. HUNTER

Clara May (Claire) Jeffs Hunter (1902-1983) was born on February 18, 1902, in Salt Lake City, the daughter of Jacob and Martha Jeffs. Claire married Howard on June 10, 1931, at the age of twenty-nine. They were married for fifty-two years and had three sons, the first of whom died in infancy. She died on October 9, 1983, after a lengthy illness, at age eighty-one.

Claire grew up in Salt Lake City and attended schools there. In 1926, she moved with her parents to Los Angeles. She was tall and elegant and worked as a fashion model.

She attended three semesters of college and later took adult education classes, as well as interior decorating and sewing classes. She read widely and was curious about the world. One summer she and a female friend took a two-month BYU-sponsored tour to France, Belgium, Netherlands, England, Italy, Switzerland, and the Riviera.

She worked as a telephone switchboard operator for more than two years in Utah and for eight years at a department store in California where she later became vice-president of the company. She also worked as personnel officer in another department store.

Claire met Howard at an M-Men and Gleaner dance at the Wilshire Ward in Los Angeles. They saw each other often at church socials and they both were members of the Thrift Chorus. Their courtship lasted for three years and they were married in the Salt Lake Temple on June 10, 1931.

Innately frugal, she sewed many of her own clothes and planned her home decor. She also kept family scrapbooks and did her husband's genealogical research. She helped her two sons, John and Richard, become Eagle Scouts.

She said in an interview: "My greatest ambition has been to be a good wife, to be a good homemaker, and to be a really good mother. I have always thought that if I could do this, I would fulfill my mission here on earth. We have worked hard to keep our boys close to the Church; the boys and I have had wonderful times together. I've gone through their scouting with them, because, well, Daddy just didn't have the time." (Knowles, *Howard W. Hunter*, p. 115.)

From the age of sixteen, Claire always held a church position, either as an officer or teacher in Young Women, Primary, or Relief Society. She was very knowledgeable about gospel principles.

Throughout her life, she showed courage, faith, and endurance. As her health began to deteriorate, she could no longer travel with President Hunter.

In 1972, she developed diabetes, suffered a cerebral hemorrhage, and was confined to a wheelchair. She was lovingly tended by her husband through years of affliction. Before her death, she ultimately spent months in a coma in a nursing home.

Three children: Howard William (died at six months), **John,** and **Richard** (both attorneys)

Inis Bernice Egan Hunter (1914-present) was born on August 14, 1914, in Thatcher, Utah, the daughter of Anna Bernhardena and Horace W. Egan. She married Howard on April 10, 1990, at age seventy-five. They were married for five years before his death. She was single for twenty-two years before her marriage to President Hunter.

Inis is an articulate woman with a sparkling and outgoing personality, great faith, hope, and an optimistic outlook. She loves the scriptures, music, travel, and literature. She has sung with such groups as the Pasadena Choral Ensemble and the Southern California Mormon Choir. She is also an accomplished soloist. She traveled widely with President Hunter and spoke at regional and stake conferences.

She has had a firm testimony of the gospel since she was a young girl. She said her favorite place to be, other than at home or in the temple, is in general conference or in another church meeting. "I love to feel the spirit of the people." Her favorite scripture is D&C 76:22-24—Joseph's testimony of seeing Christ on the right hand of God.

She worked at Church headquarters for thirteen years, beginning in 1968. The last few years before retiring, she worked as a receptionist in the lobby of the Church Office Building, where she also served, unofficially, as a missionary and an ambassador of goodwill to non-LDS visitors and to foreign tourists.

She has a large collection of dolls with expressive faces and meticulously-designed costumes; she restores dolls as a hobby. She is an excellent seamstress.

Her message to single adults is: "I know something they are feeling. I tell them that what kept me going was the fact that I knew that God loved me, that He was watching over me and knew my every thought, my every need, and that I knew He would provide for me. Sure I was lonesome, but I read the scriptures and went to the temple every week of my life, sometimes I went more than once a week. Prayer kept me going. That and knowing the Lord loved me. I came to know He was not allowing me to be single to punish me, but

He was preparing me for something. I always knew that I wouldn't be left holding the bag, that something was coming to me. I just didn't know what it was."

She first met Howard Hunter in 1945 when her family moved into the El Sereno Ward in California where he was bishop.

Sister Hunter counsels: "I follow the philosophy that you should do your best wherever you are. Set your goals, and through diligence, faith, perseverance and patience you will gradually gravitate toward that which you righteously desire, and you will eventually reach your goal." (*CN*, June 25, 1994, p. 6.)

GORDON B. HINCKLEY

Marjorie Pay Hinckley was born on November 23, 1911, in Nephi, Utah, the daughter of Phillip LeRoy and Georgetta Paxman Pay. She married Gordon Hinckley on April 29, 1937, in the Salt Lake Temple, at the age of twenty-five. They have five children.

Gordon and Marjorie grew up in the same ward, and his earliest recollection of her was in a Primary program where she gave a reading; he thought she was a "cute little girl."

Marjorie's sister, Ramona H. Sullivan, said this about her: "How polished and impressive she was, even as a young girl, in giving readings and performances in the meetings and activities of our old First Ward. . . . Marjorie was downright professional. She had all of the elocution and all of the movements. I still remember those readings she gave." (Jeffrey R. Holland, "President Gordon B. Hinckley," *Ensign*, June 1995, p. 10.)

Sister Hinckley recalls when, at age sixteen, she was called to teach Junior Sunday School. "I felt a real obligation to have a personal testimony of what I was going to teach those children before I said one word to them. That was a time when I really began to read, ponder and pray. . . . My father instructed me to read through again the story of Joseph Smith's first vision. I think if I had to pinpoint a moment when I gained

a personal testimony, it would be during that particular reading of the story that I'd heard and read since my early childhood. That experience bore testimony to me that what Joseph Smith was saying was true. When you know that, everything seems to fall into place." (*CN*, Feb. 8, 1975, p. 5.)

Marjorie graduated from East High School in 1930. Following high school, she had planned to attend the University of Utah, but her father's company folded and she immediately sought full-time work as a secretary to help her family financially. She worked at the Owens Illinois Pacific Coast Glass Company in Salt Lake City.

President and Sister Hinckley's first date was a Gold and Green Ball. "There was a large group of young people in our ward and stake, so most of our earlier dates revolved around the Church. We went to a lot of ward picnics and MIA dances." Elder Hinckley's mission call to England interrupted their courtship; they were married in 1937.

After her marriage, Marjorie attended LDS Institute classes at the University of Utah to help fulfill her desire to deepen her gospel knowledge. Her love of learning has given her a zest for life and a positive attitude—she is energetic and full of fun and life. She is happy, enthusiastic, friendly, and supportive of her husband; she loves people and reaches out to bring comfort to those in distress. She, like her husband, is an excellent public speaker. She loves the scriptures, music, literature, and art. In the midst of turmoil, discomfort, or challenge, she maintains her composure and her happy disposition.

Now that her children are grown, she devotes her time to civic service, homemaking, genealogy, and temple service. On the local level, she has taught and presided in Primary, Young Women, and Relief Society. She travels worldwide with her husband, speaking at regional and stake conferences, mission seminars, and missionary meetings. She has the remarkable distinction of having spoken at the dedicatory services of more than thirty temples. She enjoys meeting Latter-day Saints throughout the world and interacting with those from different cultures.

"It's not surprising that President Hinckley and the Hinckley children think Sister Hinckley is wonderful, too. 'Mom is guileless,' says oldest daughter Kathleen.

'She is absolutely pure. She is a friend to all and can't give enough praise to people, whether that be the milkman, the mailman, the garbage man—everyone.'"

Her daughter Jane calls her their head cheerleader. "She knew everything we were doing and everything we were interested in, and now knows the same about all her grandchildren. She loved having us home after school and couldn't wait for summer vacation to arrive. Other mothers were only too happy to see school start again in the fall, but not Mom—she would weep! She would grieve that we were leaving her." (*Ibid.*, p. 11.)

Another daughter, Kathy, said, "I remember the beautifully vivid description she gave of the events associated with the dedication of the Seoul Korea Temple. . . . She was reliving all of it—and helping us to live it—with an enthusiastic, bright-eyed account of every aspect of the experience, particularly that of these women's beautiful [national] apparel and appearance. Right in the middle of that mesmerizing description, my father looked up and said, 'What costumes?' That is the difference between my mother and my father." (Jeffrey R. Holland, "President Gordon B. Hinckley," *Ensign*, June 1995, pp. 11-12.)

Sister Hinckley said of her parents, "My father and mother were humble people but our home was filled with faith." (Gerry Avant, "Prophet's Surprise Visit Delights Branch," *CN,* Dec. 21, 1995, p. 6.)

Regarding parenting, Sister Hinckley believes that "there were certain kinds of things that didn't merit intervention, anxiety or, worse, punishment; most definitely they weren't worth creating conflict between parent and child. 'I learned that I needed to trust my children,' she said later, 'so I tried to never say no if I could possibly say yes.

"'When we were raising a family, it was a matter of getting through every day and having a little fun along the way. As I could see that I wasn't going to be able to make all of my children's decisions anyway, I tried not to worry about every little thing. I think that came from my parents, because they had absolute confidence in me and my siblings. As hard as it has been at times, Gordon and I tried to have the same confidence in our children.'"

"We tried not to take ourselves too seriously. We learned that you get in trouble when you do that. . . . Humor became the trademark in a family when the ability to laugh at oneself was required for survival." The Hinckley children often heard their mother say, "The only way to get through life is to laugh your way through it." "Marjorie Hinckley took that approach with her husband and family, refusing to take offense where none was intended and filtering daily events through an attitude of good humor." (Dew, *GBH,* pp. 173-75.)

Marjorie's granddaughter, Holly Hinckley, says her grandmother is a "quiet strength" to the Hinckley family. "She is always gentle, always loving, always kind." Her "pragmatic and humorous" view of life has allowed her to be happy in any situation. One of Sister Hinckley's mottos is: "Expect the worst, and if it doesn't happen, you will be pleasantly surprised."

"All of the grandchildren adore their grandparents. Marjorie is well known throughout the family as the 'groovy grandma,' a reputation earned after countless shopping trips, sleep overs and grand-children parties. Even in her eighties she planned Christmas celebrations with activities for all ages." (Dew, *GBH,* p. 476.)

Sister Hinckley loves her grandchildren, and she is very special to them. When asked what their grandmother is like, the grandchildren all have the same reaction: "We always say that we love Grandpa so much because he married Grandma. Everybody loves her so much. She never stops smiling."

Other comments from her grandchildren are, "She's never in a grumpy mood. She's always happy. The whole way she looks at the world is so real and unpretentious. She is a fun grandma . . . . You go anywhere with her, and it's fun." (*NE*, April 1997, pp. 30-31.)

On February 28, 1996, students at BYU gave Sister Hinckley the highest honor given by the university and student body, the Exemplary Womanhood Award, calling her a "special individual whose life has exemplified the teachings of Jesus Christ." Sister Hinckley said, "If this gospel is anything at all, it is a gospel of love and I am grateful for it." She explained that the Church has made her what she is today. "I am what I am because of my activity in the Church.

President Hinckley stated that he has never found, in all his travels, someone who doesn't like his wife. "She speaks and she gets letters constantly telling her how much people enjoy what she had to say," he noted. "Then they add a little postscript at the bottom that says, 'We also enjoyed your husband.'"

President Hinckley describes his wife as a leader. "She has been a great mother, a remarkable companion and a wonderful servant of the Lord. She has been active and done much in the Church and in the community." He has also commented that he is "constantly amazed at what a voracious reader she is. She reads two newspapers a day, goes through magazines, is an ardent student of the Book of Mormon and the Doctrine and Covenants and I saw her the other evening reading a lengthy biography." (*Ensign,* March 1997, p. 62.)

Sister Hinckley says she believes it is important for women in the Church "to keep the faith" and "set an example of kindness and excellence."

Elder Bruce Hafen commented that Sister Hinckley's entire life reflects the five aims of BYU: "spiritually strengthening, intellectually enlarging, character building, lifelong learning and serving." BYUSA President Wesley McDougal added, "She has filled her life with service, with love, with caring stewardship, and with being a woman of God. She is pure and clear. We have all been touched by her light." (Sarah Jane Weaver, *CN*, Mar. 9, 1996, pp. 3, 10.)

"Sister Hinckley complements her husband with her warm manner, sense of humor, and sincere expression of testimony. Without exception the Saints enjoy the exchanges between the two. In one meeting President Hinckley introduced her by saying, 'I am going to exercise my prerogative and call on Sister Hinckley to speak. This is something for which I will pay a dear price, but so be it.' Sister Hinckley countered with: 'What would you do if you were married to a man like that? There used to be two important men in my life—my husband and the President of the Church. Now, all of a sudden, there's only one.' Typically her friendly manner and wit were but a prelude to the bearing of sincere testimony." (Dew, *GBH*, pp. 548-49.)

Sister Hinckley's family history is filled with examples of faith that helped her gain a testimony. "I grew up on pioneer stories. . . . On the 24th of July, our father would take us up on the mountain where our grandmother's handcart company entered the valley. He'd have us sit down and then he would tell us the story of these pioneers. It gave us a feeling of reality and it was something for us to live up to.

I think I must have been born with a testimony, but I have to give my parents credit for it. We had a beautiful Latter-day Saint home where the gospel was a way of life. We had family home evenings long before they were called that. They always consisted of gospel discussions, and we played lots of games because that was an inexpensive form of family recreation." (Gerry Avant, *CN*, Feb. 8, 1995, p. 5.)

Church News writer Gerry Avant said, "Elder and Sister Hinckley reared their two sons and three daughters in a home in the suburbs of Salt Lake City, where working, playing and praying together was a daily routine. The acre and a half lot had a garden, an orchard, broad lawns and many trees. Close ties were bound as the family plowed the earth and planted seeds in their garden, and picked fruit from peach, apple, apricot, and cherry trees.

"Many evenings were spent together as either Elder or Sister Hinckley read aloud to the children, who even today, talk about their favorite books that the family read together. 'They're always coming to our home to find the books we read together so they can read them to their children.'" (*Ibid*., p. 6.)

President Hinckley said of Sister Hinckley on the day he was ordained and set apart as President of the Church: "She is a woman of great faith. She is a wonderful mother. How I love her." (*Ensign*, May 1995, p. 74.)

Five children: **Kathleen H. Barnes**, **Richard Gordon** (business, controller), **Virginia H. Pearce**, **Clark Bryant** (bank officer), and **Jane H. Dudley**.

Quotations by Marjorie Hinckley

Church Membership. I am happy to be a member of this Church. Every day of my life I pray that I may be worthy to be one of you. The gospel is true. Every day of my life I realize more than ever that this is truly the work of the Lord. I've seen far too much in my lifetime to ever deny this is His work and His glory. I'm thankful I learned as early as I did anything that the Church of Jesus Christ is true. I am grateful for this. It is wonderful to grow up knowing where you came from, why you are here and where you hope to go. (*CN*, Oct. 21, 1995, p. 6.)

Decisions. I love the scripture from Doctrine and Covenants 10:4: "Do not run faster or labor more than you have strength." Choose carefully each day that which you will do and that which you will not do, and the Lord will bless you to accomplish the important things that have eternal consequences. (Stovall and Madsen, *As Women of Faith*, p. 7.)

Friendship. Sisters, we are all in this together. We need each other. Oh, how we need each other. Those of us who are old need you who are young. And, hopefully you who are young need some of us who are old. It is a sociological fact that women need women. We need deep satisfying and loyal friendships with each other. These friendships are a necessary source of sustenance. We need to renew our faith every day. We need to lock arms and help build the kingdom so that it will roll forth and fill the whole earth. (*Ibid.*, p. 11.)

Jesus Christ. He was divine, the Prince of Peace, the King of Glory. He was mortal. He lived on the same earth we live on. He had to overcome even as you and I. He had to discipline Himself to get up in the morning and do His chores. He had to study and learn to get along with His peers and learn obedience. My love for Him knows no bounds. *(Ibid.,* p. 4.)

Jesus Christ. My love for my Savior began at an early age. Hanging on our bedroom wall when I was a child was a very large print of a famous painting of the boy Jesus teaching the wise men in the temple. Mother had positioned the picture so that the first thing our eyes saw when we awakened each morning was the beautiful face of Jesus. I was grown and long gone from the home before I realized what a profound effect this had had on my life. (*Ibid.*, p. 3.)

Motherhood. Motherhood is the noblest and greatest of all callings. . . . When you teach children to love

their Heavenly Father, you have done one of the greatest things you will ever do. (*Ibid.*, p. 5.)

Prayer. I think family prayer had a great deal to do with the way our children responded to us. Even though Gordon didn't preach to them, they heard everything we wanted them to hear in family prayer. (Dew, *GBH*, p. 171.)

Service. There is so much we can do to be an influence, perhaps not in ways we have once known, but in many other ways. Last year in the Upland Terrace School in the Granite School District, which three of my grandchildren attend, grandparents gave the equivalent of two hundred hours of volunteer service. Who can measure the worth of a grandmotherly or grandfatherly influence in the classroom? (Dew, *GBH*, p. 10.)

Testimony. I know [Gordon B. Hinckley] is a prophet of God. I have seen the power of the Lord magnify him. I have seen him solve problems that seemed to be almost unsolvable because the Lord has given him the inspiration and the answers he needed to move the work along. . . . He bears the mantle of the prophet. (Dew, *GBH*, pp. 533-34.)

Values. I believe we sometimes have a tendency to think that America has a corner on things that are good—that the American way of life is the only right way. I've learned that people of other lands have a great deal to offer us in many areas. It's interesting and valuable to note that their interests and values are similar to our own. We all want our children educated. It gives one a great feeling to realize that we're all one—that we're striving for the same things; that we're sons and daughters of God with similar aspirations. (Gerry Avant, "Sister Hinckley Talks About Her Church Life," *CN*, Feb. 8, 1975, p. 5.)

Women. Our women bring to the corporate world a firm but soft touch. Hardly realizing it, they bring a special quality of friendship, flexibility, love and understanding to the professional environment. They are making this a better place for all of us, as their faith and integrity and their understanding of right and wrong flavor everything they do. (Stovall and Madsen, *As Women of Faith*, p. 10.)

IMPORTANT PRINCIPLES ON HOW TO LIVE A MORE CHRIST-CENTERED LIFE
(From the Teachings of the Church Presidents)
Compiled by Emerson R. West

The Savior beckons, "Come follow me." As we learn of Him, we are invited to follow the Savior's example to love, obey, forgive and give of ourselves. Following are suggestions for accomplishing that end.

- Seek to know, love, and commune with your Heavenly Father through regular and sincere prayer. Strive to develop a close personal relationship with Him. He loves you no matter who or where you are.

- Be submissive to the Savior, build and focus your life on His teachings. Study and live to understand the character of the Lord. It will influence you in all aspects of life. Manifest your discipleship in civility, gentility, cheerfulness, and optimism.

- Strive to feel the Holy Ghost throughout each day. Think of what the Savior would do as circumstances arise, ask for guidance, and then follow the promptings of the Spirit.

- Search, read and ponder the scriptures and apply what you learn to your daily life.

- Be kind, humble, merciful, and helpful in communicating with others.

- Forgive without condition, limitation, or exception. God forgives those who forgive others. Then forgive yourself so you may have inner peace.

- Be patient with yourself and with others. Be patient during adversity, trusting in the Lord and having hope through Him.

- Be a peacemaker. Endeavor to love others, even those who see themselves as your enemies.

- Serve others willingly and generously. Achieve the proper balance between contentment and ambition.

- Be diligent and consistent in your duties toward God, your fellowmen, and yourself.

- Be honest and maintain high ethical standards.

- Repent of your sins to qualify for the beautiful promises that He will forgive, forget, and never mention the sins of which we have truly repented. Never stop repenting; it is a life-long process.

- Control your temper and tongue or lose the Spirit.

- Accept the divine worth of others regardless of race, origin, background, beliefs, or culture.

- Partake of the sacrament worthily, in humility and in gratitude for the Lord's mercy, love, and forgiveness. Make it an opportunity to renew covenants previously made and to commit to regular improvement.

- Seek to achieve true worship and acknowledge the Lord's blessings.

- Build genuine spirituality into your life by developing a foundation of faith, hope, charity, gratitude, meekness, and courage.

- Perform temple ordinances often and keep all of your temple covenants.

- Seek the Spirit in understanding and implementing the counsel of the prophets and local leaders.

- Follow the counsel in your patriarchal blessing.

- Keep a journal as a reference to review past actions, to appreciate the Lord's involvement in your life, and to maintain an eternal perspective.

- Seek righteousness and daily improvement. Cleave unto truth. Be clean in thought and action. Avoid anything that would offend the Spirit.

Christ has given us a pattern of life—principles by which to live. Make time for the Savior and accept His great love. Let all that He represents abide in our hearts. If we stray from His example, we must repent and come unto Him again. The true measure of a Christ-centered life is the treatment of our family, friends, and others; these actions will show our true character and the quality of our faith.

THOUGHTS ABOUT JESUS CHRIST BY OUR CHURCH PRESIDENTS

Joseph Smith

The Son, who was in the bosom of the Father, [is] a personage of tabernacle, made or fashioned like unto man, or being in the form and likeness of man, or rather man was formed after his likeness and in his image; he is also the express image and likeness of the personage of the Father, possessing all the fullness of the Father, or the same fullness of the Father; being begotten of him, and ordained from before the foundation of the world to be a propitiation for the sins of all those who should believe on his name, and is called the Son because of the flesh, and descended in suffering below that which man can suffer; or, in other words, suffered greater sufferings, and was exposed to more powerful contradictions than any man can be.

But, notwithstanding all this, he kept the law of God, and remained without sin, showing thereby that it is in the power of man to keep the law and remain also without sin; and also, that by him a righteous judgment might come upon all flesh, and that all who walk not in the law of God may justly be condemned by the law, and have no excuse for their sins. And he being the Only Begotten of the Father, full of grace and truth, and having overcome, received a fullness of the glory of the Father. (*Lectures on Faith*, p. 49; see also *JSH* 25; "Articles of Faith" 1, 3-4; D&C 76:11-24.)

Brigham Young

The Lord has revealed to us a plan by which we may be saved both here and hereafter. God has done everything we could ask, and more than we could ask. The errand of Jesus to earth was to bring his brethren and sisters back into the presence of the Father; he has done his part of the work, and it remains for us to do ours. There is not one thing that the Lord could do for the salvation of the human family that he has neglected to do; and it remains for the children of men to receive the truth or reject it; all that can be accomplished for their salvation, independent of them, has been accomplished in and by the Savior. It has been justly remarked this afternoon that "Jesus paid the debt; he atoned for the original sin; he came and suffered and died on the cross." He is now King of kings and Lord of lords, and the time will come when every knee will bow and every tongue confess, to the glory of God the Father, that Jesus is the Christ. That very character that was looked upon, not as the Savior, but as an outcast, who was crucified between two thieves and treated with scorn and derision, will be greeted by all men as the only Being through whom they can obtain salvation. (*DBY*, p. 27.)

John Taylor

It was necessary, when the Savior was upon the earth, that he should be tempted in all points, like unto us, and "be touched with the feeling of our infirmities," to comprehend the weaknesses and strength, the perfections and imperfections of poor fallen human nature. And having accomplished the thing he came into the world to do; having to grapple with the hypocrisy, corruption, weaknesses, and imbecility of man; having met with temptation and trial in all its forms, and overcome, he has become a faithful High Priest to intercede for us in the everlasting kingdom of His Father. He knows how to estimate and put a proper value upon human nature, for he having been placed in the same position as we are, knows how to bear with our weaknesses and infirmities, and can fully comprehend the depth, power and strength of the afflictions and trials that men have to cope within this world, and thus understandingly and by experience, he can bear with them as a father and an elder brother. (*JD* 1:148-49.)

Wilford Woodruff

I have always looked upon the life of our Savior—who descended beneath all things that he might rise above all things—as an example for his followers. And yet it has always, in one sense of the word, seemed strange to me that the Son of God, the First Begotten in the eternal worlds of the Father, and the Only Begotten in the flesh, should have to descend to the earth and pass through what he did—born in a stable, cradled in a manger, persecuted, afflicted, scorned, a hiss and byword to almost all the world, and especially to the inhabitants of Jerusalem and Judea. There was apparently nothing that the Savior could do that was acceptable in the eyes of the world; anything and almost everything he did was imputed to an unholy influence. When He cast out devils the people said he did it through the power of Beelzebub, the prince of devils. . . .There is something about all this that appears sorrowful; but it seemed necessary for the Savior to descend below all things that he might ascend above all things. (*JD* 23:327.)

Lorenzo Snow

Jesus Christ the Son of God was once placed in a condition that it required the highest effort in order to accomplish what was necessary for the salvation of millions of the children of God. It required the highest effort and determination that had to be exercised before the Son of God could pass through the ordeal, the sacrifice that was necessary. I believe that his Father had educated him, had passed him through scenes that were a very serious character, of great trials, and he knew just what he could depend upon from the facts that were illustrated and shown by his experience. (*CR*, Oct. 1900, p. 2.)

Joseph F. Smith

Christ himself was not perfect at first; he received not a fullness at first, but he received grace for grace, and he continued to receive more and more until he received a fullness. . . . It is the Spirit of God which proceeds through Christ to the world, that enlightens every man that comes into the world, and that strives with the children of men, and will continue to strive with them, until it brings them to a knowledge of the truth. (*IE*, Nov. 1907-1908, pp. 380-83.)

Heber J. Grant

The story of Jesus Christ is a story of old that ever remains new. The oftener I read of His life and labors the greater are the joy, peace, the happiness, the satisfaction that fill my soul. . . . We all know that no one ever lived upon the earth that exerted the same influence upon the destinies of the world as did our Lord and Savior Jesus Christ; and yet He was born in obscurity, cradled in a manger. He chose for His apostles poor, unlettered fishermen. More than nineteen hundred years have passed and gone since His crucifixion, and yet all over the world, in spite of all strife and chaos, there is still burning in the hearts of millions of people a testimony of the divinity of the work that He accomplished. (*GS*, pp. 22-23.)

George Albert Smith

When Christ came to instruct the people, he told them that there must be faith in God and righteousness in life or they would not please our Heavenly Father. And so the Savior of the world came with kindness and love. He went among the people healing the sick, unstopping the ears of the deaf, and restoring sight to those who were blind. They saw these things done by the power of God. Comparatively few of them could understand or believe that he was the Son of God. . . . And when the time came for him to die, and he hung upon the cross, and was cruelly tortured by those of his own people, his own race, he did not become angry, he did not resent the unkindness. The people of the world do not understand some of these things, and particularly, many men cannot understand how the Savior felt when in the agony of his soul, he cried to His Heavenly Father, not to condemn and destroy those who were taking his mortal life, but he said, " Father, forgive them; for they know not what they do." (Luke 23:44.)

That should be the attitude of all the members of The Church of Jesus Christ of Latter-day Saints. . . . And would be, it seems to me, if they fully understood the plan of Salvation. (*CR*, Oct. 1945, pp. 167-69.)

David O. McKay

The highest of all ideals are the teachings and particularly the life of Jesus of Nazareth, and that man is most truly great who is most Christlike. What you sincerely in your heart think of Christ will determine what you are, will largely determine what your acts will be. No person can study this divine personality, can accept his teachings without becoming conscious of an uplifting and refining influence within himself. . . . None, however, is so vital, so contributive to the peace and happiness of the human family as the surrendering of our selfish, animal-like natures to the life and teachings of our Lord and Savior, Jesus Christ. (*GI,* pp. 34-35.)

Joseph Fielding Smith

This is what he did: He carried, in some way that I cannot understand and you cannot understand, the burden of the combined weight of the sins of the world. It is hard enough for me to carry my own transgressions, and it is hard enough for you to carry yours. . . . Can you comprehend the suffering of Jesus Christ when he carried, not merely by physical manifestation but in some spiritual and mental condition or manner, the combined weight of sin. . . . It was in the Garden of Gethsemane that the blood oozed from the pores of his body. . . . Now I cannot comprehend that pain. . . . A mortal man could not have stood it—that is, a man such as we are. . . . He carried that load for us if we will only accept him as our Redeemer and keep his commandments. . . . If we are rebellious, we will have to pay the price ourselves. (*DS* 1:129-131.)

Harold B. Lee

Today we should ask ourselves the question in answer to what the Master asked of those in His day, "What think ye of Christ?" (Matt. 22:42.) We ought to ask as we would say it today, "What think we of Christ?" and then make it a little more personal and ask, "What think I of Christ?" Do I think of Him as the Redeemer of my soul? Do I think of Him with no doubt in my mind as the one who appeared to the prophet Joseph Smith? Do I believe that He established this church upon the earth? Do I accept Him as the Savior of this world? Am I true to my covenants, which in the waters of baptism, if I understood, meant that I would stand as a witness of Him at all times, and in all things, and in all places, wherever I would be, even until death? (*THBL*, p. 8.)

Spencer W. Kimball

Jesus said many times, "Come, follow me." His was a program of "do what I do," rather than "do what I say." His innate brilliance would have permitted him to put on a dazzling display, but that would have left his followers far behind. He walked and worked with those he was to serve. His was not a long-distance leadership. He was not afraid of close friendships; he was not afraid that proximity to him would disappoint his followers. The leaven of true leadership cannot lift others unless we are with and serve those to be led. . . .The Savior's leadership was selfless. He put himself and his own needs second and ministered to others beyond the call of duty, tirelessly, lovingly, effectively. . . .

Jesus had perspective about problems and people. He was able to calculate carefully at long range the effect and impact of utterances, not only on those who were to hear them at the moment, but on those who would read them 2,000 years later. So often, secular leaders rush in to solve problems by seeking to stop the present pain, and thereby create even greater difficulty and pain later on. . . .

Jesus was not afraid to make demands of those he led. His leadership was not condescending or soft. The most important thing I can say about Jesus Christ . . . is that he lives. He really does embody all those virtues and attributes the scriptures tell us. . . . We will find it very difficult to be significant leaders unless we recognize the reality of the perfect leader, Jesus Christ, and let his be the light by which we see the way! (*Ensign*, Aug. 1979, pp. 5-7.)

Ezra Taft Benson

Nearly two thousand years ago, a perfect man walked the earth—Jesus the Christ. He was the Son of a Heavenly Father and an earthly mother. He is the God of this world, under the Father. In His life, all the virtues were lived and kept in perfect balance; He taught men truth—that they might be free; His example and precepts provide the great standard—the only sure way—for all mankind. Among us He became the first and only one who had the power to reunite His body with His spirit after death.

By His power all men who have died shall be resurrected. Before Him one day we all must stand to be judged by His laws. He lives today, and in the not too distant future shall return, in triumph, to subdue His enemies, to reward men according to their deeds, and to assume His rightful role and reign in righteousness over the entire earth. (*TETB*, p. 8.)

Howard W. Hunter

The great thing he did was to set a perfect example of right living, of kindness and mercy and compassion, in order that all of the rest of mankind might know how to live, know how to improve, and know how to become more godlike. Let us follow the Son of God in all ways and in all walks of life. Let us make him our exemplar and our guide. We should at every opportunity ask ourselves, "What would Jesus do?" and then be more courageous to act upon the answer. We must follow Christ, in the best sense of that word. We must be about his work as he was about his Father's. We should try to be like Him, even as the Primary children sing, "Try, try, try" (*Children's Songbook,* p. 55).

To the extent that our mortal powers permit, we should make every effort to become like Christ—the one perfect and sinless example this world has ever seen. . . .We must know Christ better than we know him; we must remember him more often than we remember him; we must serve him more valiantly than we serve him. Then we will drink water springing up unto eternal life and will eat the bread of life. What manner of men and women ought we to be? Even as he is. (*Ensign*, May 1994, p. 64.)

Gordon B. Hinckley

I believe in the Lord Jesus Christ, the Son of the eternal, living God. I believe in Him as the Firstborn of the Father and the Only Begotten of the Father in the flesh. I believe in Him as an individual, separate and distinct from His Father. . . .

I believe that in His mortal life He was the one perfect man to walk the earth. I believe that in his words are to be found that light and truth which, if observed, would save the world and bring exaltation to mankind. . . .

I believe that through His atoning sacrifice, the offering of His life on Calvary's Hill, He expiated the sins of mankind, relieving us from the burden of sin if we will forsake evil and follow Him. I believe in the reality and the power of His resurrection. . . .

None so great has ever walked the earth. None other has made a comparable sacrifice or granted a comparable blessing. He is the Savior and the Redeemer of the world. I believe in Him. I declare His divinity without equivocation or compromise. I love Him. I speak His name in reverence and wonder. I worship Him as I worship His Father, in spirit and in truth. I thank Him and kneel before His wounded feet and hands and side, amazed at the love He offers me. (*Ensign*, Nov. 1986, pp. 50-51.)

THE FIRST PRESIDENCY OF THE CHURCH (1832-1997)

First Counselor	President	Second Counselor
Sidney Rigdon[1] 1832-44 Age 39-52	**#1 Joseph Smith**[2] First Elder 1830-1832 (1 year 9 months) Age 24-26 President 1832-1844 (12½ years) Age 26-38	**Jesse Gause**[1] 1832 Age 48
		Frederick G. Williams[1] 1833-1837 Age 45-50
		Hyrum Smith[2] 1837-1841 Age 37-41
		William Law[2] 1841-1844 Age 31-34
	Oliver Cowdery[2] Associate President 1834-1837 Age 27-30	
	Hyrum Smith[2] Associate President 1841-44 Age 41-44	
Heber C. Kimball 1847-1868 Age 46-67	**#2 Brigham Young** 1847-1877 (30 years) Age 46-76	**Willard Richards** 1847-1854 Age 43-49
George A. Smith 1868-1875 Age 51-58		**Jedediah M. Grant**[2] 1854-1856 Age 38-40
John W. Young[2] 1876-1877 Age 32-33		**Daniel H. Wells**[2] 1857-1877 Age 42-62
George Q. Cannon 1880-1887 Age 53-60	**#3 John Taylor** 1880-1887 (7 years) Age 71-78	**Joseph F. Smith** 1880-1887 Age 41-48
George Q. Cannon 1889-1898 Age 62-71	**#4 Wilford Woodruff** 1889-1898 (9½ years) Age 82-91	**Joseph F. Smith** 1889-1898 Age 50-59
George Q. Cannon 1898-1901 Age 71-74	**#5 Lorenzo Snow** 1898-1901 (3 years) Age 84-87	**Joseph F. Smith** 1898-1901 Age 59-62
Joseph F. Smith[3] 1901 Age 62		**Rudger B. Clawson**[3] 1901 Age 44
John R. Winder[1] 1901-1910 Age 79-88	**#6 Joseph F. Smith** 1901-1918 (17 years) Age 62-80	**Anthon H. Lund** 1901-1910 Age 57-65
Anthon H. Lund 1910-1918 Age 65-74		**John Henry Smith** 1910-1911 Age 61-63
		Charles W. Penrose 1911-1918 Age 79-86

First Counselor	President	Second Counselor
Anthon H. Lund 1918-1921 Age 74-76	**#7 Heber J. Grant** 1918-1945 (26½ years) Age 62-88	**Charles W. Penrose** 1918-1921 Age 86-89
Charles W. Penrose 1921-1925 Age 89-93		**Anthony W. Ivins** 1921-1925 Age 68-72
Anthony W. Ivins 1925-1934 Age 72-82		**Charles W. Nibley**[1] 1925-1931 Age 76-82
		J. Reuben Clark, Jr.[4] 1933-1934 Age 61-63
J. Reuben Clark, Jr.[4] 1934-1945 Age 63-73		**David O. McKay** 1934-1945 Age 60-71
J. Reuben Clark, Jr. 1945-1951 Age 73-78	**#8 George Albert Smith** 1945-1951 (6 years) Age 75-81	**David O. McKay** 1945-1951 Age 71-77
Stephen L Richards 1951-1959 Age 71-79	**#9 David O. McKay** 1951-1970 (19 years) Age 77-96	**J. Reuben Clark, Jr.** 1951-1959 Age 79-87
J. Reuben Clark, Jr. 1959-1961 Age 87-90		**Henry D. Moyle** 1959-1961 Age 70-72
Henry D. Moyle 1961-1963 Age 72-74		**Hugh B. Brown** 1961-1963 Age 77-79
Hugh B. Brown 1963-1970 Age 79-86		**N. Eldon Tanner** 1963-1970 Age 65-71
Harold B. Lee 1970-1972 Age 71-73	**#10 Joseph Fielding Smith** 1970-1972 (2½ years) Age 93-95	**N. Eldon Tanner** 1970-1972 Age 71-74
N. Eldon Tanner 1972-1973 Age 74-75	**#11 Harold B. Lee** 1972-1973 (1½ years) Age 73-74	**Marion G. Romney** 1972-1973 Age 75-76
N. Eldon Tanner 1973-1982 Age 75-84	**#12 Spencer W. Kimball** 1973-1985 (12 years) Age 78-90	**Marion G. Romney** 1973-1982 Age 76-85
Marion G. Romney 1982-1985 Age 85-88		**Gordon B. Hinckley** 1982-1985 Age 72-75
Gordon B. Hinckley 1985-1994 Age 75-83	**#13 Ezra Taft Benson** 1985-1994 (8½ years) Age 86-94	**Thomas S. Monson** 1985-1994 Age 58-66
Gordon B. Hinckley 1994-1995 Age 83-84	**#14 Howard W. Hunter** 1994-1995 (9 months) Age 86-87	**Thomas S. Monson** 1994-1995 Age 66-67
Thomas S. Monson 1995- Age 67-	**#15 Gordon B. Hinckley** 1995- Age 84-	**James E. Faust** 1995- Age 74-

1   Called as counselor to the President but was never ordained an apostle.
2   Ordained an apostle but was not a member of the Quorum of the Twelve.
3   At the death of George Q. Cannon, Joseph F. Smith was sustained as first counselor on October 6, 1901, with Rudger Clawson as second counselor. They were sustained but not set apart because this First Presidency was dissolved four days later by the death of President Snow.
4   J. Reuben Clark, Jr., U.S. Ambassador to Mexico, was called on December 19, 1931, to be the second counselor, but due to complications with ambassadorial assignments, he was unable to begin his service until October 1933.

ASSOCIATE PRESIDENTS OF THE CHURCH

Oliver Cowdery - (1834-37)
Hyrum Smith - (1841-44)

Oliver Cowdery (ordained an apostle in 1829 by Peter, James, and John) was Associate President of the Church, but in a spirit of rebellion he lost his position and was excommunicated. **Hyrum Smith** (to whom Joseph Smith gave all priesthood authority formerly held by Oliver Cowdery, including office of apostle) was selected to take Oliver Cowdery's position as Associate President. The deaths of the two most prominent men in the Church, Joseph and Hyrum Smith, are the effectual sealing of their testimonies.

President Joseph Fielding Smith (grandson of Hyrum Smith) said, "Hyrum Smith, Associate President of the Church, held the keys conjointly with his younger brother, the Prophet Joseph Smith. . . . Had Hyrum Smith escaped martyrdom, he would have been President of the Church. However, it was just as essential that Hyrum Smith lay down his life as the Second Witness as it was for the Prophet Joseph Smith." (Pearson H. Corbett, *Hyrum Smith, Patriarch*, pp. xiii-xvi.)

ADDITIONAL COUNSELORS IN THE FIRST PRESIDENCY
(when the First Presidency had more than two counselors)

Other Counselors in the First Presidency		Assistant Counselors in the First Presidency	
John C. Bennett[1]	1841-42	Oliver Cowdery[2]	1837-38
Amasa M. Lyman	1843-44	Joseph Smith, Sr.[1]	1837-40
Joseph F. Smith	1866-77	Hyrum Smith[2]	1837
Lorenzo Snow	1873-74	John Smith[1]	1837-44
Brigham Young, Jr.	1873-74	Lorenzo Snow	1874-77
Albert Carrington	1873-74	Brigham Young, Jr.	1874-77
John W. Young[1]	1873-74	Albert Carrington	1874-77
George Q. Cannon	1873-74	John W. Young[2]	1874-76
Hugh B. Brown	1961	George Q. Cannon	1874-77
Joseph Fielding Smith	1965-70		
H. Thorpe B. Isaacson[1]	1965-70		
Alvin R. Dyer[2]	1968-70		
Gordon B. Hinckley	1981-82		

[1] Called as counselor to the President but never ordained an apostle.
[2] Ordained an apostle but was not a member of the Quorum of the Twelve.

APOSTLES IN THE QUORUM OF THE TWELVE (1835-1997)

(Dates refer to period of service in the Quorum; age at time of ordination is also listed)

1.	Thomas B. Marsh[1,6]	(1835-39)	35
2.	David W. Patten	(1835-38)	35
3.	**Brigham Young**[1]	(1835-47)	33
4.	Heber C. Kimball[2]	(1835-47)	33
5.	Orson Hyde[1,3]	(1835-39; 39-78)	30
6.	William E. M'Lellin[6]	(1835-38)	29
7.	Parley P. Pratt	(1835-57)	27
8.	Luke S. Johnson[6]	(1835-38)	27
9.	William B. Smith[3,6]	(1835-39; 39-45)	23
10.	Orson Pratt[4]	(1835-42; 43-81)	23
11.	John Boynton[6]	(1835-37)	23
12.	Lyman E. Johnson[6]	(1835-38)	23
13.	John E. Page[6]	(1838-46)	39
14.	**John Taylor**[1]	(1838-80)	30
15.	**Wilford Woodruff**[1]	(1839-89)	32
16.	George Albert Smith[2]	(1839-68)	21
17.	Willard Richards[2]	(1840-47)	36
18.	Lyman Wight[6]	(1841-48)	44
19.	Amasa M. Lyman[2,6]	(1842-43; 44-67)	29
20.	Ezra T. Benson	(1846-69)	35
21.	Charles C. Rich	(1849-83)	39
22.	**Lorenzo Snow**[1,2]	(1849-98)	34
23.	Erastus Snow	(1849-88)	30
24.	Franklin D. Richards[1]	(1849-99)	27
25.	George Q. Cannon[2]	(1860-80)	33
26.	**Joseph F. Smith**[2]	(1867-80)	28
27.	Brigham Young Jr.[1]	(1868-03)	31
28.	Albert Carrington[6]	(1870-85)	57
29.	Moses Thatcher[6]	(1879-96)	37
30.	Francis M. Lyman[1]	(1880-16)	40
31.	John Henry Smith[2]	(1880-10)	32
32.	George Teasdale	(1882-07)	50
33.	**Heber J. Grant**[1]	(1882-18)	25
34.	John W. Taylor[6]	(1884-05)	25
35.	Marriner W. Merrill	(1889-06)	57
36.	Anthon H. Lund[1,2]	(1889-01)	45
37.	Abraham H. Cannon[5]	(1889-96)	30
38.	Matthias F. Cowley[6]	(1897-05)	39
39.	Abraham O. Woodruff	(1897-04)	24
40.	Rudger Clawson[1,2]	(1898-43)	41
41.	Reed Smoot	(1900-41)	38
42.	Hyrum Mack Smith	(1901-18)	29
43.	**George Albert Smith**[1]	(1903-45)	33
44.	Charles W. Penrose[2]	(1904-11)	72
45.	George F. Richards[1]	(1906-50)	45
46.	Orson F. Whitney	(1906-31)	50
47.	**David O. McKay**[1,2]	(1906-34)	32
48.	Anthony W. Ivins[2]	(1907-21)	55
49.	**Joseph Fielding Smith**[1,2]	(1910-70)	33
50.	James E. Talmage	(1911-33)	49
51.	Stephen L Richards[2]	(1917-51)	37
52.	Richard R. Lyman[6]	(1918-43)	47
53.	Melvin J. Ballard	(1919-39)	45
54.	John A. Widtsoe	(1921-52)	49
55.	Joseph F. Merrill	(1931-52)	63
56.	Charles A. Callis	(1933-47)	68
57.	J. Reuben Clark[2,5]	(1934-61)	63
58.	Alonzo A. Hinckley	(1934-36)	64
59.	Albert E. Bowen	(1937-53)	61
60.	Sylvester Q. Cannon[5]	(1938-43)	62
61.	**Harold B. Lee**[1,2]	(1941-70)	42
62.	**Spencer W. Kimball**[1]	(1943-73)	48
63.	**Ezra Taft Benson**[1]	(1943-85)	44
64.	Mark E. Petersen	(1944-84)	43
65.	Matthew Cowley	(1945-53)	48
66.	Henry D. Moyle[2]	(1947-59)	57
67.	Delbert L. Stapley	(1950-78)	53
68.	Marion G. Romney[1,2,5]	(1951-72; 85-88)	54
69.	LeGrand Richards[5]	(1952-83)	66
70.	Adam S. Bennion	(1953-58)	66
71.	Richard L. Evans[5]	(1953-71)	47
72.	George Q. Morris[5]	(1954-62)	80
73.	Hugh B. Brown[2,5]	(1958-61; 70-75)	74
74.	**Howard W. Hunter**[1]	(1959-94)	51
75.	**Gordon B. Hinckley**[1,2,5]	(1961-81)	51
76.	N. Eldon Tanner[2,5]	(1962-63)	64
77.	Thomas S. Monson[1,2]	(1963-85)	36
78.	Boyd K. Packer[5]	(1970-)	45
79.	Marvin J. Ashton[5]	(1971-94)	56
80.	Bruce R. McConkie[5]	(1972-85)	57
81.	L. Tom Perry[5]	(1974-)	51
82.	David B. Haight[5]	(1976-)	69
83.	James E. Faust[2,5]	(1978-95)	58
84.	Neal A. Maxwell[5]	(1981-)	55
85.	Russell M. Nelson	(1984-)	59
86.	Dallin H. Oaks	(1984-)	51
87.	M. Russell Ballard[5]	(1985-)	57
88.	Joseph B. Wirthlin[5]	(1986-)	69
89.	Richard G. Scott[5]	(1988-)	59
90.	Robert D. Hales[5]	(1994-)	61
91.	Jeffery R. Holland[5]	(1994-)	53
92.	Henry B. Eyring[5]	(1995-)	61

---

[1] Served as President of the Quorum of the Twelve Apostles.
[2] Served as a counselor in the First Presidency.
[3] Dropped from Quorum; restored to Quorum. (See *Deseret News 1997-98 Church Almanac*, p. 49.)
[4] Excommunicated in 1842; rebaptized and re-ordained an apostle in 1843; seniority adjusted to date of second entry into the Quorum. (*Deseret News 1997-98 Church Almanac*, pp. 49-50.)
[5] Served as a General Authority prior to calling to the Quorum of the Twelve.
[6] Excommunicated, disfellowshipped, resigned, or dropped from Quorum. In some cases, were rebaptized.

Quorum of the Twelve Apostles at the Beginning of
Each Church President's Administration

The date in parentheses indicates when each member of the Quorum of the Twelve was ordained and set apart **except** for members of the first Quorum of the Twelve. Members of the first Quorum, chosen by the Three Witnesses in 1835, were assigned seniority in the Quorum by the Prophet Joseph Smith according to their ages. Dates adjacent to the names of members of the first quorum are birth dates.

Joseph Smith
February to April 1835

Thomas B. Marsh	(Nov. 1, 1799)
Age 35	
David W. Patten	(Nov. 14, 1799)
Age 35	
Brigham Young	(Jun. 1, 1801)
Age 33	
Heber C. Kimball	(Jun. 14, 1801)
Age 33	
Orson Hyde	(Jan. 8, 1805)
Age 30	
William E. M'Lellin	(Jan. 18, 1806)
Age 29	
Parley P. Pratt	(Apr. 12, 1807)
Age 27	
Luke S. Johnson	(Nov. 3, 1807)
Age 27	
William B. Smith	(Mar. 13, 1811)
Age 23	
Orson Pratt	(Sep. 19, 1811)
Age 23	
John F. Boynton	(Sep. 20, 1811)
Age 23	
Lyman E. Johnson	(Oct. 24, 1811)
Age 23	

Brigham Young
December 27, 1847

Orson Hyde	(1835)
Parley P. Pratt	(1835)
Orson Pratt	(1835)
John Taylor	(1838)
Wilford Woodruff	(1839)
George A. Smith	(1839)
Lyman Wight	(1841)
Amasa M. Lyman	(1842)
Ezra T. Benson	(1846)

*See p. 145, Apostle No. 10

John Taylor
October 10, 1880

Wilford Woodruff	(1839)
Orson Pratt*	(1843)
Charles C. Rich	(1849)
Lorenzo Snow	(1849)
Erastus Snow	(1849)
Franklin D. Richards	(1849)
Brigham Young, Jr.	(1868)
Albert Carrington	(1870)
Moses Thatcher	(1879)
Francis M. Lyman	(1880)
John Henry Smith	(1880)

Wilford Woodruff
April 7, 1889

Lorenzo Snow	(1849)
Franklin D. Richards	(1849)
Brigham Young, Jr.	(1868)
Moses Thatcher	(1879)
Francis M. Lyman	(1880)
John Henry Smith	(1880)
George Teasdale	(1882)
Heber J. Grant	(1882)
John W. Taylor	(1884)
Marriner W. Merrill	(1889)
Anthon H. Lund	(1889)
Abraham H. Cannon	(1889)

Lorenzo Snow
September 13, 1898

Franklin D. Richards	(1849)
Brigham Young, Jr.	(1868)
Francis M. Lyman	(1880)
John Henry Smith	(1880)
George Teasdale	(1882)
Heber J. Grant	(1882)
John W. Taylor	(1884)
Marriner W. Merrill	(1889)
Anthon H. Lund	(1889)
Matthias F. Cowley	(1897)
Abraham O. Woodruff	(1897)
Rudger Clawson	(1898)

Joseph F. Smith
October 17, 1901

Brigham Young, Jr.	(1868)
Francis M. Lyman	(1880)
John Henry Smith	(1880)
George Teasdale	(1882)
Heber J. Grant	(1882)
John W. Taylor	(1884)
Marriner W. Merrill	(1889)
Matthias F. Cowley	(1889)
Abraham O. Woodruff	(1897)
Rudger Clawson	(1898)
Reed Smoot	(1900)
Hyrum Mack Smith	(1901)

Heber J. Grant
November 23, 1918

Rudger Clawson	(1898)
Reed Smoot	(1900)
George Albert Smith	(1903)
George F. Richards	(1906)
Orson F. Whitney	(1906)
David O. McKay	(1906)
Anthony W. Ivins	(1907)
Joseph Fielding Smith	(1910)
James E. Talmage	(1911)
Stephen L Richards	(1917)
Richard R. Lyman	(1918)
Melvin J. Ballard	(1919)

George Albert Smith
May 21, 1945

George F. Richards	(1906)
Joseph Fielding Smith	(1910)
Stephen L Richards	(1917)
John A. Widtsoe	(1921)
Joseph F. Merrill	(1931)
Charles A. Callis	(1933)
Albert E. Bowen	(1937)
Harold B. Lee	(1941)
Spencer W. Kimball	(1943)
Ezra Taft Benson	(1943)
Mark E. Petersen	(1944)
Matthew Cowley	(1945)

David O. McKay
April 9, 1951

Joseph Fielding Smith	(1910)
John A. Widtsoe	(1921)
Joseph F. Merrill	(1931)
Albert E. Bowen	(1937)
Harold B. Lee	(1941)
Spencer W. Kimball	(1943)
Ezra Taft Benson	(1943)
Mark E. Petersen	(1944)
Matthew Cowley	(1945)
Henry D. Moyle	(1947)
Delbert L. Stapley	(1950)
Marion G. Romney	(1951)

Joseph Fielding Smith
January 23, 1970

Spencer W. Kimball	(1943)
Ezra Taft Benson	(1943)
Mark E. Petersen	(1944)
Delbert L. Stapley	(1950)
Marion G. Romney	(1951)
LeGrand Richards	(1952)
Richard L. Evans	(1953)
Hugh B. Brown	(1958)
Howard W. Hunter	(1959)
Gordon B. Hinckley	(1961)
Thomas S. Monson	(1963)
Boyd K. Packer	(1970)

Harold B. Lee
July 7, 1972

Spencer W. Kimball	(1943)
Ezra Taft Benson	(1943)
Mark E. Petersen	(1944)
Delbert L. Stapley	(1950)
LeGrand Richards	(1952)
Hugh B. Brown	(1958)
Howard W. Hunter	(1959)
Gordon B. Hinckley	(1961)
Thomas S. Monson	(1963)
Boyd K. Packer	(1970)
Marvin J. Ashton	(1971)
Bruce R. McConkie	(1972)

Spencer W. Kimball
December 30, 1973

Ezra Taft Benson	(1943)
Mark E. Petersen	(1944)
Delbert L. Stapley	(1950)
LeGrand Richards	(1952)
Hugh B. Brown	(1958)
Howard W. Hunter	(1959)
Gordon B. Hinckley	(1961)
Thomas S. Monson	(1963)
Boyd K. Packer	(1970)
Marvin J. Ashton	(1971)
Bruce R. McConkie	(1972)
L. Tom Perry	(1974)

Ezra Taft Benson
November 10, 1985

Marion G. Romney	(1951)
Howard W. Hunter	(1959)
Boyd K. Packer	(1970)
Marvin J. Ashton	(1971)
L. Tom Perry	(1974)
David B. Haight	(1976)
James E. Faust	(1978)
Neal A. Maxwell	(1981)
Russell M. Nelson	(1984)
Dallin H. Oaks	(1984)
M. Russell Ballard	(1985)
Joseph B. Wirthlin	(1986)

Howard W. Hunter
June 5, 1994

Boyd K. Packer	(1970)
L. Tom Perry	(1974)
David B. Haight	(1976)
James E. Faust	(1978)
Neal A. Maxwell	(1981)
Russell M. Nelson	(1984)
Dallin H. Oaks	(1984)
M. Russell Ballard	(1985)
Joseph B. Wirthlin	(1986)
Richard G. Scott	(1988)
Robert D. Hales	(1994)
Jeffery R. Holland	(1994)

Gordon B. Hinckley
March 12, 1995

Boyd K. Packer	(1970)
L. Tom Perry	(1974)
David B. Haight	(1976)
Neal A. Maxwell	(1981)
Russell M. Nelson	(1984)
Dallin H. Oaks	(1984)
M. Russell Ballard	(1985)
Joseph B. Wirthlin	(1986)
Richard G. Scott	(1988)
Robert D. Hales	(1994)
Jeffery R. Holland	(1994)
Henry B. Eyring	(1995)

Average Age of Quorum

Joseph Smith	28
Brigham Young	39
John Taylor	55
Wilford Woodruff	49
Lorenzo Snow	52
Joseph F. Smith	50
Heber J. Grant	52
George Albert Smith	60
David O. McKay	62
Joseph Fielding Smith	67
Harold B. Lee	67
Spencer W. Kimball	66
Ezra Taft Benson	67
Howard W. Hunter	68
Gordon B. Hinckley	68

Youngest at Ordination

George A. Smith	21
William B. Smith	23
Orson Pratt	23
John Boynton	23
Lyman E. Johnson	23
Heber J. Grant	25
John W. Taylor	25

Oldest at Ordination

George Q. Morris	80
Hugh B. Brown	74
Charles W. Penrose	72
David B. Haight	69
Joseph B. Wirthlin	69

PRESIDENTS OF THE CHURCH AND THEIR APOSTLESHIP

Peter, James and John
were ordained apostles by the Lord Jesus Christ (John 15:16)

President	Apostle No.	Date Ordained	Ordained By	Served As Senior Apostle[1]	Served As President
Joseph Smith	Not a member of the Twelve	1829, age 23 (D&C 20:2; 27:12)	Peter, James, and John	—	First Elder, 1830-32 (1 yr. 9 mos.) age 24-26 President, 1832-44 (12½ yrs.), age 26-38
Brigham Young	3	Feb. 14, 1835, age 33	Three Witnesses[2]	Jun. 27, 1844 - Dec. 17, 1847 (3½ yrs.)	1847-77 (30 yrs.), age 46-76
John Taylor	14	Dec. 19, 1838, age 30	Brigham Young and Heber C. Kimball[3]	Aug. 29, 1877 - Oct. 10, 1880 (3 yrs.)	1880-87 (7 yrs.), age 71-78
Wilford Woodruff	15	Apr. 26, 1839, age 32	Brigham Young	Jul. 25, 1887 - Apr. 1889 (2 yrs.)	1889-98 (9½ yrs.), age 82-91
Lorenzo Snow	22	Feb. 12, 1849, age 35	Heber C. Kimball	Sep. 2-13, 1898 (11 days)	1898-1901 (3 yrs.), age 84-87
Joseph F. Smith	26	Jul. 1, 1866, age 27[5]	Brigham Young	Oct. 10-17, 1901 (7 days)	1901-18 (17 yrs.), age 62-80
Heber J. Grant	33	Oct. 16, 1882, age 25	George Q. Cannon[4]	Nov. 19-23, 1918 (4 days)	1918-45 (26½ yrs.), age 62-88
George Albert Smith	43	Oct. 8, 1903, age 33	Joseph F. Smith	May 14-21, 1945 (7 days)	1945-51 (6 yrs.), age 75-81
David O. McKay	47	Apr. 9, 1906, age 32	Joseph F. Smith	Apr. 4- 9, 1951 (5 days)	1951-70 (19 yrs.), age 77-96
Joseph Fielding Smith	49	Apr. 7, 1910, age 33	Joseph F. Smith	Jan. 18-23, 1970 (5 days)	1970-72 (2½ yrs.), age 93-95
Harold B. Lee	61	Apr. 10, 1941, age 42	Heber J. Grant	Jul. 2-7, 1973 (5 days)	1972-73 (1½ yrs.), age 73-74
Spencer W. Kimball	62	Oct. 7, 1943, age 48	Heber J. Grant	Dec. 26-30, 1973 (5 days)	1973-85 (12 yrs.), age 78-90
Ezra Taft Benson	63	Oct. 7, 1943, age 44	Heber J. Grant	Nov. 5-10, 1985 (5 days)	1985-94 (8½ yrs.), age 86-94
Howard W. Hunter	74	Oct. 15, 1959, age 51	David O. McKay	May 30-June 2, 1994 (4 days)	1994-95 (9 mos.), age 86-87
Gordon B. Hinckley	75	Oct. 5, 1961, age 51	David O. McKay	Mar. 3-11, 1995 (9 days)	1995 - present, age 84-

[1] Served as presiding officer of the Church as Senior Apostle until the reorganization of the First Presidency

[2] The Three Witnesses (Oliver Cowdery, David Whitmer, and Martin Harris) were called by revelation to choose the Twelve Apostles. On February 14, 1835, they were "blessed by the laying on of hands by the First Presidency" (Joseph Smith, Jr., Sidney Rigdon, and Frederick G. Williams) to ordain the Twelve Apostles (HC 2:187-88.)

[3] Ordained by the Three Witnesses, Oliver Cowdery, David Whitmer, and Martin Harris

[4] Ordained by Brigham Young in 1860. [5] Joseph F. Smith, apostle, became a member of the Quorum of the Twelve on October 8, 1867, age 28.

PROFILES OF THE PRESIDENTS

President	Age at Ordination / Years in Quorum	Age Ordained President	Age at Death	Years as President	Years as President of the Twelve	Years as General Authority
Joseph Smith, Jr. 1805-1844	23 / 3 years (Not member of Twelve)	1st Elder - 24 (1830-32) President - 26 (1832)	38	1830-44 / 14 years	—	14 years
Brigham Young 1801-1877	33 / 12½ years	46	76	1847-77 / 30 years	7 years	42½ years
John Taylor 1808-1887	30 / 41 years	71	78	1880-87 / 7 years	3 years	48½ years
Wilford Woodruff 1807-1898	32 / 50 years	82	91	1889-98 / 9½ years	9 years	59½ years
Lorenzo Snow 1814-1901	34 / 49½ years	84	87	1898-01 / 3 years	9½ years	52½ years
Joseph F. Smith 1838-1918	28 / 35 years	62	80	1901-18 / 17 years	No record of ordination	52½ years
Heber J. Grant 1856-1945	25 / 36 years	62	88	1918-45 / 26½ years	2 years	62½ years
George Albert Smith 1870-1951	33 / 42 years	75	81	1945-51 / 6 years	2 years	47½ years
David O. McKay 1873-1970	32 / 45 years	77	96	1951-70 / 19 years	6 months	64 years
Joseph Fielding Smith 1876-1972	33 / 60 years	93	95	1970-72 / 2½ years	19 years	62 years
Harold B. Lee 1899-1973	42 / 31 years	73	74	1972-73 / 1½ years	2½ years	32½ years
Spencer W. Kimball 1895-1985	48 / 30 years	78	90	1973-85 / 12 years	1½ years	42 years
Ezra Taft Benson 1899-1994	44 / 42 years	86	94	1985-94 / 8½ years	12 years	50½ years
Howard W. Hunter 1907-1995	51 / 35 years	86	87	1994-95 / 9 months	6 years	35½ years
Gordon B. Hinckley 1910-	51 / 34 years	84		1995-	9 months	39 years (as of Apr. 1997)

CAPSULE PORTRAITS OF THE PROPHETS

President	Date and Place of Birth	Occupation	Education	Special Interests and Hobbies	Date, Place, Age and Cause of Death
Joseph Smith 1805-1844	December 23, 1805 Sharon, Vermont	Farmer, banker, city builder, merchant, public servant	Grade school, heavenly tutors, home study, and School of the Prophets	Wrestling, jumping at a mark, pulling sticks, horseback riding, and ice skating	June 27, 1844 Nauvoo, Illinois Age 38 Murdered
Brigham Young 1801-1877	June 1, 1801 Whitingham, Vermont	Carpenter, business-man, glazier, pioneer, colonizer, public servant	Self-educated, School of the Prophets, and apprenticeship	Acting in plays, dancing, attending theater, singing duets with his brother Joseph	August 29, 1877 Salt Lake City, Utah Age 76 Ruptured appendix
John Taylor 1808-1887	November 1, 1808 Milnthorpe, England	Farmer, publisher, wood-turner, prolific writer, public servant	English private schools, School of the Prophets, and self-educated	Carpentry, architecture, engineering, construction, writing poetry and singing hymns	July 25, 1887 Kaysville, Utah Age 78 Kidney failure
Wilford Woodruff 1807-1898	March 1, 1807 Farmington (now Avon), Connecticut	Farmer, miller, public servant	Private schools, School of the Prophets, and self-educated	Hunting, fly fishing, cultivating and improving strains of vegetables, nuts, fruits and keeping a diary	September 2, 1898 San Francisco, California Age 91 Bladder infection
Lorenzo Snow 1814-1901	April 3, 1814 Mantua, Ohio	Educator, farmer, businessman, public servant	Oberlin College, School of the Prophets, private schools, and self-educated	Reading poetry, attending and promoting all forms of high class entertainment, learning in wide variety of subjects, singing, playing checkers, and riding horses	October 10, 1901 Salt Lake City, Utah Age 87 Pneumonia
Joseph Fielding Smith 1838-1918	November 13, 1838 Far West, Missouri	Church worker, farmer, public servant	Ward schools and self educated	Long car rides, golfing, attending plays and concerts, enjoying music, playing checkers, and riding horses	November 19, 1918 Salt Lake City, Utah Age 80 Bronchopneumonia
Heber Jeddy Grant 1856-1945	November 22, 1856 Salt Lake City, Utah	Entrepreneur, self-educated businessman	Private schools and self-educated	Baseball, volleyball, golf, exercising, attending sports events, attending movies and theater, reading, singing, long car rides, teaching penmanship	May 14, 1945 Salt Lake City, Utah Age 88 Heart failure
George Albert Smith 1870-1951	April 4, 1870 Salt Lake City, Utah	Businessman, public servant	Ward school, Brigham Young Academy, University of Utah	Horses, marking pioneer sites and trails, out-door activities, swimming, hunting, collecting objects of art, scouting, playing guitar and harmonica, promoting air transportation, visiting Indians	April 4, 1951 Salt Lake City, Utah Age 81 Respiratory infection

President	Date and Place of Birth	Occupation	Education	Special Interests and Hobbies	Date, Place, Age and Cause of Death
David Oman McKay 1873-1970	September 8, 1873 Huntsville, Utah	Educator (faculty member at Weber State Academy)	LDS Church Academy (Weber), University of Utah graduate	Horseback riding, swimming, debate, singing, attending theater, music, reading English literature, memorizing poetry, and playing the piano	January 18, 1970 Salt Lake City, Utah Age 96 Congestive heart failure
Joseph Fielding Smith 1876-1972	July 19, 1876 Salt Lake City, Utah	Genealogist, historian, prolific writer (author of 25 books and many articles)	Public and ward schools, LDS Business College	Writing hymns, singing duets with wife, baking pies, playing handball, swimming, flying aircraft, writing	July 2, 1972 Salt Lake City, Utah Age 95 Heart attack
Harold Bingham Lee 1899-1973	March 28, 1899 Clifton, Idaho	Educator, public servant	University of Utah (with teacher's certificate)	Gardening, playing the piano, fishing, home repairs, watching football and basketball games	December 26, 1973 Salt Lake City, Utah Age 74 Heart and lung failure
Spencer Woolley Kimball 1895-1985	March 28, 1895 Salt Lake City, Utah	Businessman (insurance and real broker)	University of Arizona (one year)	Indian mementos, playing piano, swimming, quartet singing, and keeping a diary	November 5, 1985 Salt Lake City, Utah Age 90 Heart failure
Ezra Taft Benson 1899-1994	August 4, 1899 Whitney, Idaho	Agricultural administrator, public servant	BYU (B.A.), Iowa State College (M.A.), University of California at Berkeley (graduate school)	Horse shoes, scouting, horseback riding, singing, speaking on patriotic themes, reading poetry, family reunions	May 30, 1994 Salt Lake City, Utah Age 94 Heart failure
Howard William Hunter 1907-1995	November 14, 1907 Boise, Idaho	Banker, attorney	Southwestern University Law School graduate	Scouting, music, collecting wild bird eggs, stamps, coins, archaeology, collecting classical records, playing instruments and keeping a diary	March 3,1995 Salt Lake City, Utah Age 87 Cancer
Gordon Bitner Hinckley 1910-	June 23, 1910 Salt Lake City, Utah	Church business executive	University of Utah graduate	Reading English literature and Church history, planting flowers and trees, carpentry, writing of text for hymns, music	

GROWTH DURING ADMINISTRATIONS OF THE PRESIDENTS (By End of Term)

President	Members[1]	Stakes	Missions	Missionaries[2]	Temples	General Authorities[5]
Joseph Smith 1830-1844	26,146	2	3	1844 586	1[3]	29
Brigham Young 1847-1877	115,065	20	8	1869 250	2[4]	26
John Taylor 1880-1887	173,029	31	12	1887 282	2	28
Wilford Woodruff 1889-1898	267,251	40	20	1898 1,059	4	26
Lorenzo Snow 1898-1901	292,931	50	21	1900 796	4	26
Joseph F. Smith 1901-1918	495,962	75	22	1906 1,015	4	26
Heber J. Grant 1918-1945	954,004	149	22	1925 1,313	7	31
George Albert Smith 1945-1951	1,111,314	184	43	1950 5,800	8	31
David O. McKay 1951-1970	2,807,456	500	88	14,387	13	40
Joseph Fielding Smith 1970-1972	3,218,908	581	102	16,367	15	41
Harold B. Lee 1972-1973	3,306,658	630	110	17,258	15	44
Spencer W. Kimball 1973-1985	5,920,000	1,570	195	29,265	37	78
Ezra Taft Benson 1985-1994	8,688,511	1,980	295	47,311	45	104
Howard W. Hunter 1994-1995	9,025,914	2,029	303	48,631	47	97
Gordon B. Hinckley 1995-	9,900,000 Aug. 1997	2,325	318	56,000	50	103

[1] Year-end total for last year of President's life.

[2] The highest annual number set apart during each president's administration is the number used from Joseph Smith to George Albert Smith. Beginning with David O. McKay, the number represents the highest total number of missionaries in the field at the end of the President's administration

[3] Kirtland Temple no longer in use by The Church of Jesus Christ of Latter-day Saints

[4] Nauvoo Temple no longer stands

[5] General Authorities serving at end of each administration

Sources: *Deseret News 1997-98 Church Almanac*; Church Affairs Office, March 14, 1997.
Church membership: Over one-half reside outside the United States as of February 26, 1996.

JESUS CHRIST AND HIS APOSTLES

After much prayer, Jesus called His faithful, devoted, and loyal disciples to Him and chose twelve whom He ordained as apostles. (See Matt. 10:1-4; Luke 6:14-16.) Those selected were:

Simon Peter	Matthew Levi
Andrew	Thomas Didymus
James Boanerges	James
John	Simon
Philip	Jude Thaddaeus
Bartholomew Nathaniel	Judas Iscariot

(See Acts 1:23-26, 14:14; Romans 1:1, 16:7; 2 Cor. 1:1; Gal. 1:19.) The Twelve were the Savior's most important representatives. They were charged by Him to go forth in His name, bearing witness of His divinity and His resurrection.

After Jesus' resurrection, He visited the American continent and selected twelve disciples (apostles) to carry out His work of the ministry in the western hemisphere. (See 4 Ne. 1:14.) The Prophet Joseph said: "He (Christ) planted the gospel here in all its fulness . . . they had Apostles . . . the same priesthood, gifts, powers and blessings, as were enjoyed on the eastern continent." (*HC* 4:538; see also heading to Moroni, chapter 2.) These Nephites ministered in an ordained apostolic capacity (see 3 Ne. 19:4). The original twelve were:

Nephi	Kumenonhi
Timothy	Jeremiah
Jonas*	Shemnon
Mathoni	Jonas*
Mathonihah	Zedekiah
Kumen	Isaiah

*Two apostles were named Jonas.

Elder James E. Talmage said: "The Holy Apostleship is an an office and calling belonging to the Higher or Melchizedek Priesthood, at once exalted and specific, comprising a distinguishing function, that of personal and special witness to the divinity of Jesus Christ as the one and only Redeemer and Savior of mankind. The apostleship is an individual bestowal, and is conferred only through ordination. (Talmage, *Jesus the Christ*, p. 227.) When a vacancy occurred with the death of Judas Iscariot, Matthias was divinely appointed to that special office as a member of the quorum. (See Acts 1:15-26.) Today twelve men with this same divine calling and ordination constitute the Quorum of the Twelve Apostles in The Church of Jesus Christ of Latter-day Saints.

The number twelve refers to the number of tribes of Israel whom the apostles are to judge. (See Matt. 19:28; Luke 22:30.) The Twelve apostles were the organizational foundation of the early Christian church. (Eph. 2:20-21; 4:11-14.)

Jesus is referred to as an apostle in Hebrews 3:1-2, a designation meaning that He is the personal and select representative of the Father. As the Father sent Him, so Jesus sent His apostles. (See John 20:21.)

President Harold B. Lee said, "At the commencement of His ministry, the Master chose twelve men whom He separated from the rest by the name apostles. These were to be special witnesses of the sanctity of His life and of His divine mission, and to be responsible for transmitting to the latest posterity a genuine account of His doctrines, principles, and ordinances essential to the salvation of the human soul." (Lee, *SYHP*, p. 41.)

President J. Reuben Clark said, "The Lord, being possessed of all power, gave power and authority to the Apostles; He did not pray the Father to give it, that is, it was a present bestowal of power, not a prayer for power." (Clark, *On the Way to Immortality and Eternal Life*, p. 34; see also Matt. 28:18-20.)

After the death of the Savior, the apostles has supreme authority in the Church, holding all the Keys of the Kingdom. They possessed and exercised the right and authority to endow others by ordination. They ordained other apostles (see Acts 1:15) and endowed others with the authority to exercise certain priesthood powers; for example, the calling and ordination of subordinate officers. (See Titus 1:5.)

At the head of the Quorum of Christ's original church were the apostles Peter, James, and John. They had been with or near Jesus on sacred occasions, including Jesus' raising of the daughter of Jairus from the dead (see Mark 5:35-43), his glorification on the Mount of Transfiguration (see Mark 9:2-9), and His suffering in Gethsemane (see Mark 14:32-34). It is commonly understood that at the death, resurrection, and ascension of Christ, Peter became the chief apostle, or president, of the Lord's Church. Many Christian churches believe that Peter was the head of the church after the ascension of Jesus.

Most Christian churches do not understand that when the Lord told Peter—"Thou art Peter, and upon this rock I will build my church" (Matt. 16:18-19), that it was *revelation* to which Jesus was referring. The Church proclaims that *revelation* was the rock referred to by Jesus. (See *TPJS*, p. 274.)

Modern revelation adds additional information. The apostolic office and authority were conferred on the Prophet Joseph Smith and Oliver Cowdery by the resurrected apostles Peter, James, and John. After the Church was restored, the Three Witnesses—Oliver Cowdery, David Whitmer, and Martin Harris—were blessed by the laying on of hands by the First Presidency—Joseph Smith, Jr., Sidney Rigdon, and Frederick G. Williams—to select and ordain the Twelve Apostles, which they did in February of 1835.

The Twelve Apostles hold the keys of the priesthood. (See D&C 124:128.) Of their priesthood authority, President Brigham Young stated, "Could he [Joseph Smith] have built the kingdom of God without first being an apostle? No, he never could. The keys of the eternal Priesthood, which is after the order of the Son of God, are comprehended by being an Apostle. All the Priesthood, all the keys, all the gifts, all the endowments, and everything preparatory to entering into the presence of the Father and of the Son, are in, composed of, circumscribed by, or I might say incorporated within the circumference of the apostleship." *(MS, July 23, 1853, p. 489.)* Apostle is an office in the Melchizedek Priesthood. The members of the Quorum of the Twelve Apostles are sustained as prophets, seers, and revelators. This quorum is next in authority to the quorum of the First Presidency.

Today, apostles are chosen through inspiration by the President of the Church, sustained by the general membership of the Church, and ordained by a member of the First Presidency, usually the President, by the laying on of hands. The Lord instructed that the number of apostles in the Quorum of the Twelve be maintained. (See D&C 118:1.) New men were appointed to succeed the original members as they passed away. (See Gal. 1:19.)

According to President Joseph Fielding Smith: "The question frequently arises: 'Is it necessary for a member of the Quorum of the Twelve to see the Savior in order to be an apostle?' It is their privilege to see Him if the occasion requires, but the Lord has taught that there is a stronger witness than seeing a personage, even of seeing the Son of God in a vision. Impressions on the soul that come from the Holy Ghost are far more significant than a vision. When spirit speaks to spirit, the imprint upon the soul is far more difficult to erase." *(IE, 1966, p. 979.)*

A minister once laughed at two missionaries when they told him that apostles were necessary today in order for the true church to be upon the earth. The minister said, "Do you realize that when the apostles met to choose one to fill the vacancy caused by the death of Judas, they said it had to be one who companied with them and had been a witness of all things pertaining to the mission and resurrection of the Lord? How can you say you have apostles, if that be the measure of an apostle?" President Lee said to the missionaries: 'Go back and ask your minister friend two questions. First, how did the Apostle Paul gain what was necessary to be called an apostle? He didn't know the Lord, and had no personal acquaintance. He hadn't accompanied the apostles. He hadn't been a witness of the ministry nor of the resurrection of the Lord. How did he gain his testimony sufficient to be an apostle? And the second question you ask him is, How does he know that all who are today apostles have not likewise received that witness?'

"I bear witness to you that those who hold the apostolic calling may, and do, know of the reality of the mission of the Lord. To know is to be born and quickened in the inner man." (Lee, *SYHP*, pp. 64-65.)

JOSEPH SMITH 1830-44

By direct commission from Jesus Christ, Joseph Smith restored the original Church of Jesus Christ including the same basic offices, powers, ordinances, and doctrines. By revelation, Joseph learned the correct name of the Church, clarified the true concept of Deity, received the keys of salvation and saving ordinances for both the living and dead, received authorization for the building of the first temples in Kirtland and Nauvoo in this dispensation, published new scripture (the Book of Mormon and Book of Abraham) from records and papyri he had translated through the gift and power of God, received the Book of Moses by revelation, received revelations for this time period as recorded in the Doctrine and Covenants, and corrected at least 3,410 verses in the Bible. Joseph was persecuted and arrested many times for his religious beliefs.

1820   During fourteen-year-old Joseph Smith's First Vision, the Father and Jesus Christ answered Joseph's question about which church to join. Joseph had prayed for guidance in response to religious revivalism in the area near Manchester, New York. Joseph learned from the vision that God the Father and Jesus Christ are separate beings and that he was not to join any church.

1823   Joseph was visited many times by the ancient prophet Moroni and was told about restoring the gospel. He saw the metal plates, "having the appearance of gold," from which he eventually translated the Book of Mormon.

1824-27 The Angel Moroni visited Joseph annually.

1827   On September 22, Joseph was entrusted with the plates and commenced their translation with the aid of the Urim and Thummim.

1828   First 116 pages of the Book of Mormon were translated and the manuscript was lost; Joseph lost the gift to translate. Later, Joseph again received the plates, the Urim and Thummim, and the gift of translation.

1829   John the Baptist conferred the Aaronic Priesthood on Joseph and Oliver Cowdery, and they baptized each other. Peter, James, and John conferred on them the Melchizedek Priesthood and apostleship, thus restoring the priesthood authority that had been taken from the earth soon after the death of Jesus Christ. Joseph finished translating the Book of Mormon. Moroni showed the Three Witnesses the plates. Later, eight other witnesses were shown the plates.

1830   The Book of Mormon was published. Joseph organized the Church in Fayette, New York on April 6. The first conference was held on June 9. Joseph began a revision of the Bible. Missionary work was started.

The Church was commanded by revelation to move to Ohio.

1831   By May the majority of Saints had moved from New York to Ohio. The first bishop and the first high priests were ordained. Church membership was divided into two main bodies in Ohio and Missouri, with administrative headquarters in Ohio. The foundation of a new Zion was in Missouri.

1832   Joseph was sustained as president of the High Priesthood, and the First Presidency was organized. Missionaries were sent to Canada—the first organized missionary effort outside the U.S.

1833   Joseph Smith organized the School of the Prophets. The Word of Wisdom was given. Mobs forced the Saints from Jackson County, Missouri. The Book of Commandments was published.

1834   The first stake and first high council were organized in Kirtland, Ohio. Joseph led the Zion's Camp march from Kirtland to Missouri to give relief to the Saints expelled from Jackson County. LDS *Messenger and Advocate* was published until 1838.

1835   The twelve apostles were chosen by the Three Witnesses. First Quorum of Seventy was organized in Kirtland, Ohio. Revelation on priesthood (D&C 107) was received. Joseph commenced to translate the records of the Book of Abraham. Doctrine and Covenants was published. First hymnbook was published.

1836   Kirtland Temple was dedicated. The Savior, Moses, Elias, and Elijah appeared to Joseph and Oliver Cowdery in the Kirtland Temple (D&C 110) and gave them the keys of each of their dispensations.

1837   The British Mission was opened by members of the Quorum of the Twelve and was the first foreign mission outside North America. Much apostasy occurred within the Church.

1838   Saints left Kirtland, Ohio. The full name of the Church was revealed as "The Church of Jesus Christ of Latter-day Saints" (D&C 115:4). Law of tithing was given at Far West, Missouri. Joseph began writing the history of the Church. Lilburn Boggs, Missouri governor, issued an "extermination or expel order" against the Saints. Haun's Mill Massacre occurred. Joseph Smith and others were arrested by militia and imprisoned in Liberty Jail.

1839   Brigham Young and the Twelve conducted the removal of the Saints from Missouri to Illinois. Joseph Smith and other prisoners were allowed to escape from Missouri. Most of the Twelve left for missions to the British Isles. Joseph and other leaders appealed, without success, to President Van Buren and Congress for redress from Missouri persecutions. Saints settled in Commerce, Illinois, later called Nauvoo. *Times and Seasons* began publication in Nauvoo.

1840   First immigrants arrived from England. The *Millennial Star* was started in England (ceased in 1970). "Nauvoo Charter" was signed into law by Illinois governor.

1841   Baptism for the dead was introduced as a temple ordinance. Cornerstone was laid for Nauvoo Temple.

1842   Female Relief Society of Nauvoo was organized. The Book of Abraham was published. The Articles of Faith were published in the *Times and Seasons*. Joseph introduced the endowment. Church membership: 20,856.

1843   The *Nauvoo Neighbor* began publication for two years. Revelation on the "eternity of the marriage covenant . . . also plurality of wives" (D&C 132) was recorded.

1844   Joseph Smith became candidate for president of the United States. Joseph and Hyrum Smith were murdered at Carthage Jail. Brigham Young and the Quorum of the Twelve were sustained by vote to lead the Church.

1844   Membership: 26,146; Stakes: 2; Temple: 1
        Missions: 3; Missionaries: 586

BRIGHAM YOUNG 1844-1877

Brigham Young directed the exodus of the Saints from Nauvoo and the westward journey to Salt Lake Valley. Nauvoo Temple was dedicated (1846). Between 1847 and 1869, an estimated 70,000 pioneers made the trek to Utah. During President Young's administration, 360 villages, towns, and cities were colonized in Utah, Arizona, Idaho, Nevada, Wyoming, and California. Deseret University, now the University of Utah, was established in 1850, along with Brigham Young Academy, now Brigham Young University, in 1875; and Brigham Young College in Logan, Utah, in 1877 (closed in 1926).

1844-47 The Quorum of the Twelve, with Brigham Young as senior apostle, presided over the Church from June 27, 1844 to December 27, 1847 (3½ years).

1846   Exodus of the Saints from Nauvoo began. The ship *Brooklyn* left New York for California. Temporary settlements were established at Garden Grove, Mt. Pisgah, and Council Bluffs, in Iowa, and at Winter Quarters, Nebraska. The Mormon Battalion was organized at Council Bluffs, Iowa, and arrived in San Diego, California, in January 1847.

1847   First pioneers left Winter Quarters and arrived in Salt Lake Valley on July 24. Brigham Young returned to Winter Quarters that fall and was sustained as President of the Church on December 27, 1847.

1848   Seagulls saved the pioneers' crops from destruction by crickets (June).

1849   Church leaders organized a provisional State of Deseret, and Saints petitioned Congress for statehood but were unsuccessful. Sunday School was organized. Perpetual Emigrating Fund was established to help the poor emigrate to Utah.

1850   Territory of Utah was created, and President Millard Fillmore appointed Brigham Young as governor. *Deseret News* published its first edition.

1851   Pearl of Great Price was published in Great Britain. San Bernardino was colonized.

1852   Plural marriage, which had been taught privately by Joseph Smith, was publicly announced.

1853   Cornerstones were laid for the Salt Lake Temple.

1856   The first handcart companies left Iowa. Willie and Martin handcart disasters occurred. General "reformation" began throughout Church, with many members renewing their covenants by rebaptism as a symbol of renewed dedication.

1857   Alfred Cumming replaced Brigham Young as governor. Mountain Meadow Massacre tragedy took place. Commencement of the Utah War. Johnston's Army (federal troops) forced to remain outside Salt Lake City.

1858   Federal troops peacefully entered Salt Lake City, but later camped in Cedar Valley.

1860   The last handcart companies arrived in Salt Lake City.

1862   Antibigamy bill became federal law, designed to prevent practice of polygamy in U.S. territories.

1866   The *Juvenile Instructor*, the Sunday School magazine, began publication and in 1930 became *The Instructor*. Publication ceased in 1970.

1867   The Salt Lake Tabernacle was completed and general conference was held in it. Relief Society was reorganized as a church wide auxiliary.

1869   The transcontinental railroad was completed. Zion's Cooperative Mercantile Institution (ZCMI), a cooperative business system, was started. The Young Ladies program was organized.

1870 The "Liberal Party" was formed, which generally came to represent anti-Mormon political interests.

1872 The *Woman's Exponent* began publication and ceased in 1914.

1874 " United Orders" were organized.

1875 Young Men's MIA was organized. Brigham Young Academy (University) was founded. Church Academy movement began and eventually 35 academies were established in 7 western states, Canada and Mexico (through 1910). Salt Lake Tabernacle was dedicated.

1877 Brigham Young reorganized all priesthood quorums and commenced a more complete organization of stakes. A pamphlet of standard priesthood instructions was published. St. George Temple was dedicated.

1877 Membership: 115,006; Stakes: 20; Temple: 1
Missions: 8; Missionaries: 250

JOHN TAYLOR 1877-1887

President Taylor set the precedent of having the quorums of the priesthood sustain the new First Presidency separately in a solemn assembly. He rallied the Saints to meet the challenge of federal prosecution for plural marriages.

1877-80 The Quorum of the Twelve, with John Taylor as senior apostle, presided over the Church from August 29, 1877, until President Taylor was sustained as President on October 10, 1880 (3 years).

1878 The Primary was founded by Aurelia Rogers.

1879 The *Contributor*, the magazine of the YMMIA, began publication, continuing until 1896. The U.S. Supreme Court, in the Reynolds case, affirmed the constitutionality of the Antibigamy Act of 1862. With this ruling, prosecution became more intense.

1880 The Pearl of Great Price was formally accepted as scripture. Church Jubilee (50th anniversary) was celebrated; the Church forgave one-half the indebtedness held by the Perpetual Emigrating Fund Company debtors who were classed as "worthy poor."

1881 Weekly ward quorum and monthly stake priesthood meetings were held, but not year long. John Taylor published a treatise of priesthood instructions.

1882 Anti-polygamy legislation passed by Congress (Edmunds Law) became law, leading to the imprisonment of polygamists. Many communities practicing the United Order abandoned the project.

1884 The Logan Temple was dedicated.

1885 President Taylor and many Church leaders went into exile because of polygamy persecution. Colonies were established in Mexico.

1887 Congress passed the Edmunds-Tucker Act, disincorporated the Church, and turned its properties over to the federal government. Members appealed through the courts but lost. Colonies were established in Canada.

1887 Membership 173,029; Stakes: 31; Temples: 2
Missions: 12; Missionaries: 282

WILFORD WOODRUFF 1887-1898

The Manifesto was issued which officially discontinued Church sanction of plural marriage. The Genealogical Society was organized. Temple recommends formerly issued only by the President of the Church, became the responsibility of bishops and stake presidents. Utah was granted Statehood.

1887-89 The Quorum of the Twelve, with Wilford Woodruff as senior apostle, presided over the Church from July 25, 1887, until President Woodruff was sustained as President on April 7, 1889 (2 years).

1888-89 Manti Temple was dedicated. Bannock Academy (later Ricks College) was established. The *Young Woman's Journal* began publication (merging with *Improvement Era* in 1929).

1890 Manifesto was issued, discontinuing Church sanction of plural marriage in United States and its territories.

1893 The Salt Lake Temple was dedicated. President Benjamin Harrison issued amnesty to all polygamists who had entered into that relationship before November 1, 1890.

1894 The Genealogical Society was established. President Grover Cleveland restored all political and civil rights to those who had been disfranchised by anti-polygamy legislation.

1895 First foreign stakes were organized in Canada and Mexico.

1896 Utah granted statehood. Fast and testimony meeting was changed from the first Thursday to the first Sunday of the month.

1897 Publication of *Improvement Era* began (continuing until 1970 when replaced by the *Ensign*).

1898 The first general conference report was published in October. The first sister missionaries were called.

1898 Membership: 267,251; Stakes: 40; Temples: 4
Missions: 20; Missionaries: 1,059

LORENZO SNOW 1898-1901

President Snow established a tradition of immediate reorganization of the First Presidency upon the death of the President.

1898   Church bonds were issued to lighten the burdens of its indebtedness.

1899   Lorenzo Snow received revelation in St. George to emphasize paying a full tithe.

1901   Missionary work was re-emphasized.

1901   Membership 292,931; Stakes: 50; Temples: 4 Missions: 21; Missionaries: 796

JOSEPH F. SMITH 1901-1918

Joseph F. Smith was the first president to visit members in Europe. He told the Saints not to gather to Utah but to build Zion where they were. He also visited Mexico, Canada, and Hawaii. The Church paid all of its debts.

1902   The Church image improved by opening the Bureau of Information on Temple Square in Salt Lake City. *The Children's Friend* began publication (replaced by *The Friend* in 1970).

1903   Commencement of purchase of important Church historic sites, beginning with Carthage Jail. Apostle Reed Smoot's hearings were held.

1904   The "Second Manifesto" banned plural marriage.

1906   Classes for adults in the Sunday School were organized. Joseph F. Smith visited Europe.

1907   The Church repaid its last debts. The U.S. Senate agreed to seat Utah Senator Reed Smoot after a three-year investigation into charges of polygamy.

1908   A General Priesthood Committee revised and systematized priesthood work and instituted specific ages for Aaronic Priesthood ordinations.

1909   Regular weekly ward priesthood meetings commenced. The First Presidency issued a statement on the doctrine of origin of man, and it remains today the only official statement relating to the concept of evolution.

1911-12   The Boy Scout program was adopted. The Seminary program was established.

1914-15   The *Relief Society Magazine* began publication and ceased in 1970. The First Presidency urged members to hold regular home evenings.

1916   The First Presidency and the Quorum of the Twelve Apostles issued a "doctrinal exposition" on the Father and the Son.

1917   The Church Administration Building was completed.

1918   President Joseph F. Smith received a vision concerning the salvation of the dead and the visit of the Savior to the Spirit world after His crucifixion; it became D&C 138.

1918   Membership: 495,962; Stakes: 75; Temples: 4 Missions: 22; Missionaries: 1,015

HEBER J. GRANT 1918-1945

Heber J. Grant brought sophisticated business management methods to Church administration. He helped change the image of the Church to that of a progressive American religion. He visited Europe and Hawaii.

1919   The Hawaii Temple was dedicated.

1922   Gospel was first taught via the radio on station KZN (KSL), with a message by President Heber J. Grant.

1923   The Alberta Temple was dedicated.

1924   Radio broadcasts of General Conference began.

1926   Institute of Religion program in colleges was established. (Over 100,000 students enrolled at 1,136 colleges served by institutes in U.S. and Canada and 219,259 students worldwide in 1996.)

1927   The Arizona Temple was dedicated.

1929   The Tabernacle Choir began broadcasting on radio.

1930-31   The centennial of the Church organization was celebrated. The *Church News* section of *Deseret News* began publication.

1932   Missionary training programs were instituted in every ward.

1936   The Church Security Program (later called welfare program) was established.

1938   Deseret Industries program was established.

1939-40   First Presidency ordered an evacuation of missionaries from Europe, the Pacific, and South Africa.

1941   Assistants to the Twelve were called as General Authorities.

1942   The Church limited auxiliary and general board meetings to help comply with wartime travel restrictions.

1945   Membership: 954,004; Stakes: 149; Temples: 7
Missions: 38; Missionaries: 1,313

GEORGE ALBERT SMITH 1945-1951

At the end of World War II, President Smith's Christ-like love helped to lead the Saints on both sides of the war conflict to understand that only righteous living would heal and solve the world's problems. Missionary work was revitalized. President Smith visited Mexico.

1945   The Idaho Falls Temple was dedicated.

1946   Relief goods were sent to Saints in Europe at the conclusion of World War II.

1947   "This Is the Place" monument in Salt Lake City was dedicated. The centennial of the pioneers' arrival in the Salt Lake Valley was celebrated.

1949   The first public telecast of general conference.

1950   The first early morning seminary was held in southern California.

1951   Membership: 1,111,314; Stakes: 184; Temples: 8
Missions: 43; Missionaries: 5,800

DAVID O. McKAY 1951-1970

The worldwide mission of the Church was expanded. Stakes were organized throughout the world and temples were built in foreign countries. President McKay greatly expanded the institute program, which helped thousands of students reconcile their religious beliefs with their new secular knowledge. Jet transportation allowed President McKay to visit Saints in Europe, South Africa, South and Central America, New Zealand, and Australia. The public image of the Church improved during President's McKay's administration.

1952   The systematic missionary program for teaching the gospel was established.

1953   The Unified Church School System was organized.

1954   The Indian Placement Program began. Young men were ordained to the office of teacher at age 14 and priest at age 16; previous ages were 15 and 17.

1955   The Church College of Hawaii, now BYU-Hawaii, was established. The Swiss Temple was dedicated.

1956   The Los Angeles Temple was dedicated. The first student stake was organized at BYU.

1958   The first "overseas" stake was organized at Auckland, New Zealand. The New Zealand and London temples were dedicated.

1961   The All-Church Coordinating Council was established to correlate curriculum and activities for children, youth, and adults. The missionary program was revised with language training, a new teaching plan, and seminars for mission presidents. "Every Member a Missionary" program was introduced.

1962   General Conference was broadcast via shortwave radio. The First Presidency asked all worthy young men (nineteen and older) to serve a mission

1963   All foreign language missionaries were trained in the Language Training Mission (LTM) in Provo.

1964   A new home teaching program was inaugurated. The Oakland Temple was dedicated.

1965   The Family Home Evening manual was published for placement in every LDS home.

1966   The Uniform Church Curriculum year was inaugurated with all organizations beginning curriculum on January 1.

1967   Regional Representatives of the Twelve were called.

1970:   Membership 2,807,456; Stakes: 500; Temples: 13
Missions: 88; Missionaries: 14,387

JOSEPH FIELDING SMITH 1970-1972

The first Area Conference was held, which took the Church program to the people. With thousands of youth worldwide, the seminary program became international, operating in 90 countries and territories (136 countries, 320,648 enrolled in 1996). This period began with better trained teachers and materials and with greater emphasis in knowing and using the scriptures. Seminary helped prepare future missionaries. Emphasis was placed on scripture study for all members. President Smith visited Mexico and England.

1970   Bishop's training program (to teach responsibilities) and teacher development program were started.

1971   The first Area Conference was held at Manchester, England. Publication began on three new Church magazines: *Ensign*, *New Era*, and *Friend*.

1972   The Ogden and Provo temples were dedicated.

1972   Membership 3,218,908; Stakes: 581; Temples: 15
Missions: 102; Missionaries: 16,357

HAROLD B. LEE 1972-1973

President Lee traveled to Israel, Italy, Switzerland, Austria, Mexico, England, Greece, and Germany. He was the first prophet to visit Jerusalem in 2000 years, and his visit is regarded as a landmark of the Restoration. Sweeping organizational changes were made in preparation for rapid expansion of membership and activities. The Welfare Program served individuals and communities in many countries.

1972   MIA program was restructured into Aaronic Priesthood and Melchizedek Priesthood MIA. Single Adult Program was established. Church departments moved into new Church Office Building. Jerusalem Branch, first in Israel, was organized and President Lee authorized Saturday worship for those members. Church Music Department was started.

1973   A new set of missionary lessons was completed for use in all missions, the first since 1961. The creation of the Welfare Services Department combined the three welfare units—health, social, and welfare—into full correlation.

1973   Membership: 3,306,650; Stakes: 630; Temples: 15 Missions: 110; Missionaries: 17,258

SPENCER W. KIMBALL 1973-1985

President Kimball challenged members to "lengthen our stride." He called for more and better trained people from every land to accept mission calls. Twenty-one temples were constructed; solemn assemblies were held for several years. Area conferences were held in many foreign countries. Cable TV and satellite transmissions and public service TV announcements began. Video tapes were produced for members and nonmembers, and general conference audio tapes were made available. President Kimball traveled to every continent. There was an increase in the number of missionary couples performing proselyting, genealogical, and temple work and providing social services in undeveloped areas, including teaching at some church schools. Welfare missionaries were sent to needy and under developed countries. Greater emphasis was given on every member being a missionary. Women were authorized to give prayers in Sacrament meetings and given more opportunities to speak in general conference.

1974   Names of stakes were changed to reflect geographic localities. The Washington Temple was dedicated.

1975   The new Church Office Building was dedicated. The First Quorum of the Seventy was organized.

1976   Two revelations were added to Pearl of Great Price (later becoming D&C 137 and 138). The new missionary training complex opened in Provo, Utah. Women's Conference at BYU began, later co-sponsored by the General Relief Society. All stakes and missions were put under area supervisory program. Assistants to the Twelve and First Council of the Seventy were called to the new First Quorum of Seventy.

1977   General conference was decreased from three days to two days.

1978   A revelation was announced that extended the priesthood to all worthy male members and was added to the Doctrine and Covenants as Official Declaration-2. The Missionary Training Center (MTC) was established in Provo, Utah, for all English and foreign-speaking missionaries. The first General Women's Meeting (for Young Women and Relief Society) was held. Sao Paulo Temple was dedicated.

1979   The 1000th stake was created in Nauvoo, Illinois. The new LDS edition of the King James version of Bible, with study helps, was published. Ancestral file concept was added to Four Generation Program. Semi-annual stake conferences replaced quarterly ones. Orson Hyde Memorial Gardens on Mount of Olives in Jerusalem was dedicated.

1980   The consolidated ward meeting schedule in U.S. and Canada was established. The General Relief Society Meeting was held. The Tokyo and Seattle temples were dedicated.

1981   The new edition of the triple combination was published. A satellite network was established to carry Church programs worldwide. The Jordan River Temple was dedicated.

1982   Subtitle "Another Testament of Jesus Christ" was added to the Book of Mormon.

1983   General Women's Meeting held annually until 1993. Temples dedicated: Atlanta Georgia, Apia Samoa, Nuku'alofa Tonga, Santiago Chile, Pepeete Tahiti, and Mexico City.

1984   The 1,500th stake was organized. Area Presidencies were established. Museum of Church History and Art was dedicated. Temples dedicated: Boise Idaho, Sydney Australia, Manila Philippines, Dallas Texas, Taipei Taiwan, and Guatemala City.

1985   A new LDS hymnbook was published. Family History Library was dedicated. Temples dedicated: Freiberg Germany, Stockholm Sweden, Chicago Illinois, and Johannesburg South Africa.

1985   Membership: 5,920,000; Stakes: 1,570; Temples: 37 Missions: 195; Missionaries: 29,265

EZRA TAFT BENSON 1985-1994

There was special emphasis placed on reading the Book of Mormon and sharing it with friends of other faiths. The distribution of the book of Mormon during President Benson's administration exceeded total numbers given out during all previous years combined. Simplified manuals and materials allowed for greater local control and the incorporation of cultural diversity. A greater percentage of local missionaries and the calling of native leaders to serve as mission presidents improved the missionary and communication effort in foreign countries. President Benson traveled to Finland, Sweden, England, Germany Canada, and Puerto Rico.

1985   The Seoul Korea Temple was dedicated.

1986   New English missionary discussions focused on "teaching from the heart." Stake Seventies quorums were discontinued. Temples dedicated: Lima Peru, Buenos Aires Argentina, and Denver Colorado.

1987   The Church Genealogical Department was renamed the Family History Department. Frankfurt Germany Temple was dedicated.

1988   The first stake in which all priesthood leaders were black was organized—the Aba Nigeria Stake. The First Presidency issued a statement on AIDS, stressing chastity before marriage, fidelity in marriage, and abstinence from homosexual behavior.

1989   Second Quorum of Seventy was organized. The Portland Oregon and Las Vegas Nevada Temples were dedicated. BYU Jerusalem Center was dedicated.

1990   The Toronto Ontario Temple was dedicated.

1991   Missionaries were called to the Russian Republic. The *Encyclopedia of Mormonism* was published. The 500,000th full-time missionary was called (May 1).

1992   Gospel literacy effort (to encourage life-long gospel study) was sponsored by the Relief Society; non-readers were to be taught reading skills.

1993   The Joseph Smith Memorial Building in Salt Lake City (former Hotel Utah) was dedicated; its theater showed the new film *Legacy*. The San Diego California Temple was dedicated. The annual General Relief Society Meeting was held.

1994   First Annual General Young Women's Meeting was held. Stake Record Extraction and Family History Record Extraction programs combined into Family Record Extraction Program. Missionary Training Center was dedicated in Buenos Aires, Argentina.

1994   Membership 8,688,511; Stakes: 1,980; Temples: 45 Missions: 295; Missionaries: 47,311

HOWARD W. HUNTER 1994-1995

President Hunter emphasized temple worthiness and attendance, the temple as the symbol of membership, and becoming more Christlike. He traveled to Mexico and Switzerland.

1994   The Orlando Florida Temple was dedicated. The 2000th stake was organized in Mexico City, Mexico.

1995   The Bountiful Utah Temple was dedicated.

1995   Membership: 9,025,914; Stakes: 2,029; Temples: 47 Missions: 303; Missionaries: 48,631

GORDON B. HINCKLEY 1995-Present

The world's people understand better the Church, its standards, doctrines, and practices because of President Hinckley's many media interviews. He has traveled tens of thousands of miles to more than thirty countries and most states and has spoken to thousands of people. Technological and media advances have provided greater missionary opportunities.

1995   To decentralize leadership and management, Area Authorities were called to serve in the Church in more than 150 nations. The First Presidency and Quorum of the Twelve issued a proclamation to the world reaffirming gospel standards and practices concerning the family.

1996   Observances were held of Utah Statehood Centennial and the sesquicentennial of the Saints' forced exodus in 1846 from Nauvoo, Illinois. General Authorities were withdrawn from boards of directors of business corporations, including Church-owned corporations. Church members living outside U.S. outnumbered those living inside U.S. The profile of President Hinckley and the Church aired on the TV show *60 Minutes*. The Church launched its official Internet website. The Hong Kong and Mount Timpanogos Utah temples were dedicated.

1997   First film ever shown at General Conference (April): a sesquicentennial celebration of the pioneers' arrival in Salt Lake. Area Authorities became Area Authority Seventies and members of the Third, Fourth, and Fifth Quorums of the Seventy. The St. Louis Missouri Temple was dedicated. A new LDS CD-ROM was released that honors the Church and pioneers; it was sent to 20,000 media sources worldwide and made available to the general public. Many centers, trail sites, and parks were dedicated. The Church received nationwide media coverage of its pioneers' sesquicentennial celebration.

1997   Membership (Aug. est.): 9,900,000; Stakes: 2,325; Temples: 50; Missions: 318; Missionaries: 56,000. Missionary work is being done in 160 countries and territories and in 145 languages.

Sources: *Encyclopedia of Mormonism* 4:1652-58; *Deseret News 1997-98 Church Almanac; Church News;* and Church Public Affairs.

QUESTIONS ABOUT THE PRESIDENTS OF THE CHURCH

1. **Who was the oldest President to join the Church as a convert?**
   - *Brigham Young, age 31*

2. **Who served in civic or other Church callings while President?**
   - *Joseph Smith—Kirtland stake president, general in the Illinois state militia and mayor of Nauvoo*
   - *Brigham Young—Territorial Governor and U.S. Indian Agent*
   - *Wilford Woodruff—General Superintendent of the Young Men*
   - *Lorenzo Snow—General Superintendent of the Young Men and Sunday School*
   - *Joseph F. Smith—General Superintendent of Young Men, General Superintendent of Sunday School, and president of Salt Lake Temple*

3. **In honor of which Presidents were towns named?**
   - *Joseph City, Arizona (Joseph Smith)*
   - *Brigham City, Utah; Young, Arizona (Brigham Young)*
   - *Taylorsville, Utah; Taylor, Arizona; (John Taylor);*
   - *Woodruff, Arizona; Woodruff, Utah (Wilford Woodruff)*
   - *Snowville, Utah (Lorenzo Snow).*

4. **Who had recognized musical talent?**
   - *Brigham Young and his brother Joseph sang many duets during Zion's Camp, Kirtland, and Nauvoo at the invitation of the Prophet Joseph.*
   - *John Taylor sang for the Prophet Joseph in Carthage Jail just prior to Joseph's death.*
   - *John Taylor, Joseph Fielding Smith, and Gordon B. Hinckley wrote the text of hymns.*
   - *Lorenzo Snow had a wonderful tenor voice.*
   - *George Albert Smith played the harmonica and guitar.*
   - *David O. McKay, Joseph Fielding Smith, Harold B. Lee, Spencer W. Kimball, and Howard W. Hunter played the piano, serving as pianists. Presidents Lee and Kimball both played the piano for the meetings of the General Authorities in the Salt Lake Temple.*
   - *Ezra Taft Benson sang in a quartet composed of members of the Quorum of the Twelve.*
   - *Howard W. Hunter played many instruments and had his own band as young man. Harold B. Lee also played in a band.*

5. **Who dedicated the most temples?**
   - *Gordon B. Hinckley, as a counselor in the First Presidency and as President, has dedicated or rededicated 29 temples.*

6. **Who lived past the age of 90?**
   - *Wilford Woodruff (91), David O. McKay (96), Joseph Fielding Smith (95), Spencer W. Kimball (90), Ezra Taft Benson (94)*

7. **Who lived the longest length of time?**
   - *David O. McKay, 96*

8. **Who became an orphan as a teenager?**
   - *Joseph F. Smith (his father Hyrum died when he was six, and mother Mary died when he was thirteen)*

9. **Whose father died while the president was still an infant?**
   - *Heber J. Grant's father, Jedediah, died nine days after Heber's birth.*

10. **Who was known as the "Lion of the Lord?"**
    - *Brigham Young*

11. **Who were involved in sports?**
    - *Joseph Smith, wrestling*
    - *Joseph F. Smith, golf*
    - *Heber J. Grant, baseball and golf*
    - *David O. McKay, football*
    - *Joseph Fielding Smith, handball*
    - *Harold B. Lee and Spencer W. Kimball, basketball*

12. **Which Presidents were not born in the Church?**
    - *Joseph Smith, Brigham Young, John Taylor, Wilford Woodruff, and Lorenzo Snow*

13. **Which Presidents spent their entire adult lives in Church service?**
    - *Joseph Fielding Smith*
    - *Gordon B. Hinckley (except two years with the railroad during World War II)*

14. **Who had a special interest in the Indians?**
    - *Joseph Smith, Brigham Young, Wilford Woodruff, George Albert Smith, and Spencer W. Kimball*

15. **Who became a General Authority before becoming an apostle?**
    - *Gordon B. Hinckley, Assistant to the Twelve (1958)*

16. **Under whose direction were Assistants to the Twelve added?**
    - *Heber J. Grant, 1941*

17. **Who was the first President to visit or travel outside the United States while serving as President?**
    - Joseph Smith, Canada, October 5, 1833

18. **Who were the only father and son to serve as presidents?**
    - *Joseph F. Smith and Joseph Fielding Smith*

19. **Who lived the shortest length of time?**
    - *Joseph Smith, 38 and Harold B. Lee, 74*

20. **Who was the first President to be born in the Church?**
    - *Joseph F. Smith*

21. **Who was the first President to speak on the radio?**
    - *Heber J. Grant, 1922*

22. **Who was the first President to speak on television?**
    - *George Albert Smith, 1949*

23. **Who, as a member of the Quorum of the Twelve, helped establish the Boy Scouts of America as a program in the Church?**
    - *George Albert Smith*

24. **Who ordained their sons to the apostleship?**
    - *Brigham Young—John W. Young (1855), not a member of the Twelve; Brigham, Jr. (1864); Joseph A. (1864), not a member of the Twelve*
    - *John Taylor—John W. Taylor (1884)*
    - *Wilford Woodruff—Abraham O. Woodruff (1897)*
    - *Joseph F. Smith—Hyrum Mack Smith (1901), Joseph Fielding Smith (1910)*

25. **Who published the most books?**
    - *Joseph Fielding Smith (25)*

26. **Who served as an apostle at the same time his father was an apostle?**
    - George Albert Smith (father: John Henry Smith)

27. **Who served as a counselor in the First Presidency and also simultaneously as president of the Quorum of the Twelve?**
    - *David O. McKay, Joseph Fielding Smith, Harold B. Lee, and Gordon B. Hinckley*

28. **Who pioneered the welfare program while serving as a stake president?**
    - Harold B. Lee

29. **Who served the longest and shortest periods as President of the Quorum of the Twelve?**
    - *Joseph Fielding Smith (19 years) and David O. McKay (6 months)*

30. **Who, as a boy, walked across the plains to the Great Salt Lake Valley?**
    - Joseph F. Smith

31. **Who were the shortest and tallest presidents?**
    - *Lorenzo Snow (5 feet 6 inches), Spencer W. Kimball (5 feet 6½ inches)*
    - *Joseph Smith, Heber J. Grant, George Albert Smith, Howard W. Hunter (6 feet)*
    - *David O. McKay and Ezra Taft Benson (6 feet 1 inch)*

32. **During the first six years of which President's administration were more copies of the Book of Mormon distributed than in all the previous years of the Church combined?**
    - *Ezra Taft Benson (1986-1991)*

33. **Who was the youngest President to be ordained an apostle in the Quorum of the Twelve?**
    - *Heber J. Grant (age 25)*

34. **Under which President did the Church dedicate the most temples?**
    - *Spencer W. Kimball (21 temples)*

35. **Who was known as the "Apostle of Love?"**
    - *George Albert Smith*

36. **Who served the longest time in the First Presidency?**
    - *Joseph F. Smith (44 years) and David O. McKay (almost 36 years)*

37. **Who were very much involved in Scouting during their youth and as apostles and presidents?**
    - *George Albert Smith and Ezra Taft Benson*

38. **Who made the statement that later became a principle of eternal progression: "As man is, God once was; as God is, man may be"?**
    - *Lorenzo Snow*

39. **Who made the statement: "No other success can compensate for failure in the home"?**
    - *David O. McKay*

40. **Who was noted for helping to get the Church out of debt?**
    - *Lorenzo Snow (re-emphasized tithing)*

41. **Which two Presidents were ordained apostles on the same day?**
    - *Spencer W. Kimball and Ezra Taft Benson (October 7, 1943)*

42. **Who was the only President to have sons serve with him in the First Presidency?**
    • *Brigham Young (John and Brigham, Jr.)*

43. **Hollywood made a motion picture of which president?**
    • Brigham Young—Frontiersman *1940, with Dean Jagger as Brigham Young. Jagger later became a member of the Church in 1971.*

44. **Who appeared on the covers of weekly news magazines?**
    • *George Albert Smith,* Time, *July 24, 1947 (in conjunction with the pioneer centennial in the Great Basin); Ezra Taft Benson,* U.S. News & World Report, Time, Newsweek, *and* Business Week *(in the capacity as U.S. Secretary of Agriculture—1953-61)*

45. **Who was the first President to ride on the railroad, run for the office of President of the United States, and be a pioneer in adult education?**
    • *Joseph Smith*

46. **Who was the first President to have his voice recorded?**
    • *Wilford Woodruff*

47. **Who was the first President to drive a car, to be photographed, and to visit Europe?**
    • *Joseph F. Smith*

48. **Who was a great defender of the U.S. Constitution and gave numerous speeches honoring it, as well as gave numerous patriotic speeches?**
    • *Ezra Taft Benson*

49. **Who was the first President to visit the Holy land as President?**
    • *Harold B. Lee*

50. **Who were put in jail?**
    • *Joseph Smith, on a variety of false charges, and Lorenzo Snow, on a plural marriage charge*

51. **Who was disrupted while giving a fireside address at Brigham Young University by a man threatening to detonate a bomb?**
    • Howard W. Hunter (February 1993)

52. **Who was responsible for developing materials (audiovisual) and programs that relied on evolving communications technology to help spread the Church's message throughout the world?**
    • *Gordon B. Hinckley*

53. **Who was honored by having an agriculture and food institute established at Brigham Young University?**
    • *Ezra Taft Benson*

54. **Who, while serving in three consecutive First Presidencies, continued the work while the President was disabled?**
    • *Gordon B. Hinckley*

55. **Under which President has the Church seen the greatest membership growth?**
    • *Ezra Taft Benson (2,768,511)*

56. **Which Presidents, as young men, also converted their parents?**
    • *Joseph Smith and Brigham Young*

57. **Who made the following changes or additions: general conference (two days rather than three); consolidated meeting schedule; stake conferences held semi-annually rather than quarterly; First Quorum of Seventy reorganized; expansion of scriptures to include two visions received by Joseph Smith and Joseph F. Smith; new LDS editions of the scriptures and hymns?**
    • *Spencer W. Kimball*

58. **Who announced that priesthood is available to all worthy male members?**
    • *Spencer W. Kimball*

59. **Which two Presidents were trained as professional teachers?**
    • *David O. McKay and Harold B. Lee*

60. **Who was shot four times in Carthage Jail and witnessed the killings of Joseph Smith and Hyrum Smith?**
    • *John Taylor*

61. **Who served the shortest time?**
    • *Harold B. Lee (1½ years) and Howard W. Hunter (9 months)*

62. **Who served as counselor to four Presidents before becoming President himself?**
    • *Joseph F. Smith*

63. **Who was the first to call men from Europe, South America, and Asia to be General Authorities?**
    • *Spencer W. Kimball*

64. **Who, while serving as a missionary to the Sandwich Islands (Hawaii), was virtually raised from the dead?**
    • *Lorenzo Snow*

65. **Who was a widower when he became President?**
   - *George Albert Smith (Lucy Emily Woodruff died in 1937, and he did not remarry)*

66. **Who made this statement: "The most important work you will ever do will be within the walls of your own home."**
   - *Harold B. Lee*

67. **Who issued the Manifesto, permitting no future plural marriages?**
   - *Wilford Woodruff*

68. **Who worried about his advanced age and pleaded for a manifestation of divine will? (He testified that the Lord appeared to him in the Salt Lake Temple and affirmed that he should serve.)**
   - *Lorenzo Snow*

69. **Who served as an apostle under six Presidents prior to becoming President?**
   - *Ezra Taft Benson (served under Heber J. Grant, George Albert Smith, David O. McKay, Joseph Fielding Smith, Harold B. Lee, and Spencer W. Kimball)*

70. **Which President, as a young man, was the youngest to serve a mission?**
   - *Joseph F. Smith, age 15, to Hawaii in 1854*

71. **What has been the average age of the President when he was ordained, excluding Joseph Smith and Brigham Young?**
   - *Age 78. Presidents younger than 78 were John Taylor—71, Joseph F. Smith—62, Heber J. Grant—62, George Albert Smith—75, David O. McKay—77, Harold B. Lee—73, Spencer W. Kimball—78. Presidents older than 78 were Lorenzo Snow—84, Joseph Fielding Smith—93, Ezra Taft Benson—84, Howard W. Hunter—86, and Gordon B. Hinckley—84.*

72. **Who, while serving as an apostle, also served as U.S. Secretary of Agriculture for eight years?**
   - *Ezra Taft Benson, 1953-1961*

73. **Who wrote the texts for LDS hymns?**
   - *John Taylor, "Go, Ye Messengers of Glory" and "Go, Ye Messengers of Heaven"*
   - *Joseph Fielding Smith, "Does the Journey Seem Long?"*
   - *Gordon B. Hinckley, "My Redeemer Lives"*

74. **Who walked with a limp from the time he was seven years old?**
   - *Joseph Smith, due to surgery on his leg and the extraction of pieces of bone*

75. **Who taught at a one-room school, being younger than some of his students?**
   - *Harold B. Lee*

76. **Who organized his own orchestra that played on a ship that sailed to the Orient?**
   - *Howard W. Hunter*

77. **Who was the youngest person to serve in the First Presidency?**
   - *Joseph F. Smith, age 27, was ordained an apostle and named counselor in the First Presidency in 1866.*

78. **Who carried a bullet in his left leg throughout his life?**
   - *John Taylor*

79. **Which Presidents had fathers who served in the First Presidency?**
   - *Joseph Smith (Joseph Smith, Sr.)*
   - *Joseph F. Smith (Hyrum Smith)*
   - *Heber J. Grant (Jedediah M. Grant)*
   - *George Albert Smith (John Henry Smith)*
   - *Joseph Fielding Smith (Joseph F. Smith)*

80. **Who did not serve as counselors in First Presidency prior to becoming President?**
   - *Brigham Young, John Taylor, Wilford Woodruff, Heber J. Grant, George Albert Smith, Spencer W. Kimball, Ezra Taft Benson, and Howard W. Hunter*

81. **What was the average age of the Church Presidents when they were ordained apostles?**
   - *From Joseph Smith to Gordon B. Hinckley, the average age is 37. Note: From Joseph Smith to Joseph Fielding Smith, the average age is 29. From Harold B. Lee to Gordon B. Hinckley, the average age is 42, a difference of 13 years.*

BIBLIOGRAPHY

Books

Allen, James B. and Glen M. Leonard. *The Story of the Latter-day Saints*, Salt Lake City: Deseret Book Co., 1992.

Arrington, Leonard J. *Brigham Young: America Moses.* New York: Alfred A. Knopf, 1985.

Arrington, Leonard J., editor. *The Presidents of the Church.* Salt Lake City: Deseret Book Co., 1986. Cited as *TPC*.

Benson, Ezra Taft. *God, Family, Country: Our Three Great Loyalties.* Salt Lake City: Deseret Book Co., 1974.

Benson, Ezra Taft. *Come unto Christ.* Salt Lake City: Deseret Book Co., 1974.

Benson, Ezra Taft. *Teachings of Ezra Taft Benson.* Salt Lake City: Bookcraft, 1988. Cited as *TETB*.

Benson, Ezra Taft. *This Nation Shall Endure.* Salt Lake City: Deseret Book Co., 1977.

Black, Susan Easton and Larry C. Porter, editors. *Lion of the Lord, Essays on the Life and Service of Brigham Young.* Salt Lake City: Deseret Book Co., 1995.

Burton, Alma P., compiler. *Doctrines from the Prophets.* Salt Lake City: Bookcraft, 1970.

Cannon, Elaine, compiler. *Notable Quotables from Women to Women.* Salt Lake City: Bookcraft, 1992.

Carter, Kate B. *Our Pioneer Heritage.* Salt Lake City, Utah: Daughters of the Utah Pioneers, 1958.

Clark, James R., compiler. *Messages of the First Presidency of the Church of Jesus Christ of Latter-day Saints*, 6 vols. Salt Lake City: Bookcraft, 1965-75.

Clark, J. Reuben, Jr. *On the Way to Immortality and Eternal Life.* Salt Lake City: Deseret Book Co., 1949.

Corbett, Pearson H. *Hyrum Smith.* Salt Lake City: Deseret Book Co., 1963.

Cornwall, Spencer. *A Century of Singing—The Salt Lake Tabernacle.* Salt Lake City: Deseret Book Co., 1958.

Deseret News 1997-98 Church Almanac. Salt Lake City: Deseret News Press, 1996.

Dew, Sheri L. *Ezra Taft Benson, A Biography.* Salt Lake City: Deseret Book Co., 1987.

Dew, Sheri L. *Go Forward With Faith: The Biography of Gordon B. Hinckley.* Salt Lake City: Deseret Book Co., 1996. Cited as *GBH*.

Emerson, Ralph Waldo, as quoted in *Focus on America Literature.* Edited by Philip McFarland, Boston: Houghton Mifflin Company, 1981.

Encyclopedia of Mormonism, 4 vols. New York: Macmillan Publishing Company, 1991.

Evans, John Henry. *Joseph Smith: An American Prophet.* Salt Lake City: Deseret Book Co., 1933.

Gibbons, Francis M. *Joseph Fielding Smith, Gospel Scholar, Prophet of God.* Salt Lake City: Deseret Book Co., 1992.

Gibbons, Francis M. *Heber J. Grant: Man of Steel, Prophet of God.* Salt Lake City: Deseret Book Co., 1979.

Gibbons, Francis M. *Spencer W. Kimball: Resolute Disciple, Prophet of God.* Salt Lake City: Deseret Book Co., 1995.

Goates, L. Brent. *Harold B. Lee: Prophet & Seer.* Salt Lake City: Bookcraft, 1985.

Goates, Helen Lee. *Fern Lucinda Tanner Lee: Her Life Story* [unpublished].

Godfrey, Kenneth, Audrey Godfrey, and Jill Mulvay Derr. *Women's Voices: An Untold History of the Latter-day Saints, 1830-1900.* Salt Lake City: Deseret Book Co., 1981.

Grant, Heber J. *Gospel Standards.* Compiled by G. Homer Durham. Salt Lake City: Deseret Book Co., 1969. Cited as *GS*.

Hinckley, Bryant. *Heber J. Grant: Life of a Great Leader.* Salt Lake City: Deseret Book, 1951.

Hinckley, Gordon B. "Strengthening Each Other," in *Hope.* Salt Lake City: Deseret Book Co., 1988.

Hinckley, Gordon B. *Faith: The Essence of True Religion.* Salt Lake City: Deseret Book, 1989.

Hinckley, Gordon B. *Man of Integrity, 15th President of the Church of Jesus Christ of Latter-day Saints*, 1995 video tape.

Hinckley, Gordon B. *Be Thou an Example,* Salt Lake City, Deseret Book Co., 1981.

Hunter, Howard W. *That We Might Have Joy.* Salt Lake City: Deseret Book Co., 1994.

Jenson, Andrew. *Latter-Day Saint Biographical Encyclopedia*, 4 vols. Salt Lake City: Deseret Press, 1901-1936.

Journal of Discourses. London: Latter-day Saints Book Depot, 1855-86, 26 vols. Cited as *JD*.

Kimball, Edward L. and Andrew E. Kimball, Jr. *Spencer W. Kimball*. Salt Lake City: Bookcraft, 1977.

Kimball, Spencer W. *Faith Precedes the Miracle*. Salt Lake City: Deseret Book Co., 1972. Cited as *FPM*.

Kimball, Spencer W. *Teachings of Spencer W. Kimball*. Salt Lake City: Bookcraft, 1977. Cited as *TSWK*.

Kimball, Spencer W. *The Miracle of Forgiveness*. Salt Lake City: Bookcraft, 1969. Cited as *MF*.

Knowles, Eleanor. *Howard W. Hunter*. Salt Lake City: Deseret Book Co., 1994.

Lee, Harold B. *Decisions for Successful Living*. Salt Lake City: Deseret Book Co., 1973.

Lee, Harold B. *Stand Ye in Holy Places*. Salt Lake City: Deseret Book Co., 1974. Cited as *SYHP*.

Lee, Harold B. *Teachings of Harold B. Lee*. Compiled by Clyde Williams. Salt Lake City: Bookcraft, 1996. Cited as *THBL*.

Lee, Harold B. *Ye Are the Light of the World*. Salt Lake City: Deseret Book Co., 1974. Cited as *YALW*.

Lee, Harold B. *Youth and the Church*. Salt Lake City: Deseret Book Co., 1970.

Madsen, Carol Cornwall. *In Their Own Words*. Salt Lake City: Deseret Book Co., 1994.

McKay, David O. *Cherished Experiences*. Compiled by Clare Middlemiss. Salt Lake City: Deseret Book Co., 1955.

McKay, David O. *Gospel Ideals*. Salt Lake City: Deseret Book Co., 1953. Cited as *GI*.

McKay, David O. *Man May Know for Himself*. Compiled by Claire Middlemiss. Salt Lake City: Deseret Book Co., 1967.

McKay, David Lawrence. *My Father, David O. McKay*. Salt Lake City: Deseret Book Co., 1989.

Miner, Caroline Eyring and Edward Kimball. *Camilla*. Salt Lake City: Deseret Book, 1980.

Nibley, Preston. *The Presidents of the Church*. Salt Lake City: Deseret Book Co., 1971.

Pusey, Merlo J. Pusey. *Builders of the Kingdom*, Provo: Brigham Young University Press, 1981,

Roberts, B. H. *Life of John Taylor*. Salt Lake City: Bookcraft, 1963.

Romney, Thomas C. *The Life of Lorenzo Snow*. Salt Lake City: Deseret Book Co., 1955.

Schluter, Fred E. *A Convert's Tribute to President David O. McKay*. Salt Lake City: Deseret News Press, 1964.

Smith, Joseph. *History of the Church of Jesus Christ of Latter-day Saints*, 7 vols. Edited by B.H. Roberts. Salt Lake City: The Church of Jesus Christ of Latter-day Saints, 1932-51. Cited as *HC*.

Smith, Joseph. *Teachings of Joseph Smith*. Compiled by Larry E. Dahl and Donald Q. Cannon. Salt Lake City: Bookcraft Co., 1997.

Smith, Joseph. *Teachings of the Prophet Joseph Smith*. Compiled by Joseph Fielding Smith. Salt Lake City: Deseret Book Co., 1938. Cited as *TPJS*.

Smith, Joseph. *Lectures on Faith*. (Lectures given to the School of the Prophets) 1834-35, Kirtland, Ohio. Salt Lake City: Deseret Book Co., 1921.

Smith, Joseph Fielding. *Life of Joseph F. Smith*. Salt Lake City: Deseret Book Co., 1969.

Smith, Lucy Mack. *History of Joseph Smith*. Edited by Preston Nibley. Salt Lake City: Bookcraft, 1956.

Smith, Edna Lambson, *The Descendants of Joseph F. Smith (1838-1918)*. Compiled by the Joseph F. Smith Family Genealogical Committee [unpublished].

Smith, Joseph Fielding. *Doctrines of Salvation*, 3 vols. Compiled by Bruce R. McConkie. Salt Lake City: Bookcraft, 1954-56.

Smith, Joseph Fielding. *The Life of Joseph F. Smith*. Salt Lake City: Deseret Book Co., 1938.

Smith, George Albert. *Sharing the Gospel with Others*. Compiled by Preston Nibley. Salt Lake City: Deseret Book Co., 1948. Cited as *SGO*.

Smith, Joseph Fielding, Jr., and John Stewart. *Life of Joseph Fielding Smith*. Salt Lake City: Deseret Book, 1972.

Smith, Joseph Fielding, *Answers to Gospel Questions*, 5 Vols. Salt Lake City: Deseret Book Co., 1954-66.

Smith, Joseph F. Smith. *Gospel Doctrine*. Salt Lake City: Deseret Book Co., 1939. Cited as *GD*.

Smith, Joseph Fielding. *Church History and Modern Revelation*, 3 vols. Salt Lake City: The Church of Jesus Christ of Latter-day Saints, 1953.

Smith, Joseph Fielding. *Take Heed to Yourselves*. Salt Lake City: Deseret Book Co., 1966.

Snow, Eliza R., *Biography and Family Record of Lorenzo Snow*. Salt Lake City: Deseret News Co., 1884.

Snow, Lorenzo. *Teachings of Lorenzo Snow*. Compiled by Clyde Williams. Salt Lake City: Bookcraft, 1984. Cited as *TLS*.

Stewart, John. *Remembering the McKays.* Salt Lake City: Deseret Book Co., 1970.

Stovall, Mary E. and Carol Cornwall Madsen, editors. *As Women of Faith: Talks Selected from the BYU Women's Conferences.* Salt Lake City: Deseret Book Co., 1989.

Taylor, John. *The Mediation and the Atonement.* Salt Lake City: Deseret News Co., 1882.

Taylor, John. *The Government of God.* Liverpool, England: S.W. Richards, 1852.

Taylor, John. *Gospel Kingdom.* 4th ed. Compiled by G. Homer Durham. Salt Lake City: Bookcraft, 1943.

Teachings of the Latter-day Prophets, a publication of limited circulation. Salt Lake City: The Church of Jesus Christ of Latter-day Saints.

Young Brigham. *Discourses of Brigham Young.* Compiled by John A. Widtsoe. Salt Lake City: Deseret Book Co., 1961.

West, Emerson R. *Profiles of the Presidents.* Salt Lake City: Deseret Book Co., 1980.

Woodruff, Wilford. *The Discourses of Wilford Woodruff* Selected by G. Homer Durham. Salt Lake City: Bookcraft, 1946.

Wilford Woodruff: His Life and Labors. Compiled by Matthias F. Cowley. Salt Lake City: Bookcraft, 1964.

Magazines and Periodicals

Brigham Young University Studies

BYU Speeches of the Year

BYU Law Review, 1976.

Church News, section of the *Deseret News*. Cited as *CN*.

Conference Report of the Church of Jesus Christ of Latter-day Saint. Cited as *CR*.

Deseret News. Cited as *DN*.

Ensign

Improvement Era. Cited as *IE*.

Juvenile Instructor. Cited as *JI*.

Millennial Star. Cited as *MS*.

New Era. Cited as *NE*

Relief Society Magazine. Cited as *RS*.

Salt Lake Tribune

Utah Genealogical and Historical Magazine

Other

Address to employees of the Physical Facilities Dept. of the Church, Hotel Utah, June 1965.

Carter, Kate B., compiler, "Miriam Works Young" *Our Pioneer Heritage* (Salt Lake City, Utah: Daughters of Utah Pioneers, 1958), pp. 419-20.

Report of the Seoul Korea Area Conference, 1975.

Richards, Stephen L. "About Mormonism." Pamphlet of the Church of Jesus Christ of Latter-day Saints.

Smith, Joseph F. Smith Family Genealogical Committee, compiler *The Descendants of Joseph F. Smith* (1838-1918).

Letter from Reed Benson to Emerson R. West, May 9, 1995.

Letter from Geraldine Callister (niece of Sister Lee) to Emerson R. West, April 17, 1985.

Letters from Richard Hunter to Emerson R. West, April 27, 1995, and May 11, 1995.

Letters from Robert McKay to Emerson R. West, May 5, 1995 and April 3, 1996.

Letter from Dr. Larry C. Porter, LDS Church History Department to Emerson R. West, April 17, 1995.

Telephone conversations between Edward Kimball and Emerson West, February 24 and June 19, 1997.

Telephone conversations between Emma McKay Ashton and Emerson R. West, March 11 and May 20, 1985.

Telephone conversation between Geraldine Callister and Emerson R. West, May 15, 1985.

Telephone conversations between Helen Lee Goates, April 2, 1997 and June 21, 1997.

Telephone conversation between Inis Bernice Hunter and Emerson R. West, April 29, 1995.

Telephone conversations between Reed Benson and Emerson R. West, April 23, 1995, February 18 and June 18, 1997.

Telephone conversations between Robert McKay and Emerson R. West, April 20, 1995 and June 21, 1997.

INDEX